Miguel de Cervantes Saavedra, James Young Gibson

Journey to Parnassus

Miguel de Cervantes Saavedra, James Young Gibson

Journey to Parnassus

ISBN/EAN: 9783744798747

Printed in Europe, USA, Canada, Australia, Japan

Cover: Foto ©ninafisch / pixelio.de

More available books at **www.hansebooks.com**

JOURNEY TO PARNASSUS

COMPOSED BY

MIGUEL DE CERVANTES SAAVEDRA

TRANSLATED INTO ENGLISH TERCETS WITH
PREFACE AND ILLUSTRATIVE NOTES

BY

JAMES Y. GIBSON

TO WHICH ARE SUBJOINED THE ANTIQUE TEXT
AND TRANSLATION OF THE LETTER OF
CERVANTES TO MATEO VAZQUEZ

LONDON
KEGAN PAUL, TRENCH AND CO.
1 PATERNOSTER SQUARE
1883

Thou, who art listening, if thou heed aright
The sweet recital of this ' Journey ' grand,
Shalt hear new things of exquisite delight.
                              Ch. viii. p. 237.

TO MARGARITA.

Across the gorse-clad common, sprent with gold,
   Through lanes of black-thorn, bright with blooms of snow,
   Up sunny slopes, with daisies all aglow,
We walked, and talked of things both new and old.

In memory of those Spring-days, loved so well,
   I send to thee this tiny, modest gem,
   Dropped from a Spanish monarch's diadem,
Or, shall I say, his cross of San Miguél.

Such wealth of jewels had that poet-king,
   This little straggling pearl forgotten lay,
   And connoisseurs, who passed it on the way,
Disdained to pick it up,—the common thing!

To me it seemed to gleam with light untold,
   And so with mickle pains, and mickle fretting,
   I coaxed it into this plain English setting,
To wile its lustre forth with English gold.

Thyself a pearl, deign thou this pearl to wear,
   Mayhap the critics' glance will then be kind;
   If not, what matter? Beauty's in the mind;
I'm pleased if thou be pleased to think it fair.
                            J. Y. G.
     Tunbridge-Wells,
       April, 1882.

CONTENTS.

	PAGE
TRANSLATOR'S PREFACE	ix-lxv
OF THE PORTRAIT AND ITS PEDIGREE	lxvii-lxxv
AUTHOR'S DEDICATION, PROLOGUE, AND SONNET	1-7
JOURNEY TO PARNASSUS, SPANISH TEXT AND ENGLISH VERSION	8-261
APPENDIX TO THE "PARNASSUS"	263-297
LETTER OF CERVANTES TO MATEO VAZQUEZ DURING HIS CAPTIVITY IN ALGIERS	299-327
NOTES AND ILLUSTRATIVE PIECES	329

TRANSLATOR'S PREFACE.

"Good wine needs no bush," and a good poem should need no prologue. Cervantes was evidently of this opinion, for the single enigmatical sentence with which he introduces this delightful satire, like the piquant olive which ushers in a good Spanish dinner, was intended simply to quicken the palates of his readers. We would gladly follow his example, and allow this Parnassus-Journey of his, tricked out in the choicest English and the smoothest *Terza rima* at our command, to present itself to English readers without the formality of an Introduction. We are the more tempted to do so, inasmuch as we find, on perusing the admirable French version of the *Voyage au Parnasse* by M. Guardia, that this painstaking scholar thinks it needful to preface it with a learned and laborious Introduction of well-nigh 200 pages, and to supplement it with a long biographical dictionary of 135 pages, while the little poem of 125 pages, wedged in between two such bulky treatises, has hardly breathing-space. We humbly confess that for such a task as this we have little ability and less inclination. A satire that requires so much minute commentary is manifestly defunct, and may be regarded as a curious fossil, of interest only to the antiquarian. We make bold to say that such is not the case with this little poem of Cervantes. It needs no such extraneous aid to make it intelligible. There is enough of native vitality in it to interest and even to fascinate all readers of the right sort. Though one of the children of Cervantes' old age, produced in his sixty-seventh year, it has a sprightliness and vigour worthy of his prime. It is instinct with that peculiar humour which sparkles in his Novels, and overflows in his "Don Quixote," and which, though at times it seems to run riot, is redeemed from the charge of utter extravagance by its intensely human heartiness. And there is wisdom too combined with the wit ; for as M. Guardia truly says : " The reader, who would make this Journey of Parnassus in company with Cervantes, will find in him not only an unequalled guide, who will not allow him to sleep by the way, but also a critic of the grand school, of rare sagacity, of exquisite taste, unrivalled in that most difficult art—the art of teaching truth with a smile and of making wisdom lovable."

But that which seems to us to give this delectable poem its chief charm and value is the curious self-revelation it offers of the inner life and aspirations of the man who, after Shakespeare, was the foremost creative genius of his age, and whose life, unlike that of his great contemporary, was chequered with numberless " moving accidents by flood and field." Shakespeare, in his *Sonnets*, gives us a certain measure by which to test the nature and depth of the passion that possessed him, though the heart of the mystery is still untouched. But Cervantes is much more un-reserved and communicative. Whoever has felt the spell of this Wizard of the South must know how his personality is stamped, like a hall-mark, on everything he wrote; how the romance of his life is interwoven with the romance of his writings, so that a peculiar loving interest in the matchless story-teller is born, and increases with our love for his works. All the world knows that this is eminently the case with his *Don Quixote*. In that tale of tales, and behind the visor of the immortal knight, who seems born for no other reason than to banish "loathéd Melancholy" from the world, and replace it with "heart-easing Mirth" and "Laughter holding both his sides," we are confronted with the face of a man, whose eyes betray no spark of insanity, but a glowing enthusiasm tempered with all sorts of humorous gleamings; whose mobile lips have always a winning smile for his friends, and a light curl of irony for his foes ; whose brow, furrowed with care, and sorrow, and thought, bespeaks the man of vast experience, both of men and things, which gives him the right and power to speak on all matters that concern humanity ; in fact, one of those rare heroic characters, of gentle manners, splendid gifts, and noble thoughts, whom to know and to love is of itself a liberal education.

If such loving personal interest has grown up in any of our readers by a thoughtful study of the adventures of the Knight of La Mancha, it will certainly not be lessened by a perusal of the *Journey to Parnassus*. For herein Cervantes openly takes up the rôle of his own Don Quixote, and with a faith as simple, and a courage as undaunted, he sets himself to a task as hopeless as the most desperate of his hero's. This Herculean labour is nothing more nor less than to banish mediocrity from the realm of Spanish poesy, and to sweep from its sacred precincts, which had become as foul as an Augean stable, all shams, lies, hypocrisies, and vulgar baseness whatsoever. A Quixotic purpose truly in any age or country, but doubly Quixotic in a land which, in the time of Cervantes, was overrun with a perfect plague of poetastry! To say the truth, it is but a mild sort of interest that we take in the enterprise itself, though the

Translator's Preface. xiii

surroundings of it, and the period at which it takes place, are sufficiently fascinating. For the combined reigns of the Second and Third Philips, during which Cervantes lived, form undoubtedly the Augustan age of Spanish literature. It is adorned with a roll of names as brilliant as were ever concentrated in any one age, in any country. There is Herrera, with his sublime odes; Luis de Leon, with his heaven-inspired lyrics; Gongora, with his clear, trenchant satires, ringing romances, and new, turgid, superfine, æsthetic jargon; Lope de Vega, with his eternal flow of comedies, like the sands on the sea-shore innumerable; Quevedo, with his wonderful visions that electrified Europe, and his political satires that gave him the fame of a Spanish Junius; and, lastly, there is Calderon de la Barca, who, born in the middle of this wonderful age, winds it up with his incomparable dramas, which soar to the utmost height that Spanish dramatic genius has ever reached. If we add to these some of the minor deities, the Argensolas, Borjas, Villegas', Rebolledos, Riojas, Molinas, De Castros, and Artiedas, we have an array of multifarious talent such as the world has seldom seen in such close conjunction.

In the midst of this brilliant conclave of poets Cervantes occupies a peculiar position. He has affinity with each, but stands apart from all. As thoroughly Spanish as any in all that constitutes nationality (*Castellano á las derechas*), his genius, consciously or unconsciously, claims kinship with humanity. His works, firmly rooted in Spanish soil, are destined to bear transplanting to every region, and to be reproductive in every climate, save that of their birth. Other nations since then have had their Walter Scotts, Goethes, and Victor Hugos, heaven-inspired geniuses of the same type and earthly descent, sturdily national and intensely human, but Cervantes is childless in Spain. We may fitly compare him to one of those ancient giant oaks in some ancestral park (shall we say Herne's Oak, with all the witchery and glamour of Elf-land around it?) which stands alone in its majesty, carefully guarded and palisaded, reverenced and idolized, but round which there is a treeless waste, without a sturdy sapling to show the vigour of the parent trunk.

It was perhaps this peculiarity of Cervantes' genius that made him so solitary and unbefriended amongst his contemporaries; it was certainly this that made him so sensitive to all that passed around him, and gave him such a penetrating glance into the very heart of things. He was, therefore, neither dazzled nor blinded by the brilliancy of the period in which he lived. He neither envied it nor carped at it, though few of its outward honours descended upon him. He had within himself a standard sure and unerring by which to measure its worth and tendency. With a sort of prophetic instinct he could detect, amid all its splendid, unnatural exuberance, the sure symptoms of decay; and in that fatal feverish thirst for immediate fame, regardless of high aims and pure taste, which few of his poetic comrades were able to resist, he could descry the coming degradation and prostitution of that divine art which was dearer to him than life.

But when he turns from the magnates of the realm of Literature to the common herd whom they influenced and inspired, what a curious spectacle awaits him! It seems to his vivid imagination as if Valencia and Saragossa, Madrid and Seville, all the centres of light and thought in the kingdom, had become so many huge factories for the spinning and weaving of rhymes. Throughout the length and breadth of the land he sees poetry converted into a trade, and a very vile one. All sorts and conditions of men seem pressing into it: churchmen and courtiers and scholars, tailors and cobblers and piecers; men of good education, of half-education, of no education; puffed up with vanity and bristling with conceit, and all of them doing what may emphatically be called a roaring business. Poets are here, there, everywhere. They spring from the dust like frogs; they go hopping about in the antechambers of the great, jostling each other in the theatres and market-places, haunting the wine-shops and taverns and dens of pollution; creating everywhere a very Babel of discordant sounds, and what is worse, carrying with them over the land, into every village and hamlet, that peculiarly horrible pestilence—the plague of poetastry.

As a typical instance of the truth of this description we may quote a curious passage from Suarez de Figueroa's *El Pasagero*, published in 1617, wherein he says: "In a late poetical tournament held in honour of St. Anthony of Padua, no less than 5,000 copies of verses were sent in for competition; and the monks of the monastery where it was held, after having adorned their cloisters and the body of the church with the better class of them, found that enough remained over and above to cover 100 monasteries!" The contemporary *Annals of Seville*, lately brought to light, tell us the same tale of hideous and inordinate production. It is no wonder then that Cervantes, who was essentially an aristocrat in his poetic tastes, should look on such a state of matters with supreme disgust, and should thunder forth his displeasure in such sonorous threatenings as these:—

> O false, accursèd, troubadouring race,
>   That fain would pass for poets wise and strong,
>   Being the very scum of all that's base;
> Between the palate, tongue, and lips, your song
>   Comes surging forth in never-ending blast,
>   Affronting virtue with unmeasured wrong;
> Ye poets, in deception unsurpassed,
>   Beware, for now the awful threatened day,
>   That seals your final doom, has come at last!

Cervantes would, if he could, have been a very despot in the realm of poesy. No countenance to vulgarity and common-place, no truce with pretentious ignorance, no quarter to baseness and obscenity! As he himself tells us, through the mouth of the Canon of Toledo, he would have every comedy, before acted, pass the scrutiny of a jury of experts, and be thoroughly purged of all uncleanness, moral and artistic. And as for the fledgling poets, let them dare to plant one foot on Parnassus-hill without special passport from Apollo, countersigned by himself!

It is in this humour, half-serious and half-comic, that he sets himself to write the *Journey to Parnassus* and organize a new crusade against poetic infidels. But, as we have already said, this is not the matter that concerns us most in the book. The scene and subjects of this serio-comic warfare are too remote for modern sympathy. It is but a lukewarm interest at best that we can take in most of the characters, whose merits Cervantes epitomizes in a single sentence, or whose blots he hits with a single playful touch of his satiric foil; and even the wholesale massacre of the godless and profane, righteous retribution though it be, excites in us no very lively emotion. Not even the breath of Cervantes' wit can make the dead bones of these defunct poets live and take shape before us, nor have we any great desire they should. Herrera and Gongora, Lope de Vega and Quevedo, with some others, are still living, and we are glad to meet with them again. Arbolanché, and Lo Frasso, and the author of *La Picara Justina* have suffered a kind of resurrection, and we get to have such tender affection for them as Izaak Walton had for the worm that wriggled on his hook. As for the rest they " come like shadows, so depart." If we wish to have further knowledge of them it had better be as dried specimens in the *hortus siccus* of Spanish bibliography. But we *do* desire to know something about the noblest of them all—Cervantes himself; and to learn the various elements that make up his wonderful character. Such knowledge in part he gives us here; and, if we read the poem aright, it is such knowledge he means to give us from the very outset. All the rest is but the ingenious setting which enshrines this engaging chapter of his self-biography.

Translator's Preface.

There is confessedly no more charming writer than Cervantes when he takes us into his confidence, and speaks of himself and his doings. His prologues to *Don Quixote*, the Novels, the Comedies, and best of all to the *Persiles*, are the most chatty and delectable bits of self-revelation ever penned, worth half-a-dozen ponderous memoirs. He who can read the last of them without laughter ending in a sob must have a curious temperament. Of all these the *Journey to Parnassus* is the true complement. Stitch them together with a little running thread of connection, and we need little more to tell us how he looked, how he lived, and what he lived for; we might almost say, how he died. The *Journey* is specially valuable on this account, for it is not only self-revealing, it is intensely and often amusingly self-asserting. It throws light on two things especially; his poverty and his genius.

We know already in a rough way, just as did the people of Seville and Madrid among whom he lived, what were the externals of the life of this remarkable man, who, in an age of splendid geniuses, sets himself forth as a chief authority and reformer in matters poetic; and they are not very alluring. We know that he came of a poor but noble family; that he had but a scanty education—was, in fact, in Spanish phrase, an *injenio lego*—not entitled, as we would say, to put

B.A. after his name, in an age when graduates were plentiful as blackberries; that he served as a private soldier for seven years of his life, and suffered as a captive for five; that for fifteen years he was a sort of commissary's agent to collect corn and wine and oil for the army and navy, notably for the great Armada; that for ten years more, down to the date of this *Journey*, he had picked up a precarious living as a private notary, or scrivener, or whatever the Spanish *escribano* may denote; that during all this time he had received no mark of royal acknowledgment, save that on one occasion, in 1605, he was commissioned (seemingly as a reward of merit for his *Don Quixote*) to "chronicle the small beer" of courtly festivity at the baptism of that most high and mighty princeling, Felipe Domenico Victor, afterwards Philip IV; and finally that, while he was penning this Satire, he was a poor pensioner on the bounty of the Count de Lemos, and his Grace the Archbishop of Toledo. In fact, to all outward appearance his life was a conspicuous failure.

No one could be more conscious of this than Cervantes himself. It was a standing wonder to him, that, despite of his commanding abilities, he could not get on in the world. In the economy of the universe, at least in the Spanish portion of it, there seemed no place reserved to him, in which to

Translator's Preface. xxi

plan and toil and be prosperous, for his own and the common good. It gave him cause to philosophize, and the results of his much pondering he presents in this book. He seems to have three different theories to account for the strange phenomenon, and he presents each of them in turn in a jesting or serious way, just as the humour seizes him.

The first he gives after this fashion. He belongs to a class of human beings, of all classes notoriously the most unpractical. Poverty has ever been, and must be, the badge of all the tuneful tribe, for they are essentially a generation of dreamers. When called on to attend to sublunary affairs they are winging their way above the spheres. The world goes quickly past them while they are limning the feats of Mars, or piping, in rosy bowers, of Venus and her loves. While in the solitude of their musings they are weaving a web of beautiful fancies, or adoring their own creations, they are contracting a sublime and eternal ignorance of common things. It is little wonder then that, when Nature forces them, as it forces ordinary mortals, to descend into the every-day world, they should find that everything has gone wrong, and instead of discovering a house of their own to live in and be happy, they should be fond of lingering at a neighbour's hearth (*amigo del hogar de ajena casa*). In such merry vein does Cervantes jest about his poverty in the first chapter. He is a poet of the same order, and must bear the common lot. No doubt he had full proof of this in his life of commissary and scrivener, wherein, we can well imagine, he was more engaged in studying the humours of the men he met, and weaving little stories out of their lives, than in attending to their business. That business and clients should take flight and leave him alone to his dreams, could be no mystery. It was well for him that he could console himself with an aphorism, worthy of his countryman Seneca: "With little I'm content, although I long for much!"

His second theory is one special to himself, and he gives it with a very serious face. There seems a fatality in all that he does. Good-fortune, when she comes, comes with a timid, hesitating air, but flies from his embrace as if from a spectre's. These are the words he puts into Apollo's mouth:—

> Thyself hast fickle Fortune wooed and won,
> Oft have I seen thee with her days agone,
> But from the *imprudent* she is fain to run.

Biographers have vainly vexed their brains to find out in what this "imprudence" consisted; whether it refers to his general character, or to some single act that coloured and determined his after-life. His life, so far as we know, was eminently pure, and we may be quite sure that, if he had ever been guilty of

Translator's Preface. xxiii

any grave moral offence, his enemies would have found it out. The same idea he repeats in a more poetical form, as addressed to himself by Apollo:—

> Men's evil fortunes swell up from behind,
> Bringing their current with them from afar,
> And so are feared, but cannot be declined.

The notion of fatality is here more precisely uttered. There is some back-current, taking its rise in his very nature, or in bygone events springing directly out of it, that affects his life. Things may look bright for a time, but suddenly comes this baleful current with its accumulated force, and sweeps everything before it. This idea haunts him; and his life seems to give warrant for it. When he was twenty-eight years of age, and had done with fighting the Turks, and was returning home to well-earned rest, with glowing testimonials from his commanders that promised him certain advancement, he is suddenly arrested in mid-ocean, and, as he grimly puts it, "Fate drags him by the hair" into five years' sore captivity. In Algiers he has glorious schemes for the release of himself and comrades, which are on the eve of success, when lo! in the midst of them he is confronted by a villain, in the form of that ecclesiastic Blanco de Paz, who ruins everything. He had done this person no offence, except the offence which any loyal and virtuous man naturally gives to a traitor

c

and miscreant, and yet the shadow of that Dominican falls across his life, and rests there. He returns to Spain, and presents to Philip II. a humble petition for a petty post in that paradise of the desperate, Spanish America; his hopes are bright, but something or somebody intervenes, and the demand is fruitless. His commissary's life tells the same tale. His books will not balance, his sureties vanish and leave him in the lurch, the monks of Ecija take it into their heads to excommunicate him for trespass on their sacred lands, he finds himself in prison once and again; and yet his character is unstained, he has done nothing but what might safely be put to the score of "imprudence." And now, just at the period of this satire, when his great patron, Count de Lemos, goes as Viceroy to Naples, and founds there a noble Academy, and many brilliant promises are made to him, and a door at last seems opened to honour, it may be to affluence, a little false rumour, a little backbiting whisper takes place, and the door is shut. It is well for him again that he can take refuge in such consolation as Apollo gravely offers him:—

> The man who merits luck, which Fate denies
> Without good reason, and in mood severe,
> Is honoured more than if he won the prize.

His last theory, which is no theory, affects him most of all. Cruel fate, or his own outspoken, careless, impetuous nature, may be against him; but his worst enemies are those who ought to have been his warmest friends, viz., his comrades in the literary world. He takes up this parable against them, and his words are very bitter:—

> Envy and ignorance do dog my track,
>   And envied thus, and put to direst stress,
>   The good I hope for I must ever lack.

He had written the work of the age. He knew it, and foresaw its fame. Nor had he fault to find with its immediate effect amongst his countrymen. It circulated through the length and breadth of the land. It was read and laughed over by all classes; it was a sort of nine-days' wonder. But its real value was unknown; it was soon forgotten, and it led to nothing. All the profits he reaped from it hardly sufficed to keep the wolf from his door. But the blindest of all were those who ought to have been shrewdest. To us nowadays it seems unutterably strange, that an age of great wits should have failed to recognize the worth of *Don Quixote*, and to acknowledge that the man who wrote it was the greatest of them all. It was envied by some for the stir it created; it was carped at and deprecated by others; it was understood by none. And so it remained for an age after, until the chorus of praise that rang through Christendom came echoing slowly back to the land of its birth, and revealed to the Spaniards what a priceless treasure they possessed. It was with perfect right, then, that Cervantes in his own day puts these words into Mercury's mouth:—

> Thy works, through all the world in every part,
> Which Rozinante on his crupper bears,
> Are known, and stir to strife the envious heart.

The records of the period are so scanty and void of detail, that we can hardly appreciate the full truth of this. There is one little sentence, however, in a letter of Lope de Vega's lately brought to light, which, though a small straw, may show how the wind blew. It reads thus: "There are many poets in labour for the coming year; but none so bad as Cervantes, or so stupid as to praise *Don Quixote!*"

If the man who was glorified as the "Phœnix of Spanish wits," and Commander-in-chief, *par excellence*, of the army of poets, could say this, we can imagine what part the subalterns would play. It was certainly one of Lope's clique, whether the Dominican Aliaga or some other, who at this very time played the scurviest part of all; who, under the name of Avellaneda, had the effrontery to produce a second *Don Quixote*, and withal, the ineffable meanness to gloat over the idea, that he was thereby depriving Cervantes of the profit he might surely count on from his second part. That such a public affront

Translator's Preface. xxvii

should be possible, in an enlightened Court, clearly shows in what esteem Cervantes and his works were held by the *élite* of his countrymen, and to what dire straits he was reduced. It was reserved for a noble Frenchman, who came at this time to the Court of Madrid, to pay him the finest, subtlest compliment that poor genius ever received : "If poverty constrains him to write, please God he may never have plenty, so that, remaining poor, he may enrich the whole world with his works!" It is the same sort of consolatory phrase that he himself puts into the mouth of Poesy, addressed to himself and all poets in like condition :—

> I give you wealth in hope, and not in hand;
> A guerdon rich, replete with highest cheer
> That all the realm of Fancy can command.

But the poverty of Cervantes, whatever might be its origin, was no hindrance to his gaiety. He ever wore it, as the Spanish gentleman wears his *capa*, with ease and grace and good humour. In what a merry, sprightly way does he make it the very framework of this Satire! Like a new Don Quixote, eager for a new sally, we see him (by a slight stretch of the imagination) set forth on his *Journey*, astride the haunches of Fate, the common hack of the Universe, as if it were a second Rozinante, its belly-bands bursting with joy at the thought of fresh adventure; while in actual fact he is trudging on foot along the weary road to Carthagena, in shabby garments, with wallet on his back, whose only provender is a small loaf and eight maravedis' worth of cheese! He waves a sarcastic adieu to Madrid, that stony-hearted stepmother of the poets, at whose doors he declines to be found one day dead. He meets with a smile the mocking raillery of Mercury:—

> O Adam of the poets, O Cervantes!
> What wallets and attire be these, my friend,
> Which plainly manifest thy wit but scant is?

He has a smart repartee ready for the grave irony of Apollo, who tells him that all the laurel-shaded seats are bespoken, and it behoves him to take seat on his cloak:—

> My lord, it hath escaped you quite, I fear,
> That I possess no cloak!

And so throughout the whole tale. If our readers would have a picture of Cervantes, the poor, light-hearted son of genius, we commend to them the portrait with which we have ventured to adorn this book. The common portraits, whose authenticity is not established, represent him as a gallant of the period, arrayed in rich garments of rustling silk, and bestarched ruff, like a second Pancracio de Roncesvalles. But this is a veritable effigies of the *Viajero*, half-sailor, half-landsman, who did good service to the State both on sea and land. His felt hat and homely jerkin show him as he always was—in his working dress. And the face withal is a noble one. The large, sparkling eyes, the well-proportioned nose, slightly curved, the thin, sharply-cut lips, with just a shade of dreamy melancholy resting on them, which seem ready at any moment to flicker with humour or curl with irony, bring before us in a very real way at once the Cervantes as described by himself, and the Cervantes of our fancy. Without regard at present to the genuineness of the portrait, but with simple regard to propriety and the truth of things, we feel inclined to place beneath it part of the inscription which the poet himself attached to his own sketch in pen-and-ink: "This is the portrait of him who made the *Journey of Parnassus* in imitation of that of Cesar Caporal of Perugia: he is commonly called Miguel de Cervantes Saavedra; he was many years a soldier; and for five and a half a captive; during which he learned to have patience in adversity!"

Such was Cervantes in his outward low estate, as revealed by himself: but he has something also to tell us of his peculiar genius, which constituted the inner glory of his life. He gives us to know, that in early life his eyes were greeted by the sight of a divine vision, so beautiful and unearthly that it haunted him ever afterwards. It was none other than the vision of that heavenly maid, True Poesy, whom he describes with such rapturous eulogy and wealth of phrase in the fourth chapter of this work:—

> In rear of these, there came at length along
> A wondrous being, radiant as the light
> The sun emits amid the starry throng!
> The highest beauty pales before her sight,
> And she remains alone in her array,
> Diffusing round contentment and delight;
> She looked the likeness of Aurora gay
> When, 'mid the roses and the pearly dew,
> She wakes to life and ushers in the day;
> The garments rich, and jewels bright of hue
> Which gemmed her person, might hold rivalry
> With all the world of wonders ever knew.

And this "holy maid of loveliness complete," *Santa hermosisima doncella*, met perhaps unawares on the banks of his own Henares, as Burns met the Scottish muse near the banks of Doon, was no mere casual visitant. She followed him ever after, throughout his whole career, growing to his fancy brighter and more enchanting as years went on, until at length he loved her with a measureless passion—even to idolatry. And she, in turn, lit up within his bosom the never-dying flame of genius, inspired his thoughts and works, and made his life, that was outwardly so cheerless and loveless, a well-spring of inward gaiety.

This is perhaps too sentimental a way of putting the

matter, but it is in effect Cervantes' own. According to our way of thinking, this Parnassus-Journey exists mainly for the sake of the fourth chapter, planted in the centre of it. Therein, before Apollo and the Muses, and the congregation of his brethren, seated complacently beneath the laurels, myrtles, and oaks, while he must stand on foot, he delivers an oration such as poet never ventured on before. His words have no peculiar modesty—he claims to stand apart from the common herd. He claims to be the man, "who in creative power surpasseth many." He recites before them the scanty but precious roll-call of his writings, beginning with his romantic *Galatea*; including his *Novels*, the models of all coming fiction; his peerless *Don Quixote*, the medicine for all time of minds diseased; and winding up with the philosophical *Persiles*, which in his opinion was to crown the whole. Immediately thereafter he introduces that sublime vision of True Poesy, which to him was the embodiment of earthly beauty, truth, and purity—the sum and quintessence of human good ; as if to say to his countrymen, and through them to the world: "'These are the works by which I shall henceforth be known, and this is the divine power that inspired each and all of them, from first to last, believe it who may !" No doubt in all this there is a certain air of defiance and self-assertion ; and he had even the hardihood, a few pages before, to call on Mercury to authenticate the same:—

> For not in vain is Sire Apollo's dower
> Of gifts to thee, the rare inventor's art,
> The supernatural, instinctive power.

Many of his biographers are profuse in their apologies for such immodest boasting. But what need? Cervantes was no braggart. He believed his words to be true then; the world believes them now; and, moreover, he had to tell the truth to an unbelieving generation, who were only too ready to take his poor and low condition as the measure of his genius.

We take this fourth chapter, then, to be a kind of personal manifesto. But it is not a mere piece of self-laudation. He had arrived at a time of life (he was now sixty-seven years of age) when mere vanity or lust of fame have little sway. He was conscious of possessing a higher gift than most of his fellows, and he feels free to proclaim it. But he knew besides that his ideal of perfection was nobler than theirs, and this he would hold up in his last years as a mirror to his fellow-poets, even at the risk of self-glorification. For he was much concerned about the state of his country's literature. Strange to say, his own intellect was clearer and his fancy brighter in the three last years of his life, than ever they had been before. His *Novels*, the second part of his *Don*

Translator's Preface. xxxiii

Quixote, his *Persiles*, all concentrated within this short space, are sufficient to immortalize him. They show him in the very strength of his genius; they manifest also the exceeding loftiness of his aims. Of his Novels he affirms: " One thing I feel bold to say: that if there was a shade of possibility that these novels might excite one evil desire or fancy in the minds of their readers, I would rather cut off the hand that wrote them than give them to the public!" Of the others he might have said the same with equal truth. That ideal of beauty, truth, and purity, which first inspired him, remained with him to the last. It is this he would fain leave as his best legacy to his country. He had already done good service in finally ridding the land of the polluting books of chivalry. But there were powers for evil in the State even more potent than they. The stage had now unbounded sway: their romances and ballads had been for ages the very life-blood of the people. If these became corrupt and defiling, the nation itself was doomed to quick decay. It was therefore with no little concern that he heard it proclaimed by the brilliant wits who ruled the stage, and the masters of song who delighted the people, that the pleasure and tastes of the vulgar were their pleasure and taste, and that the true art of the poet was the art of pleasing. These were the doctrines of Lope and his school, and the results had been disastrous. There was no pure standard of taste in the land: the blind followed their blind leaders. It is no wonder that the old Cervantes, whose whole life had been a striving after art in its noblest form, should feel his spirit stirred within him at the sight of such rank idolatry. So like another Paul, in another Athens, he proclaims to the enlightened wits of Madrid that the gods they were worshipping were false gods, things of wood and clay, Mammon and Vain-glory. He tells them that the image of True Poesy, which had been the strength and glory of his own life, was the only worthy object of their worship: and with a power and authority which he could wield when he chose, he calls on all poetic pretenders, the polluters of the stage and the defilers of the wells of song, who had become the pests and plagues of the nation, to confess their follies, and bow down before that "holy maid of virgin beauty," or—die in their sins! *O sancta simplicitas!* It is the old rôle of Don Quixote and his peerless Dulcinea over again: "Sir Knight, if thou confess not that the matchless Dulcinea del Toboso exceedeth in beauty thy Casildea de Vandalia, thou diest!"

It needed not the wit of Cervantes to see the hopelessness and also the humour of the situation; that he, single-handed, should dare the unequal combat with Fashion, folly, self-seeking, and presumptuous ignorance. Others, like Artieda and Barahona de Soto, men of true discernment, had tried to cope with the degraders of art, but none took the matter so much to heart as Cervantes. And so with a melancholy weariness, born of poverty and hard toil, he throws himself down one day " worn and shattered on his bed," in his "old and sombre home," and dreams a dream—this mirthful dream of the *Journey to Parnassus;* where all his lovings and longings are realized, where the destruction of the False and the triumph of the True, and the reinstatement of Poesy on her rightful throne, are all gloriously achieved —in an allegory !

We leave it to our readers to appreciate at their worth the various incidents of the tale : the gay, fantastic, rhythmic ship that ploughs the Italian and Grecian seas, with its living freight of the good and gifted, bound with fair wind to Parnassus ; that other ship of bulk immense, crammed, poop to prow, with middling poets, tawdry merchandise fit for Calicut or Goa, that excites the wrath of Neptune and the pity of Venus; the dazzling vision of True Poesy ; the weird dream of Vain-glory ; and finally the famous Battle of Parnassus, prototype of all " Battles of the Books : " whose merry sounds of victory were reechoed in Spain from the mountains of Guadarrama, and caused Pisuerga to smile, and Father Tagus to laugh, as he rolled down to the sea his sands of gold. All these seem to us instinct with the same humorous fancy that was then engaged in discovering the impossible island of Barataria, and breathing life and spirit into Clavileño, that wondrous wooden steed. But if these content them not, we trust they will be charmed with the living portraiture of the Hero himself, that poor son of genius, so mirthful in his poverty, so proud of his creations, whom repentant Spain has now placed on a higher throne than the " rare inventor" himself ever dreamed of.

While such is our estimate of the worth of this satirical poem, it is well to warn our readers that this is not the general opinion. Mr. Ticknor, the highest authority on Spanish literature, very curtly declares: "This poem of Cervantes has little merit." He concedes that some of the episodes are of interest, but on the whole his verdict is unflattering. We cannot deny that this opinion is almost warranted by the little interest which the poem has hitherto excited. It was first published in Madrid in 1614, and passed through but one edition. A reprint was issued at Milan in 1624, and this sufficed for the wants of the Spanish colony in Italy. It was never afterwards published in a separate form. None of the pirating publishers in Valencia, Barcelona, or Medina del Campo, who reprinted Cervantes' other works by the

Translator's Preface. xxxvii

thousand, seem to have thought it worth reproducing; and the same may be said of their brethren in Lisbon and Brussels. More than a hundred years afterwards, in 1736, it was issued in company with the *Galatea*, and again in 1772. In 1784 it was brought out along with Cervantes' two newly-discovered dramas, *El Trato de Argel*, and the *Numancia*. This is the edition that had the widest circulation, and since then there has been no other. The translators also fought shy of it. Almost all the other works of Cervantes, except his Comedies, were translated into English, French, or Italian, very soon after publication; but the *Viaje* was completely ignored, until M. Guardia, in 1864, rendered it for the first time into very elegant French prose, with extreme accuracy, and was followed by Mr. Gyll, in 1870, who favoured the English public with a marvellously blundering version, in very indifferent blank verse. The present translation, therefore, is the third, and the only one in the original metre. As for the Critics, their opinion has been conflicting, but on the whole adverse. They have either passed it by with a contemptuous shrug, or have dropped on it that faint praise, which is proverbially damnatory. The only critic of note, who has shown a hearty appreciation of its worth, is Bouterwek, and we give his opinion as a counterpoise to that of Ticknor: " Next to

Translator's Preface.

Don Quixote it is the most exquisite production of its extraordinary author. . . . The poem is interspersed throughout with singularly witty and beautiful ideas, and only a few passages can be charged with feebleness or languor. It has never been equalled, far less surpassed, by any similar work, and it had no prototype." The Spaniards themselves have been the greatest sinners in their neglect of the book. It seems to have been quite forgotten till Mayans, in his *Life of Cervantes*, prefixed to Lord Carteret's splendid edition of *Don Quixote*, 1738, took the cream of it, to eke out the scanty records then existing for a good biography. Since that time it has been extensively used as a sort of quarry of building materials for the same purpose, and little scintillating fragments of it may be found in every Memoir. So neglected had it been, that no one knew till lately that the editor of the 1784 edition had altered its name, from *Viage del Parnaso*, to *Viage al Parnaso*. The real title was first restored to it in the *Biblioteca de Autores Españoles*, 1864. But even that famous " Library " does not contain the piquant little Sonnet, " The Author to his Pen," which is one of the gems of the book, but was then unknown.

The reason of such neglect seems to be, that the Spanish authorities scarcely recognize this Satire as a poem at all, and appear to have grave doubts whether

Translator's Preface. xxxix

Cervantes can be regarded as a poet, in the ordinary sense of the word; or, if so, are not sure in what category to place him. Even during the lifetime of Cervantes this issue was pending. It is he himself who tells the story, that, when he went to the publisher Villaroel to bargain for the sale of his MS. Comedies, the worthy bibliopole informed him that a certain "titled" manager had whispered in his ear: "That much might be expected of Cervantes' prose, but nothing of his verse." Cervantes professed, in his own ironical way, to be greatly shocked by such an aspersion, but the opinion nevertheless was pretty general; and certainly the *Journey to Parnassus* was never thought to have settled the matter in his favour. Thus Sedano, in his *Parnaso Español*, 1768-72, never alludes to it, nor quotes from it; though he inserts the *Canto de Caliope*, which, with reverence be it spoken, displays more good nature than poetic power. Quintana, in his *Tesoro del Parnaso Español*, 1808, solves the matter by excluding Cervantes altogether from the ranks of the *élite*. Even in the present day, in the forty-second volume of the *Biblioteca de Autores Españoles*, we find the learned Adolfo de Castro heading one of his prefatory chapters with this inquiry: "Was Cervantes a poet, or not?" (*Cervantes, ¿ fué ó no poeta?*) He answers the question in the affirmative, and quotes numerous

d

little songs from the Comedies, and scraps of declamation from the *Numancia*, to prove his point, but gives not even the tiniest quotation from the *Viaje*. We thought to have gained fresh light on the matter, when we stumbled on a little modern tractate, by Luis Vidart, entitled, *Cervantes Epico Poeta;* but found only a grave argument to prove that *Don Quixote* is the Spanish *Iliad*, and Cervantes its Homer—in prose.

In fact, after patient research we have come to the conclusion, that the Spanish critics either do not think satire to be poetry, or do not think Cervantes' Satire to be poetical. It is certainly not for a foreigner to intervene in such a delicate affair, and decide what constitutes, or does not constitute, true Spanish poetry. Whether Cervantes comes up to the standard of purism in such matters as smoothness, melodious cadence, rich variety of rhymes or assonance, our Northern ears may not be sensitive enough to determine. Nor is this essential in the case before us. It may be, that the genius of Cervantes did not take kindly to the fetters of rhyme, or the rigid rules of art; but the spirit of " rare invention " which he declares to be the living principle of all poetic excellence, and of his own specially, is there in rich abundance; and that is sufficient. If we compare Lope de Vega's *Laurel de Apolo* with the *Parnassus-Journey*, which it was intended to rival, we feel how flat and flavourless become at length his ceaseless flow of sparkling words and exuberance of imagery, just for want of the divine spark of originality which distinguishes the other. The fresh nature of Cervantes is more precious than the sickly art of Lope.

But there is one part of the *Journey* which has been praised without a dissenting voice, viz., the *Adjunta* or Appendix, in prose. For purity of language, for piquancy of style, for rare quality of humour, it has been reckoned one of the masterpieces of Cervantes. And it is so. The sketch of Master Pancracio de Roncesvalles, slight though it be, is so inimitably portrayed that it may take a place, and no mean one, in the gallery of Cervantic portraits. That the whole conception is instinct with Quixotic humour need excite no surprise, when we consider that the mind which planned it was engaged at the very time in calling into being that unique character, the Governor of Barataria! This is proved to a demonstration by the fact, that the letter which Roncesvalles brought from Apollo, and the letter which Sancho Panza sent to his wife Teresa, from the Ducal palace, have for their dates the same year, the same month, and almost the same day of the month. Those who are curious may verify the fact at their leisure. In Duffield's translation, however, they will find an unfortunate misprint of 26th *June* for 26th July, 1614. The prologue to Cervantes' Comedies, published in 1615, furnishes the best commentary on the subject-matter of the Appendix. There our readers may learn how it fared with Cervantes, when he went to dispose of his Comedies to Villaroel, the publisher: "He paid me reasonably, and I gathered up my money pleasantly, without any low-comedy higglings or wranglings!" It may also interest them to know that the scurrilous Sonnet, enclosed in the letter taken in unwarily, and paid for, by his niece, Doña Constanza de Ovando, is still extant. It is supposed to have been written by one of the clique of Lope's admirers, or by the great man himself. It is worthy of a place amongst the *Amenities of Spanish Literature.*

The Dedication, Prologue, and Introductory Sonnet are also worthy of note for various reasons.

The Dedication has this peculiarity, that it is addressed to a young man, of whom nothing is known except that he was the son of his father, a personage holding an important post in the Holy Office. It is conjectured then, that Cervantes at this period of his life was reduced to such straits, that he thought it wise to place himself in this roundabout way under the protection of the higher powers.

Translator's Preface.

What is more certainly known is, that some cloud had come over his relations with his great patron and protector, the Count de Lemos. To this distinguished nobleman he had dedicated his Novels, published the year before; and his subsequent works, down to the very last of all, were also addressed to him. Why, then, this break in the connection? The Count, in 1610, had been sent as Viceroy to Naples, and had taken with him those two distinguished poets, the Argensolas, to found an Academy of Wits in that city. These brothers, early friends of Cervantes, had promised to secure for him some honourable post in the Court of the Viceroy; but nothing came of it, and hope deferred had made Cervantes' heart sick. In the third chapter of this Poem he gives his own account of the matter, in a very curious and humorous way. The dignified words with which he concludes are striking enough:—

> I hoped for much, when much protest they made,
> But it may be, that strange affairs and new
> Have caused them to forget the words they said.

Whatever might be the ground of coolness, it did not last; and Cervantes certainly bore no malice, for in this very poem we are assured that, out of the nine laureate wreaths adjudged by Apollo, three went to Naples; on whose brows to be placed may be easily conjectured.

The Prologue is distinguished by its oracular brevity; and for obvious reasons. To venture upon a critical review of existing poets was not only a novelty, but, as Cervantes well knew, a very hazardous undertaking. Just thirty years before he had attempted a similar ungrateful task in his *Canto de Caliope*, inserted in the *Galatea*, and the result, though his eulogies were uniform and unbounded, was not satisfactory. He felt that it would be true now, as it was then:—

> Some scowl on me, because I put them in,
> Others resolve, because I left them out,
> To make me feel the burden of my sin.

The best way, therefore, was to say little; and in a single ingeniously-worded sentence he contrives to convey the idea, that the compliments about to be bestowed were of such doubtful quality, that those excluded might hold themselves equally lucky with the elect. To be called a Homer or a Tasso might, under certain circumstances, be quite as depressing as to be ignored altogether. Even in the praises heaped on such men as Gongora, Herrera, and Lope de Vega, we do not feel sure that a "pinch or two of salt" is not mingled with the abounding sugar of compliment. That to Quevedo, however, seems as heartily sincere, as it is humorously conceived. It is this peculiar quality of Cervantic satire that makes the rendering of those crisp little sentences of praise or blame so difficult. To miss the point of a single word may alter the complexion of the whole.

The Sonnet almost explains itself. It is the utterance of Cervantes, for the time being lonely and isolated. There is a certain ring of defiance in it intended for his enemies, and just a shade of melancholy protest against the coldness of his friends. In curious corroboration of this, it is worth remembering that just at this very time (July, 1614) the spurious *Don Quixote* was passing through the press, and Avellaneda (whoever he might be) was giving the last caustic touches to his infamous preface, wherein occur these words: "Miguel de Cervantes is now as old as the Castle of San Cervantes, and so peevish through weight of years, that everything and everybody disgust him; and hath such a lack of friends, that when he wishes to adorn his books with turgid sonnets, he has to father them on Prester John or the Emperor of Trebizond, seeing he can find no person of title in Spain, who would not be offended that he should mouth his name." This gives the necessary touch of reality to the situation. Everyone knows how this anonymous libeller was absolutely extinguished by merciless laughter, in Cervantes' preface to the second part of his *Don Quixote*. The Sonnet, however, was suppressed while the *editio princeps* was passing through the press, and only part of the impression contains it. A floral woodcut supplies the place of the cancelled lines. Whether his own better second thoughts, or the advice of friends, conduced to this end, we know not; but certain it is that the Sonnet was reprinted in none of the subsequent editions, and passed out of the knowledge of Spanish critics. It found its proper place for the first time in the collected edition of Cervantes' works, 1863-4; and the notes of Sr. Barrera give an account of the collation he made of various copies of the poem in Madrid, establishing the above facts. The British Museum has two copies of the original edition, both of which contain the Sonnet. In the sonnetless copies the catch-word for it still remains at the bottom of the previous page— a standing memorial of a bit of curious history.

It may be of interest to indicate some of the sources of which Cervantes availed himself in this poem. Bouterwek says it had no prototype. This is true in the main, though Cervantes himself tells that his journey was fashioned after that of Cesare Caporali, of Perugia, an Italian poet of the school of Berni. Caporali was born in 1531, and died in 1601. In his youth he was passionately fond of reading and translating Horace. He was essentially a *bon vivant*, and throughout the seventy years of his life, so far as appears, he followed no more useful occupation than that of hanger-on in the houses of several noble families, where his sparkling talents and witty conversation made him always a welcome guest. He was a member of the Academy of Insensates, in Perugia, where he passed by the name of *Il Stemperato* (the Rake). To this Academy he contributed most of his poems, and, amongst others, the *Viaggio di Parnaso*. To his credit it may be said, that his poems are free from the gross licentiousness of his school. Spanish critics praise his versification as superior to that of Cervantes, but award to the latter the palm for superior invention. Cervantes, in fact, borrowed little from him except the title of his book, and the bare idea of such a romantic journey. Caporali's plan is altogether different from that of Cervantes, and is somewhat after this fashion. He embarks with his mule on board of a merchant vessel bound to Messina; thence he proceeds by way of Corfu to the Gulf of Corinth, and so to the foot of Mount Parnassus. There he finds crowds of poets, trying to scale the steep hill by the curious process of knitting MSS. into long cords, which they send whizzing to the summit, so as to attach them to some projecting rock; but their efforts are fruitless, and they are repelled by Disdain and other allegorical personages. Caporali is more fortunate, for he happens to have with him a passport signed by Ferdinando de Medici, afterwards Grand

Duke of Florence, which he carries on his breast, after the manner of the Algerine captives. At sight of this every barrier falls, and every gate is thrown open, and he finds himself on the summit in sight of the Temple of Apollo, with its four gateways, the Hebrew, Greek, Roman, and Tuscan. The entry to it is through several gardens. To explore these he takes for his guide Poetic Licence, who makes him leave his mule behind, lest the plants and flowers should be endangered, and says to him: "Let us enter: march boldly, and if thy feet play thee false, lose not thy head: say that this concerns thee not, and lay the blame on the correctors of the press!" In the first, or common garden, he meets his comrades of the Burlesque school, Berni, Lasca, Varchi, and others, who spend their time jovially. Thereafter he leaves Poetic Licence behind, and through the Elysian gate he reaches the place of noble delights, where Petrarch dwells with the other deities of the Tuscan Parnassus. This is the most delightful part of the Satire, and is worth perusing. While Caporali is gazing, awe-struck, on the wondrous scene, a mighty clamour is heard from without. He rushes back to find that a curious affair of love has arisen between an ass, the Pegasus of the bad poets, and his insulted mule. He intervenes, and begins to beat his enraged brute. She takes to her heels, he runs after, and, as he humor-

Translator's Preface. xlix

ously adds, he has run ever since, without being able to re-enter the Paradise of the Poets, or penetrate, as he wished, to the Sanctuary of the Muses. All this is sufficiently comic, but it is not the Comedy of Cervantes.

But there is a Spanish author to whom Cervantes is more indebted than to Caporali, viz., Juan de la Cueva. He was a distinguished playwright, epic poet, critic, and ballad writer of the latter half of the sixteenth century. A native of Seville, he published in that town, in 1587, a book of Romances, which is now excessively rare, but a copy of which is in the British Museum. It is entitled, *Coro Febeo de Romances Historiales*. It is divided into ten books, severally dedicated to Apollo and the Nine Muses. In the tenth book, dedicated to Calliope, occur two romances, which evidently suggested to Cervantes a number of his ideas. The first is entitled: "How the poets pursued Poesy, and what came of it." In this we have a most extraordinary description of the ragged regiment of, what Cervantes calls, "the seven-month poets, twenty thousand strong;" and also a curious speech of Poesy to the bad poets, which reminds one of the speech of Poesy to the victors of Parnassus, in the eighth chapter of this *Journey*. The second romance is more suggestive still. It is entitled : "How the poets stormed Parnassus, and captured it, and how Apollo and the Muses fled therefrom." This is no fight between the bad poets and the good, as with Cervantes, but a direct attack of the scurvy race against Apollo and the Muses. In fact it degenerates at the close into a fearful scrimmage. The poets let fly at Apollo their Ballad-books and Novel-books:—

> Cual le arroja el Cancionero,
> Cual le tira el Novelario.

Apollo seizes the trunk of a huge oak as a weapon of offence. The Muses ply the heads of the storming-party with sticks, and awful bloodshed ensues. But overwhelming numbers prevail, and the heights of Parnassus are stormed and won. Apollo, seeing "that all is lost and his Muses in danger, harnesses his four steeds, bids the Muses mount his car, and without more ado he wings his flight to heaven, and leaves Parnassus in the hands of the profane barbarians." Cervantes was in Seville when this book appeared, and no doubt enjoyed it and took note of it for further use.

There is another little book which we fancy must have been used by Cervantes, viz., the first Spanish translation of the Odyssey, by Gonzalo Pérez. It was published in Venice, 1553, under the title of *La Ulyxea de Homero*, but contained only thirteen books; the complete poem was issued at Antwerp, in 1556. It is a bald, unpretending translation; but clear, and

Translator's Preface. li

interesting for its quaint simplicity. It may well have found its way as a "crib" into the *Estudio* of Juan Lopez de Hoyos in Madrid, where Cervantes learned his "little Latin and less Greek." Be that as it may, there is no doubt that many portions of this *Journey*, and the third chapter especially, are modelled after the Odyssey. The passage of the straits between Scylla and Charybdis, with the humorous episode of Lofraso; the description of the heights of Parnassus, presenting a faint reminiscence of the gardens of Alcinoüs; the deep sleep during which Cervantes is transported from Parnassus to Naples; his entry into Madrid in the garb of a pilgrim; all these are incidents taken from the adventures of the great Grecian hero, and many of the phrases and similes used remind us of the language of Perez' version. For rapid, vivid description, for Homeric picturesqueness of incident, we commend this third chapter to our readers, as one of the most noteworthy and interesting in the book. The Spaniards have always lamented that Providence, which has been bountiful to them in other matters, has denied to their literature a great epic poem. Ercilla's *La Araucana*, though full of poetic beauties, is lacking in world-wide interest; the *Poema del Cid*, though a glorification of their national hero, is a fragment, and its language and versification, albeit racy and vivid, are antique and uncouth. Their last resource is in the *Don Quixote,* universal in its interest, and quite Homeric both in grasp and fancy, but this alas! is in prose. Might we suggest, that if they desire a first-rate burlesque Epic, a veritable humorous Odyssey, they have it ready to hand in this little poem of Cervantes, if they will only re-christen it, and call it: "*La Cervantea,* or the Journey of Cervantes in search of his proper place in the literature of his country." This, in fact, is the true aim and intent of the Satire, and as such it will never lack interest nor admirers.

The Spanish text which accompanies this translation is, in the main, that given in the *Biblioteca de Autores Españoles,* 1864, purged of its numerous misprints. We have collated it with that found in the collected edition of Cervantes' works, 1863-4, which professes to have corrections from the notes of the late learned Sr. Gallardo. The spelling is modernized, the punctuation is rectified, and a few alterations are made which the sense seems to demand, but otherwise the text is essentially that of the first edition of 1614. For valuable advice, and cordial assistance rendered in these matters, and in the interpretation of the obscurer passages, we have to acknowledge with gratitude our indebtedness to Don Pascual de Gayangos, the true "friend in need" of all English Cervantistas.

Translator's Preface. liii

With regard to the Title of the book, we have of course retained for the Spanish text that given by Cervantes himself, *Viaje del Parnaso* (altered in the edition of 1784 to *Viaje al Parnaso*), though that title seems a little inappropriate. *Viaje del Parnaso*, and the analogous titles, *Viaje del Jerusalen*, *Viaje de la Tierra Santa*, are expressive of the ordinary tour or round (*peregrinatio*) which pilgrims made on their visit to holy cities or places; but of such tour or peregrination there is little or no trace in the *Journey* of Cervantes. It is simply a journey, partly by sea and partly by land, to Parnassus for a definite object, the extermination of the bad poets. We have therefore thought it better to translate it into English, not by *Journey of Parnassus*, which would be vague and equivocal, nor by *Tour of Parnassus*, which would be misleading to English readers; but by *Journey* to *Parnassus*, which expresses with sufficient accuracy the main contents of the book. Mr. Duffield authoritatively informs us that *Travels in Parnassus* is the only correct title of the book. How he arrives at this conclusion he does not tell us. It has the double defect of being at once a mistranslation and a misnomer. *Travels in Vesuvius* would be quite as intelligible as *Travels in Parnassus*, and much more feasible.

Finally, it has been our endeavour to present to

English readers a readable and enjoyable version of this much-neglected Satire. We have striven, as far as possible, to stick to the letter of the text, and to preserve its spirit always. It has been our aim above all to imitate the easy, unconstrained, yet subtle style of the great master of modern humour. If there be shortcomings in this respect, it has not been through want of patient endeavour; but, unfortunately, such gift is not the fruit of effort. Cervantes himself tells us (*Don Quixote*, Part II., ch. 62) that he has but a poor opinion of translators in general; that the art of translating from easy tongues implies no great amount of wit, or gift of language; but he at the same time throws them this little crumb of comfort, that they might easily be employed in much worse and less profitable occupations.

As this translation was undertaken mainly for the purpose of allowing English readers to judge of the life, character, and aims of Cervantes under the light which he himself has given, we think this a fitting place to say a word or two on certain theories that have been lately broached concerning them, and especially by Mr. Duffield in the preface to his new translation of *Don Quixote*. Of the merits of this translation we would fain speak with all respect, as we had much to do with it in various ways. It is fairly accurate, and is purged of much of the

Translator's Preface.

grossness of former versions, and for these two good things we are thankful. If it had been purged likewise of the added archaisms, which are so profusely scattered over it, we should have been more thankful still. As it is, we feel sometimes, on travelling through it, as if we were jolting over some old, rough, rutty country road, instead of bounding over the smooth, easy-going, delightful Cervantic highway. But its most serious fault is its over-accentuation of the humour of the book. Whoever knows anything of the peculiar quality of Cervantic humour will feel, that there is a certain limit of reserve (difficult to define) over which it is quite fatal to pass. When we find, therefore, the somewhat vulgar eccentricities of the translator blended (as they constantly are) with the glorious extravagances of the Knight and Squire, we feel in a sort of quandary, and are tempted to ask, in no very good humour: "Is this the glory of Mambrino's helmet, or is it the glitter of the barber's basin?" In short, it is a sensational translation, the worst luck that could befall a classical masterpiece.

But what concerns us most is, that the translator has carried this overstrained, sensational manner of his into his estimate of the purpose of Cervantes in writing *Don Quixote*. We are no longer, it seems, to look upon it as a book of pleasant pastime, as this *Journey* tells us it is; nor merely as a book designed to replace and exterminate certain bad, corrupting books, as Cervantes himself assures us; but as one of those peculiar books, whose real contents must be read between the lines. If we are very observant, and especially if we wear our instructor's spectacles, we shall find things, it may be little things, constantly cropping up, which clearly show that Cervantes was a great priest-hater, and had a deadly horror of priestly ways and things—was in fact somewhat of a freethinker in matters ecclesiastic, and would have been a thorough root-and-branch reformer, if only Fate, or the Inquisition, had allowed. 'Throughout the book he may, to our simple eyes, be only trying to excite innocent and wholesome mirth; but in reality he is slyly infusing certain little drops of explosive spirit which, at the proper time, will give a shake to the foundations of the church, and cause the throne of the Queen of Heaven to topple over! In fact, if we are to believe our guide, Cervantes is playing all the while the somewhat shady part of a Spanish Guy Fawkes.

In proof of all this we are gravely requested to observe, how Don Quixote's housekeeper implores the good Curate to sprinkle the Knight's enchanted library with holy water to exorcise the demons; how the New Amadis, doing penance in the Sierra Morena, knots the end of his shirt-tail to make a rosary withal;

Translator's Preface. lvii

and how Sancho Panza, in loving converse with his chum, Tomé Cecial, makes this remark, "*In* the sweat of our brows we eat bread;" thereby becoming heterodox, seeing he has been using the Spanish Reformers' rendering of a Bible phrase, whereas he ought to have said, "*With* the sweat," in good orthodox fashion. These, and sundry matters of like importance, excite Mr. Duffield's admiration for the daring contempt they show of Holy Church on Cervantes' part. It is a standing wonder to him, so he informs us, why the "cold-blooded and relentless myrmidons of the mangling Inquisition" did not burn the author of that pestilent book on the Plaza del Sol (?); and, may we be permitted to add, with the Reformers' Bible tied to his neck, and a leaf turned down at the noxious passage, "In the sweat!" In such fashion are we asked to believe, that the mighty wit of the reforming Cervantes pounced like an eagle on such small game as this!

But the utterance of Cervantes, which most excites his astonishment for its daring defiance of orthodoxy, is that placed in the mouth of Don Quixote when he says to Sancho: "We cannot all be friars; and many are the ways by which God carries his own to heaven." We also rub our eyes in astonishment, and ask ourselves what awful mystery underlies this plain theological truism, to which the Pope of Rome himself might nod a grave assent. As Mr. Duffield does not seem to comprehend the plain sense of plain words, we offer him a Spanish Commentary of the period, which may clear his vision. While lately reading Guillen de Castro's *Mocedades del Cid*, we lighted on the following lines, which are not only pat to the point, but quaint and beautiful in themselves. They are put in the mouth of the Cid, on his pilgrimage to Santiago, in answer to the jeerings of his fellow-pilgrims, for appearing in the gay attire of a knight :—

CID *loquitur:*

Precious boon to mortals given,
 God, whose guiding hand is o'er us,
 Sets a thousand roads before us,
Leading each and all to Heaven!

Whoso, in this world of vision,
 Would as pilgrim safe be guided,
 Hath to choose the path provided
Best befitting his condition.

So, with honest soul and good,
 And the light of Heaven upon it,
 May the Cleric don his bonnet,
And the Friar wear his hood.

'Neath his cloak of double plies
 May the sturdy ploughman burrow,
 And it may be thro' his furrow
Strike a straight road to the skies.

Translator's Preface.

And the Soldier-Knight mayhap,
  If his aims be good and pure,
  With his golden garniture,
And with feather in his cap,

Will, if so he keep the road,
  On his steed, with spur of gold,
  Gallant of celestial mould,
Reach at last the home of God.

Now with tears, and now with song,
  Suffering some, and fighting others,
  To the land where all are brothers
One by one they march along!

Guillen de Castro was a poor and neglected man when he died, but it was not for saying, "God has a thousand ways of leading men to heaven." He did not mean that these thousand ways lay outside of the Church. Neither did Cervantes, as our critic ignorantly insinuates. Such an idea was quite foreign to their Spanish minds; they had no occasion to speculate upon it, or if they did they kept their speculations to themselves.

But does not the author of these childish attempts to prove Cervantes to have been a covert sceptic, or a sort of glorified Tom Paine, see that in proving this he is proving too much? He is simply demonstrating that Cervantes was a hypocrite, and his life a lie. Has he never read the glowing account which Doctor Antonio de Sosa gives as to his religious bearing in Algiers, when his character was being moulded and settled for life? He claims to have read *Don Quixote* twenty times, has he ever read *Persiles and Sigismunda* once? That book, written when the hand of death was upon Cervantes, proves him to have been to the last the good Catholic and simple Christian, that Doctor de Sosa affirms him to have been thirty-six years before. To tell us, moreover, that the secret of his poverty was, that he was hunted down by the clergy as the enemy of their order and faith, is simply to tell us to shut our eyes to the light. Let us take the following plain facts from the closing years of his life.

It was a priest, in the person of the licentiate Marquez Torres, who, in his official censure of the second part of *Don Quixote*, bestowed on him and his works, from a Christian point of view, the most glowing and hearty eulogium he ever received in his lifetime. It was a priest, in the person of the Cardinal Archbishop of Toledo, who saved him from starvation, and made his last hours peaceful. It was to this benefactor that Cervantes addressed the following touching letter, which has only lately come to light:—
" A few days ago I received the letter of your most illustrious Grace, and therewith new favours. If the malady under which I labour could be cured, the repeated proofs of favour and protection, which your

lordship dispenses, would suffice for that purpose. But the end advances so rapidly, that I think it will soon be over with me, but not with my gratitude. May God our Lord preserve you as executor of so many holy works, that you may enjoy the fruits thereof in His holy glory." This is dated, Madrid, twenty-sixth March, 1616; a month before his death. And, finally, it was a *Tercero* brother who laid the only wreath, save one, that was placed upon his tomb. It has generally been reckoned a very poor, unworthy one; but the simple brother gave his best, while the men of light and leading gave nothing! It is thus entitled:—

D. Francisco de Urbina to Miguel de Cervantes:
A famous Christian genius of our day:
Whom the members of the Third Order of St. Francis carried
to his grave, with uncovered face, as one
of their brethren.

EPITAPH.

Tread gently, O thou passer-by,
  This is the rare Cervantes' shrine;
His body 'neath the earth doth lie,
  But not his name, for that's divine.
His earthly pilgrimage is sped,
But not his fame, nor works are dead;
  As pledge whereof he had this grace,
That when he sallied forth from this
To find the world of endless bliss,
  He journeyed with uncovered face.

So much for the clerical rancour which was showered on Cervantes. As for the attitude which he in turn assumed towards the Church and Ritual of his country, it is perhaps not generally known, that the last long poem he wrote was a Hymn in praise of the Virgin, and the last sonnet that dropped from his pen was in honour of Christian Rome. They are to be found in the *Persiles and Sigismunda*, but not in the castrated English versions, from which they have been quietly dropped. They are not the finest specimens of his genius, but they are characteristic. The Hymn to the Virgin breathes the subtle essence of mystical theology. It is too long to quote, but the following stanza may show its spirit:—

> Justice and peace to-day in thee unite,
>   Most blessed Virgin, and in loving trust
> The kiss of peace they give with fond delight,
>   Pledge of the advent of the King august.
> Thou art the Dawn that ushers in the light
>   Of that pure Sun, the glory of the just,
> The sinner's hope and stay, the gentle breeze
> That soothes to rest the old tempestuous seas.

The Sonnet, striking in itself, is more striking still for the curious lines which follow it :—

> O powerful, grand, thrice-blessed, and passing fair
>   City of Rome ! To thee I bend the knee,
> A pilgrim new, a lowly devotee,

Translator's Preface. lxiii

> Whose wonder grows to see thy beauty rare!
> The sight of thee, past fame, beyond compare,
>   Suspends the fancy, soaring though it be,
>   Of him who comes to see and worship thee,
> With naked feet, and tender loving care.
> The soil of this thy land which now I view,
>   Where blood of martyrs mingles with the clod,
>   Is the world's relic, prized of every land;
> No part of thee but serves as pattern true
>   Of sanctity; as if the City of God
>   Had been in every line its model grand!

The curious words that follow are these: "When the pilgrim had finished reciting this sonnet, he turned to the bystanders and said: 'A few years ago there came to this holy city a Spanish poet, a mortal enemy to himself and a disgrace to his nation, who made and composed a sonnet, reviling this illustrious city and its noble inhabitants; but his throat will pay the fault of his tongue, should they catch him. I, not as a poet, but as a Christian, as if to make amends for his crime, composed what you have heard.'" The romance of *Persiles and Sigismunda* has never yet been well translated, nor adequately interpreted. Perhaps the critic, who has so ignorantly mistaken the character of Cervantes and made him pose before the British public as a priest-hater and iconoclast, may, like the pilgrim poet, *en discuento de su cargo*, undertake the work. We warn him, however, that at the end of the fifth chapter of the fourth book, he will find a full exposition of the Catholic creed of Cervantes, which, for beauty of expression and sonorousness of language, will tax his powers, but will also tend to his enlightenment.

But enough on this point. We are not greatly concerned to prove that Cervantes was a good Catholic. Our Scottish proclivities might have inclined us in the contrary direction, had the truth of things warranted. We are content to know that he was an upright and honest man, whose religion was simply the creed of his country and his comrades; a part of his second nature; never obtrusive, never bigoted, but always sincere. The great avocation of Cervantes was that of a man of letters. His own chief pride was to be ranked among the diviner order of poets, who have enriched the world with their creations. From this lofty elevation he was free to use the immense resources of his brilliant wit to strike at folly, vice, and ignorance, wherever he met them, in Church or State, or in the world of Literature; and through his laughter the world has grown merrier and wiser. But his wit was ever genial and void of malice:—

> My humble pen hath never winged its way
> Athwart the field Satiric, that low plain
> Which leads to foul rewards, and quick decay.

And, better still, amid all the keenest flashings of his

Translator's Preface.

humour, he had no covert designs; his irony might be subtle, but his aims were straightforward :—

> Whate'er betide, my steps are ne'er inclined
> Where travel falsehood, fraud, and base deceit,
> The total wreck of honour in mankind.

In whatever he did or wrote he remained true to the instincts of his own noble nature, and to the best traditions of his country and faith.

JAMES Y. GIBSON.

ADDENDUM.

OF THE PORTRAIT AND ITS PEDIGREE.

A portrait of Cervantes by Francisco Pacheco was for a long time a desideratum. Tradition will have it, that such a sketch was made by Pacheco during the residence of Cervantes in Seville (1587-1600?), and inserted by him in his famous portfolio, entitled: " Book of Description of genuine portraits of illustrious and memorable men: the likenesses and lives of all the most distinguished persons which Seville contained." After Pacheco's death this precious volume went a-missing, and its contents were supposed to have been dispersed, or destroyed.

In the Spring of 1864, however, that well-known Cervantista, Don José Maria Asensio y Toledo, of Seville, had the good luck to light on the much-coveted volume of MS. and drawings; but in a very imperfect condition. The original portfolio was

Of the Portrait.

known to contain a hundred and seventy sketches in black and red pencilling; but of these fifty-six alone remained, and the portrait of Cervantes was not amongst them. It contained, however, one portrait, that of Fray Juan Bernal, Father and General of the Order of Mercy, in 1601, which gave an unexpected clue to the spot, where a copy at least of the missing sketch might be found. The curious chain of evidence by which this is established, or supposed to be established, does infinite credit to the ingenuity, perhaps a little too imaginative, of Sr. Asensio. The whole details are set forth in his interesting brochure, entitled: " New documents to illustrate the Life of Miguel de Cervantes Saavedra, &c.—Seville, 1864." His arguments may be thus condensed:

1. In the Spring of 1850, while overhauling a roll of MS., belonging to Don Rafael Monti of Seville, entitled *Papeles curiosos*, he came upon one professing to be a *Narrative of Events in Seville from* 1590 *to* 1640, wherein he found the following important entry: " In one of the six pictures, painted in competition by Francisco Pacheco and Alonso Vazquez for the cloisters of the Convent of Mercy (Casa grande de Merced), is sketched the head of Cervantes, with other persons who had been in Algiers, and the picture represents the Fathers of Redemption, with other captives." The *Casa Grande de Merced* is

Of the Portrait. lxix

now the provincial Museum of Seville, and these six pictures are still to be seen on its walls. Two of them are signed with the initials of the respective artists. The one that most nearly corresponds with the description of the old chronicler is No 19, thus labelled: "S. Pedro Nolasco in one of the passages of his life." This Redemptorist Father and Saint, in company with another Father, is represented as embarking from Algiers in a small launch, for an off-lying vessel. Three Spanish captives, and a small lad, are lending assistance; while at the prow, with boat-hook in his hand to steady the launch, stands the *barquero*—a noble, striking figure—such a model boatman as the artist never found loitering on the quays of Seville. This picture is unsigned, but is proved to be Pacheco's by the following evidence:

2. In Pacheco's "Book of Description" there is attached to the sketch of Fray Juan Bernal, an account of his life and redemptive labours in Algiers; of the many captives he brought home with him to Seville; of his election as General of the Order in 1601; and of his death in the *Casa Grande de Merced* that same year. Pacheco narrates that he painted him after death: "He lay in a chapel of the cloister, where all the religious assembled, and I took his portrait. It is one of my *felicities,* as it is also one, that he himself had chosen me before any other for the

pictures of this cloister; and so, as in honour bound, I painted him to the life in one of them."

This portrait, painted under such peculiar circumstances, Sr. Asensio found, to his great delight, to be identical with that of S. Pedro Nolasco, in the picture (No. 19) to which we have referred. The face of the modern General was made to do duty for that of the older Father and Saint of the Order. The picture, therefore, is by Pacheco; its subject corresponds exactly with that mentioned by the old chronicler; and here, if anywhere, may we expect to find the alleged portrait of Cervantes; a transcript, probably, of the missing sketch.

3. If all this be true, the matter is narrowed almost to a point—to the identification of one out of *three* portraits in the picture. Sr. Asensio, with a due sense of the importance of the inquiry, assembled around him some of the most distinguished artists and littérateurs of Seville, and proceeded with them to solve the question on the spot. The artists decided at once, as artists only can, that all the heads in the picture were portraits. The Cervantistas, with the famous description of the prologue to the *Novelas* in their hands, compared the handiwork of Pacheco with the graphic delineation of Cervantes himself. After much discussion *pro* and *con.* they came at last to the unanimous verdict, that all the peculiar traits

Of the Portrait. lxxi

and lineaments of that piquant description were to be found, and found only, in the face of the noble *barquero*, who looks with such a keen and kindly eye on the embarcation of the Redemptorist Fathers. And so the question was settled to the satisfaction of the Sevilian experts; and Seville was declared to be the happy possessor of the noblest portrait of the noblest genius of Spain. How Cervantes himself would have revelled in the idea of such a solemn inquest on his likeness! What a subject for another piquant colloquy between Scipio and Berganza, the immortal dogs of Mahudes!

One of the company then assembled, D. Eduardo Cano, a distinguished artist, afterwards took a careful drawing of the head, which has been photographed, and circulated throughout the land, with much acclaim. Our etching is a faithful transcript of the drawing; except, perhaps, that the curve of the nose (the *nariz corva aunque bien proporcianada* of Cervantes,) is hardly so sharply defined as in the original.

These are the bare facts of this somewhat romantic search after Pacheco's missing portrait. The special pleadings of Sr. Asensio and his fellow-enthusiasts, as well as the sceptical criticisms of their opponents, we leave for the consideration of the curious. That the genuineness of the likeness is demonstratively proved we do not aver; that there is strong probability in its favour is sufficiently obvious. If absolute certainty be demanded, we must be content to remain without any portrait of Cervantes whatever.

The courtly likeness, tricked out in all the bravery of the period, which now adorns the walls of the Academy of Madrid—the fruitful parent of the countless progeny of engravings that circulate throughout the world—has a pedigree still more precarious. The artists of San Fernando have indeed declared it to be of the school of Carducho or of Cajes, in the reign of Philip IV.—a copy of a more perfect original—and presumably of that which Cervantes himself declared to have been painted by his friend and fellow poet, Don Juan de Jáuregui, of Seville. Its actual history, however, is somewhat perplexing. That it is a likeness of Cervantes at all depends mainly on the dictum of the dealer, F. Bracho, who (somewhere in the middle of the eighteenth century) sold it as such to the Conde del Águila, of Seville, and affirmed it to be the work of Alonso del Arco, an artist who died in 1700. The Count presented it to the Academy of Madrid to adorn their magnificent illustrated edition of the "Don Quixote;" and convinced that it was much older and more authentic than represented, they had it sumptuously

Of the Portrait. lxxiii

engraved, and presented it to the world in 1780. But, to make confusion worse confounded, this engraving, with such distinguished vouchers, was found to be almost a facsimile of the portrait prefixed to the illustrated London Edition (Lord Carteret's), published in 1738, just forty-two years before! As all the world knows, this likeness was avowedly a pure invention of the clever designer, Kent, who conjured it out of his own brain ; with nothing but the description of Cervantes to guide him. Dr. Oldfield, the editor, affirms that this was necessary, inasmuch as the whole of Spain had been ransacked for an authentic portrait, but without success. This perplexing mystery still awaits unravelment, and no doubt there has been hard swearing somewhere.

Madrid and Seville were among the seven cities that once contended for the glory of being the birthplace of Cervantes. The discovery of the baptismal register of Alcalá de Henares has settled that point for ever. They are now in friendly rivalry for the possession of the true likeness of Cervantes; the one swearing by Jáuregui, the other by Pacheco. The light of certainty rests on neither. But if a choice must be made (as we have had the privilege of seeing both), we feel tempted to affirm, that the weight of evidence, and the force of attraction, incline equally in the direction of Pacheco's noble *barquero*.

Of the Portrait.

This, at least, we may affirm with confidence, that no more admirable portraiture need be desired of the captive-poet who wrote the famous letter to Mateo Vazquez from Algiers; or of him who, when the gold of his beard had changed to silver (to use his own words), essayed the adventurous journey to Parnassus. In its homely garb, and manly bearing, it forms a perfect illustration of the mingled pride and modesty which characterize Cervantes' pithy speech to Mercury—the epitome, in fact, of his whole literary life:—

> My lord, I'm poor, and to Parnassus bound,
> And, thus accoutred, seek my journey's end!

In conclusion, to broach a kindred subject, may we remind our Spanish readers (if such there be) that the long-talked-of Memorial to Cervantes, on a scale of befitting grandeur, is still one of the *cosas de España?* A certain enthusiastic but critical Scotsman, while lately loitering on the *Plaza de las Córtes* of Madrid, and looking up at the puny statue, with its appendages, which affects to represent the grandest genius of Spain in the very face of its enlightened Parliament—and remembering at the same time, with no little pride, what a veritable poem in stone his own romantic town has created in honour of the Scottish Cervantes—could not help indulging in the following

Of the Portrait.

simple soliloquy, on the contrasted honours paid to national genius in

EDINBURGH AND MADRID.

To thee, Cervantes, Spain more glory true
    Owes, than to monarch, priest, or statesman vain;
    More wealth, than ever o'er the Spanish main
Her stately galleons brought from far Peru!
A true-born son of thine in him we view,
    Our Wizard of the North, whose teeming brain
    Did make poor Scotland rich, and struck the vein
Which drained the Old World, to enrich the New!
Scott sits, a King, beneath his Gothic shrine,
    And proud Edina guards the sculptured stone;
    Can grand Madrid afford no kinglier throne
For thee to grace, whose works she deems divine?
    O soul sublime! O name without a blot!
    Receive this tribute from a kindly Scot.

                    J. Y. G.

VIAGE
DEL PARNASO,
COMPVESTO POR

Miguel de Ceruantes

Saauedra

*Dirigido a don Rodrigo de Tapia,
Cauallero del Habito de Santiago,
hijo del señor Pedro de Tapia Oy-
dor de Cōsejo Real, y Consultor
del Santo Oficio de la Inqui-
ficion Suprema.*

Año   1614

CON PRIVILEGIO
EN MADRID

Por la viuda de Alonso Martin

JOURNEY TO PARNASSUS.

DEDICATORIA

A

D. RODRIGO DE TAPIA,

CABALLERO DEL HÁBITO DE SANTIAGO, HIJO DEL SEÑOR D. PEDRO DE TAPIA, OIDOR DEL CONSEJO REAL, Y CONSULTOR DEL SANTO OFICIO DE LA INQUISICION SUPREMA.

DIRIJO á vuesa merced este *Viaje* que hice *al Parnaso*, que no desdice á su edad florida, ni á sus loables y estudiosos ejercicios. Si vuesa merced le hace el acogimiento que yo espero de su condicion ilustre, el quedara famoso en el mundo, y mis deseos premiados. Nuestro Señor, etc.

MIGUEL DE CERVANTES SAAVEDRA.

DEDICATION

TO

DON RODRIGO DE TAPIA,

KNIGHT OF THE ORDER OF ST. JAMES, SON OF SEÑOR DON PEDRO DE TAPIA, AUDITOR OF THE ROYAL COUNCIL, AND ASSESSOR TO THE HOLY OFFICE OF THE SUPREME INQUISITION.

I DEDICATE to your Worship this Journey which I made to Parnassus, as one not ill-suited to your vigorous age, or to your praiseworthy and studious pursuits. If your Worship gives it the reception I expect from your noble generosity, it will become famous in the world, and my wishes be amply gratified. May our Lord, &c.

MIGUEL DE CERVANTES SAAVEDRA.

PROLOGO AL LECTOR.

Si por ventura, lector curioso, eres poeta, y llegare á tus manos (aunque pecadoras) este *Viaje*; si te hallares en él escrito y notado entre los buenos poetas, da gracias á Apolo por la merced que te hizo; y si no te hallares, tambien se las puedes dar. Y Dios te guarde.

D. AUGUSTINI DE CASANATE ROJAS.

EPIGRAMMA.

Excute cæruleum, proles Saturnia, tergum,
 Verbera quadrigæ sentiat alma Tethys.
Agmen Apollineum, nova sacri injuria ponti,
 Carmineis ratibus per freta tendit iter.
Proteus æquoreas pecudes, modulamina Triton,
 Monstra cavos latices obstupefacta sinunt.
At caveas tantæ torquent quæ mollis habenas,
 Carmina si excipias nulla tridentis opes.
Hesperiis Michaël claros conduxit ab oris
 In pelagus vates. Delphica castra petit.
Imò age, pone metus, mediis subsiste carinis,
 Parnassi in litus vela secunda gere.

PROLOGUE TO THE READER.

If haply, curious reader, thou art a poet, and this "Journey," should come (be it even stealthiwise) into thy hands, and thou find thyself inscribed therein and noted as one of the good poets, give thanks to Apollo for the grace he hath given thee; and if thou do not so find thyself, in like manner mayest thou give thanks. And God be with thee.

EL AUTOR Á SU PLUMA.

Pues veys que no me han dado algun soneto
   Que ilustre deste libro la portada,
   Venid vos, pluma mia mal cortada,
Y hazedle aunque carezca de indiscreto;
Hareys que escuse el temerario aprieto
   De andar de una en otra encruzijada,
   Mendigando alabanzas, escusada
Fatiga é impertinente, yo os prometo.
Todo soneto y rima allá se avenga,
   Y adorne los umbrales de los buenos,
   Aunque la adulacion es de ruyn casta;
Y dadme vos que este Viaje tenga
   De sal un panezillo por lo menos,
   Que yo os le marco por vendible, y basta.

THE AUTHOR TO HIS PEN.

To deck this frontispiece, since thou dost see
  No friend hath offered me a sonnet, none,
  Come thou, my ill-cut pen, and make me one,
If not so high-flown as it ought to be;
From grave anxiety thou'lt set me free,
  I need not then through court and alley run
  To beg eulogiums; for I'd rather shun
Such vain and humbling search, I promise thee.
Let rhymes and sonnets go, for aught I care,
  To deck the door-posts of the upper few,
  Though flattery is at best but common stuff;
And grant me that this "Journey" have its share
  Of pungent salt, at least a pinch or two,
  I warrant thee 'twill sell; and so enough.

VIAJE DEL PARNASO.

CAPITULO PRIMERO.

Un quidam caporal italiano,
   De patria perusino, á lo que entiendo,
   De ingenio griego, y de valor romano,
Llevado de un capricho reverendo,
   Le vino en voluntad de ir á Parnaso,
   Por huir de la corte el vario estruendo.
Solo y á pié partióse, y paso á paso
   Llegó donde compró una mula antigua,
   De color parda y tartamudo paso:
Nunca á medroso pareció estantigua
   Mayor, ni ménos buena para carga,
   Grande en los huesos, y en la fuerza exigua,
Corta de vista, aunque de cola larga,
   Estrecha en los ijares, y en el cuero
   Mas dura que lo son los de una adarga.
Era de ingenio cabalmente entero,
   Caia en cualquier cosa fácilmente
   Asi en abril, como en el mes de enero.

JOURNEY TO PARNASSUS.

CHAPTER I.

A certain Corporal[1], as I am told,
   Italian, and by birth a Perusine,
   In wit a Greek, and like a Roman bold,
Led by a whim, a worthy one, I ween,
   To mount Parnassus fain would set his face,
   To flee the court, its turmoil and chagrin.
Alone, on foot, he slowly reached a place
   Where an old mule[2] he bought him for the tour,
   Of steel-grey colour, and of jog-trot pace;
So gaunt a spectre ne'er met timid boor,
   Nor one less fit to carry weight along,
   Its bones colossal, and its action poor;
Short was its vision, though its tail was long,
   Lean were its flanks, and eke its hide more tough
   Than those which to an ancient targe belong;
Its wit and temper were of such rare stuff,
   That, be it April month or January,
   It fell to work right pleasantly enough.

En fin, sobre ella el poeton valiente
    Llegó al Parnaso, y fué del rubio Apolo
    Agasajado con serena frente.
Contó, cuando volvió el poeta solo
    Y sin blanca á su patria, lo que en vuelo
    Llevó la fama deste al otro polo.
Yo, que siempre trabajo y me desvelo
    Por parecer que tengo de poeta
    La gracia, que no quiso darme el cielo,
Quisiera despachar á la estafeta
    Mi alma, ó por los aires, y ponella
    Sobre las cumbres del nombrado Oeta.
Pues descubriendo desde allí la bella
    Corriente de Aganipe, en un saltico
    Pudiera el labio remojar en ella,
Y quedar del licor süave y rico
    El pancho lleno, y ser de allí adelante
    Poeta ilustre, ó al ménos manífico.
Mas mil inconvenientes al instante
    Se me ofrecieron, y quedó el deseo
    En cierne, desvalido é ignorante.
Porque en la piedra que en mis hombros veo,
    Que la fortuna me cargó pesada,
    Mis mal logradas esperanzas leo.
Las muchas leguas de la gran jornada
    Se me representaron que pudieran
    Torcer la voluntad aficionada,

On this our poet, riding valiantly,
    Did reach Parnassus, and Apollo there
    With beaming visage gave him welcome free.
When to his home alone he did repair,
    Without a plack, from this to t'other pole
    Fame bore the tale he told on wings of air.
I, who do toil and strain my being whole
    To shew, what Heaven's grace will not allow,
    The semblance of a poet's gracious soul,
Was minded greatly to dispatch mine now
    By post or through the air, and so to take
    And plant it on far-famed Oeta's brow;
Thence haply spying, through the tangled brake,
    Where Aganippe's charming current flows,
    I might take one short leap, and forthwith slake
My lips with rich sweet draughts, and in repose
    Might fill my paunch right full, and henceforth be
    A poet grand, or leastways grandiose:
But thousand stumbling-blocks appeared to me
    To bar the way, and made my purpose slack—
    A fruitless, powerless, senseless thing to see;
For in the load I bear upon my back,
    Which Fortune there has placed with heavy hand,
    I read the hopes which all fruition lack.
The leagues full many of the journey grand
    Might well have filled my bosom with dismay,
    And brought my darling project to a stand:

Si en aquel mismo instante no acudieran
   Los humos de la fama á socorrerme,
   Y corto y fácil el camino hicieran.
Dije entre mí: Si yo viniese á verme
   En la difícil cumbre deste monte,
   Y una guirnalda de laurel ponerme;
No envidiaria el bien decir de Aponte,
   Ni del muerto Galarza la agudeza,
   En manos blando, en lengua Rodamonte.
Mas como de un error siempre se empieza,
   Creyendo á mi deseo, dí al camino
   Los piés, porque dí al viento la cabeza.
En fin, sobre las ancas del destino,
   Llevando á la eleccion puesta en la silla,
   Hacer el gran viaje determino.
Si esta cabalgadura maravilla,
   Sepa el que no lo sabe, que se usa
   Por todo el mundo, no solo en Castilla.
Ninguno tiene, ó puede dar excusa
   De no oprimir desta gran bestia el lomo,
   Ni mortal caminante lo rehusa.
Suele tal vez ser tan lijera, como
   Va por el aire el águila ó saeta,
   Y tal vez anda con los piés de plomo.
Pero para la carga de un poeta,
   Siempre lijera, cualquier bestia puede
   Llevarla, pues carece de maleta.

Had not the fumes of Fame come in to play
    Their part, to make me realize my vow,
    And point me out a short and easy way:
I inly said: "Could I succeed but now
    Upon the top of that steep hill to stand,
    And press a laurel wreath upon my brow,
I'd envy not APONTE'S diction grand,
    Nor the acumen of GALARZA dead,
    With Rodomonte's tongue and woman's hand!"
But as at first we ever are misled,
    Urged on by my desire, my feet I gave
    The road, for to the wind I gave my head:
And so in fine, upon Fate's haunches grave,
    And perched upon its saddle with free-will,
    I made resolve the journey grand to brave.
If such a mount should men with marvel fill,
    Let him who knows not know, that it is used
    The whole world round, not merely in Castile;
No one can be, nor ever is excused
    From taking seat upon that wondrous brute,
    Nor mortal traveller has e'er refused:
At times 'tis wont to go so swift, and shoot
    Like shaft or eagle through the upper air,
    And then at times to jog with leaden foot;
But for the poet's travelling weight to bear
    The task is light, and any beast is good
    To carry it; for no valise is there.

Que es caso ya infalible, que aunque herede
    Riquezas un poeta, en poder suyo
    No aumentarlas, perderlas le sucede.
Desta verdad ser la occasion arguyo,
    Que tú, ó gran padre Apolo, les infundes
    En sus intentos el intento tuyo.
Y como no le mezclas ni confundes
    En cosas de agibilibus rateras,
    Ni en el mar de ganacia vil le hundes;
Ellos, ó traten burlas, ó sean veras,
    Sin aspirar á la ganancia en cosas,
    Sobre el convexo van de las esferas,
Pintando en la palestra rigurosa
    Las acciones de Marte, ó entre las flores
    Las de Vénus mas blanda y amorosa.
Llorando guerras, ó cantando amores,
    La vida como en sueño se les pasa,
    O como suele el tiempo á jugadores.
Son hechos los poetas de una masa
    Dulce, süave, correosa y tierna,
    Y amiga del hogar de ajena casa.
El poeta mas cuerdo se gobierna
    Por su antojo baldío y regalado,
    De trazas lleno, y de ignorancia eterna.
Absorto en sus quimeras, y admirado
    De sus mismas acciones, no procura
    Llegar á rico, como á honroso estado.

Yea, 'tis God's truth, that though a poet should
   Inherit wealth, he straightway doth incline
   To lose it, not increase it; 'tis his mood.
The reason of this fact I do divine,
   That thou, great Sire Apollo, dost infuse
   Into their minds a goodly share of thine;
And as thou dost not mingle, nor confuse
   The same with business matters of the day,
   Nor on the sea of commerce vile dost cruise;
So they, whate'er their themes, severe or gay,
   Concern them not with trade or balance-sheet,
   But o'er the spheres prefer to wing their way;
Limning, perchance, of Mars some bloody feat
   On foughten field, or else among the flowers
   The deeds of Venus, amorous and sweet;
Bewailing wars, or piping in Love's bowers,
   With them life passes like a dream of earth,
   Or as the gamblers spend the fleeting hours.
Poets are made of clay of dainty worth,
   Sweet, ductile, and of delicacy prime,
   And fond of lingering at a neighbour's hearth;
For e'en the wisest poet of his time
   Is ruled by fond desires and delicate,
   Of fancies full and ignorance sublime;
Wrapped in his whimsies, with affection great
   For his own offspring, he is not designed
   To reach a wealthy, but an honoured state.

Vayan pues los leyentes con lectura,
  Cual dice el vulgo mal limado y bronco,
  Que yo soy un poeta desta hechura :
Cisne en las canas, y en la voz un ronco
  Y negro cuervo, sin que el tiempo pueda
  Desbastar de mi ingenio el duro tronco :
Y que en la cumbre de la varia rueda
  Jamas me pude ver solo un momento,
  Pues cuando subir quiero, se está queda.
Pero por ver si un alto pensamiento
  Se puede prometer feliz suceso,
  Seguí el viaje á paso tardo y lento.
Un candeal con ocho mis.ª de queso
  Fué en mis alforjas mi reposteria,
  Util al que camina, y leve peso.
—Adios, dije á la humilde choza mia,
  Adios, Madrid, adios tu Prado, y fuentes
  Que manan néctar, llueven ambrosia.
Adios, conversaciones suficientes
  A entretener un pecho cuidadoso,
  Y á dos mil desvalidos pretendientes.
Adios, sitio agradable y mentiroso,
  Do fuéron dos gigantes abrasados
  Con el rayo de Júpiter fogoso.
Adios, teatros publicos, honrados
  Por la ignorancia que ensalzada veo
  En cien mil disparates recitados.

So let my patient readers henceforth mind—
    As saith the vulgar impolite and coarse—
    That I'm a poet of the self-same kind;
With snowy hairs of swan, with voice of hearse
    And jet-black crow, the rough bark of my wit
    To polish down Time vainly spends its force;
Upon the top of Fortune's wheel to sit,
    For one short moment, hath not been my fate,
    For when I'd mount, it fails to turn a whit;
But yet to learn if one high thought and great
    Might not some happier occasion seize,
    I travelled on with slow and tardy gait.
A wheaten-loaf, with eight small scraps of cheese,
    Was all the stock my wallet did contain,
    Good for the road, and carried with great ease;
" Farewell," quoth I, " my humble home and plain!
    Farewell, Madrid, thy Prado, and thy springs
    Distilling nectar and ambrosial rain!
Farewell, ye gay assemblies, pleasant things
    To cheer one aching bosom, and delight
    Two thousand faint, aspiring underlings!
Farewell, thou charming and deceitful site,
    Where erst two giants great were set ablaze
    By thunderbolt of Jove, in fiery might!
Farewell, ye public theatres, whose praise
    Rests on the ignorance I see becrown
    The countless follies of unnumbered plays!

Adios de San Felipe el gran paseo,
    Donde si baja ó sube el turco galgo
    Como en gaceta de Venecia leo.
Adios, hambre sotil de algun hidalgo,
    Que por no verme ante tus puertas muerto,
    Hoy de mi patria y de mi mismo salgo.—
Con esto poco á poco llegué al puerto,
    A quien los de Cartago dieron nombre,
    Cerrado á todos vientos y encubierto.
A cuyo claro y singular renombre
    Se postran cuantos puertos el mar baña,
    Descubre el sol, y ha navegado el hombre.
Arrojóse mi vista á la campaña
    Rasa del mar, que trujo á mi memoria
    Del heróico Don Juan la heróica hazaña.
Donde con alta de soldados gloria,
    Y con propio valor y airado pecho
    Tuve, aunque humilde, parte en la vitoria.
Allí con rabia y con mortal despecho
    El otomano orgullo vió su brio
    Hollado y reducido á pobre estrecho.
Lleno pues de esperanzas, y vacio
    De temor, busqué luego una fragata,
    Que efetüase el alto intento mio.
Cuando por la, aunque azul, líquida plata
    Vi venir un bajel á vela y remo,
    Que tomar tierra en el gran puerto trata.

Farewell, St. Philip's broadway of the town,[5]
    Where, as in Venice fly-sheet, I can know
    Whether the Turkish dog be up or down !
Farewell, some lordling's hunger, keen and slow ;
    For sooner than drop dead beside thy door,
    This day from country and from self I go ! "
At last I reached the port, with travail sore,
    To which the men of Carthage gave their name,
    Shut in from all the winds that scourge the shore :
Before whose clear renown and peerless fame
    Bow down whatever ports the sea doth lave,
    The sun illumes, or sailors make their aim.
And, as I cast mine eyes across the wave,
    The briny plain brought back to mind and heart
    The glorious action of Don Juan the brave ;
Wherein, with soldier's fire, and soldier's art,
    And valour of mine own, on that great day
    I bore a certain though a humble part ;
When, with a baffled rage they could not stay,
    And mortal spite, the haughty Ottoman
    Saw power and prestige shattered in the fray.
All hopeful, then, and fearless, I began
    To look about to find some frigate near,
    Wherein to carry out my lofty plan ;
When on the sea, so blue and silvery clear,
    I saw approach a barque, with sail and oar,
    Which right into the grand old port did steer.

Del mas gallardo, y mas vistoso extremo
De cuantos las espaldas de Neptuno
Oprimieron jamas, ni mas supremo.
Cual este, nunca vió bajel alguno
El mar, ni pudo verse en el armada,
Que destruyó la vengativa Juno.
No fué del vellocino á la jornada
Argos tan bien compuesta y tan pomposa,
Ni de tantas riquezas adornada.
Cuando entraba en el puerto, la hermosa
Aurora por las puertas del oriente
Salia en trenza blanda y amorosa;
Oyóse un estampido de repente,
Haciendo salva la real galera,
Que despertó y alborotó la gente.
El son de los clarines la ribera
Llenaba de dulcísima armonía,
Y el de la chusma alegre y placentera.
Entrábanse las horas por el dia,
A cuya luz con distincion mas clara
Se vió del gran bajel la bizarría.
Ancoras echa, y en el puerto para,
Y arroja un ancho esquife al mar tranquilo
Con música, con grita y algazara.
Usan los marineros de su estilo,
Cubren la popa con tapetes tales
Que es oro y sirgo de su trama el hilo.

Of all that Neptune's shoulders ever bore,
  More gallant and more sightly none, I wis,
  None that could rank beside it or before:
Yea, never on the main swam barque like this,
  Not even in the Armada's proud array,
  Which vengeful Juno whelmed in the abyss:
Not Argo's self, upon that famous day
  It went to fetch the fleece, was rigged so rare,
  Or with such wealth of grandeur made display!
As into port she sailed, Aurora fair
  Passed through the Eastern gates the world to cheer,
  With amorous locks and sweetly waving hair;
When lo! a loud report struck on mine ear,
  The royal galley giving welcome roar
  That woke the town, and filled the folk with fear.
The clanging sound of clarions filled the shore
  With sweetest harmony, wherewith did blend
  The merry songs of those who plied the oar;
The rosy Hours did on the day attend,
  Whose light a great distinctness and more clear
  Did on the barque and all its splendour send.
The men dropped anchor, and made fast their gear,
  And launched a spacious skiff on the calm sea,
  To sound of music, shouts, and lusty cheer.
With such array as sailors love to see
  They crowned the poop with carpets o'er and o'er,
  All woven with silk and gold embroidery;

Tocan de la ribera los umbrales,
    Sale del rico esquife un caballero
    En hombros de otros cuatro principales.
En cuyo traje y ademan severo
    Vi de Mercurio al vivo la figura,
    De los fingidos dioses mensajero.
En el gallardo talle y compostura,
    En los alados piés, y el caduceo,
    Símbolo de prudencia y de cordura,
Digo, que al mismo paraninfo veo,
    Que trujo mentirosas embajadas
    A la tierra del alto coliseo.
Vile, y apénas puso las aladas
    Plantas en las arenas venturosas
    Por verse de divinos piés tocadas;
Cuando yo revolviendo cien mil cosas
    En la imaginacion, llegué á postrarme
    Ante las plantas por adorno hermosas.
Mandóme el dios parlero luego alzarme,
    Y con medidos versos y sonantes,
    Desta manera comenzo á hablarme:
—¡Oh Adan de los poetas, oh Cervantes!
    ¿Qué alforjas y qué traje es este, amigo,
    Que así muestra discursos ignorantes?—
Yo, respondiendo á su demanda, digo:
    —Señor, voy al Parnaso, y como pobre
    Con este aliño mi jornada sigo.—

Soon as the wealthy skiff had touched the shore,
    There sallied forth a man of high degree,
    Whom four great chiefs upon their shoulders bore;
In whose attire, and gesture firm and free,
    Mercurius' living figure I divined,
    The envoy of the gods of fable he ;
With gallant mien, and bearing most refined,
    With wingèd feet, Caduceus in his hand,
    Symbol of prudence and of wit combined ;
It was the self-same paranymph so bland,
    Who, from the lofty Empyrean seat,
    Brought lying messages to many a land.
Scarce had I seen him plant his wingèd feet
    Upon the yellow sands, that smiled in glee
    The treading of such feet divine to greet,
When hundred thousand fancies came to me,
    As there I stood, and straightway I was fain
    To kneel before that form, so grand to see.
The spokesman god quick bade me rise again,
    And, in sonorous measured verse like Dante's,
    Began to parley with me in this strain :
" O Adam of the poets ! O Cervantes !
    What wallets and attire be these, my friend,
    Which plainly manifest thy wit but scant is ! "
I blandly said, that I might not offend :
    " My lord, I'm poor, and to Parnassus bound,
    And thus accoutred seek my journey's end ! "

Y él á mí dijo: ¡Sobrehumano, y sobre
　　Espíritu cilenio levantado!
　　Toda abundancia y todo honor te sobre.
Que en fin has respondido á ser soldado
　　Antiguo y valeroso, cual lo muestra
　　La mano de que estás estropeado.
Bien sé que en la naval dura palestra
　　Perdiste el movimiento de la mano
　　Izquierda, para gloria de la diestra.
Y sé que aquel instinto sobrehumano
　　Que de raro inventor tu pecho encierra,
　　No te le ha dado el padre Apolo en vano.
Tus obras los rincones de la tierra,
　　Llevándolas en grupa Rocinante,
　　Descubren, y á la envidia mueven guerra.
Pasa, raro inventor, pasa adelante
　　Con tu sotil disinio, y presta ayuda
　　A Apolo; que la tuya es importante:
Antes que el escuadron vulgar acuda
　　Demas de veinte mil sietemesinos
　　Poetas, que de serlo estan en duda.
Llenas van ya las sendas y caminos
　　Desta canalla inútil contra el monte,
　　Que aun de estar á su sombra no son dinos.
Armate de tus versos luego, y ponte
　　A punto de seguir este viaje
　　Conmigo, y á la gran obra disponte.

"O superhuman mind," he cried, "and sound,
   Raised high above Cyllenian spirit too,
   May fame and plenty aye with thee abound!
Thine is the answer of a soldier true,
   Of antique valour, testified aright
   To all by that maimed hand which now I view:
I know that, in the naval bloody fight,
   Thy left hand shattered lost the active power
   It once possessed, for glory of the right!
Yet not in vain is Sire Apollo's dower
   Of gifts to thee, the rare inventive art,
   The instinct which transcends the passing hour;
Thy works, through all the world in every part,
   Which Rozinante on his crupper bears,
   Are known, and stir to strife the envious heart.
Pass, rare inventor, subtle in affairs,
   Pass on before, and to Apollo lend
   Thy timely aid, so needful in his cares;
Before the vulgar squadron thither wend
   Of seven-month poets, twenty thousand told,
   Whose being is a riddle without end.
Already doth this useless rabble bold
   Throng all the paths and roads, to storm the hill
   Whose shade they are not worthy to behold.
So arm thee with thy verses and thy skill,
   And make thee ready to embark with me,
   And gird thee for the service with good will;

Conmigo segurísimo pasaje
  Tendrás, sin que te empaches, ni procures
  Lo que suelen llamar matalotaje.
Y porque esta verdad que digo, apures,
  Entra conmigo en mi galera, y mira
  Cosas con que te asombres y asegures.—
Yo, aunque pensé que todo era mentira,
  Entré con él en la galera hermosa,
  Y ví lo que pensar en ello admira.
De la quilla á la gavia, ¡oh extraña cosa!
  Toda de versos era fabricada,
  Sin que se entremetiese alguna prosa.
Las ballesteras eran de ensalada
  De glosas, todas hechas á la boda
  De la que se llamó Malmaridada.
Era la chusma de romances toda,
  Gente atrevida, empero necesaria,
  Pues á todas acciones se acomoda.
La popa de materia extraordinaria,
  Bastarda, y de legítimos sonetos,
  De labor peregrina en todo, y varia.
Eran dos valentísimos tercetos
  Los espaldares de la izquierda y diestra,
  Para dar boga larga muy perfetos.
Hecha ser la crujía se me muestra
  De una luenga y tristísima elegía,
  Que no en cantar, sino en llorar es diestra.

With me thy passage shall be safe and free,
 No pother needst thou make, nor question raise,
 About thy needful provender at sea ;
And to convince thee that I do not phrase,
 Come with me to my galley, and strange sight
 Thou'lt see, to fill thy fancy with amaze!"
I, though I deemed the whole fictitious quite,
 Went on with him into the galley fair,
 And saw what thrilled my senses with delight.
From keel to main-mast top, O wonder rare,
 A swarm of verses[7] formed the whole array,
 No single bit of prose did mingle there !
The port-holes were a curious compound gay
 Of Glosses, made to order and designed
 To grace Malmaridada's[8] wedding day;
The bank of oars was with Romances lined,
 A daring folk, but needful as a change,
 And fit for active work of every kind ;
The poop was of material wondrous strange,
 Of Sonnets[9] bastard and legitimate,
 Of cunning work withal, and varied range ;
Two Tercets, each of power exceeding great,
 Composed the stroke oars of the left and right,
 A wider oar-sweep to effectuate ;
The rowers' gangway came before my sight,
 Formed of a long-drawn Elegy and drear,
 Designed for wailing, not for song's delight ;

Por esta entiendo yo que se diria
   Lo que suele decirse á un desdichado,
   Cuando lo pasa mal, pasó crujía.
El árbol hasta el cielo levantado
   De una dura cancion prolija estaba
   De canto de seis dedos embreado.
El, y la entena que por él cruzaba,
   De duros estrambotes, la madera
   De que eran hechos clara se mostraba.
La racamenta, que es siempre parlera,
   Toda la componian redondillas,
   Con que ella se mostraba mas lijera.
Las jarcias parecian seguidillas
   De disparates mil y mas compuestas,
   Que suelen en el alma hacer cosquillas.
Las rumbadas, fortísimas y honestas
   Estancias, eran tablas poderosas,
   Que llevan un poema y otro á cuestas.
Era cosa de ver las bulliciosas
   Banderillas que al aire tremolaban,
   De varias rimas algo licenciosas.
Los grumetes, que aquí y allí cruzaban,
   De encadenados versos parecian,
   Puesto que como libres trabajaban.
Todas las obras muertas componian
   O versos sueltos, ó sextinas graves,
   Que la galera mas gallarda hacian.

So might I understand what strikes the ear,
    When sorrows on some wretch's head do pour :
    " He runs the gangway!" 'tis the phrase we hear:
The solid main-mast, that aloft did soar,
    Was fashioned of a stiff and prolix Lay,
    Six fingers deep, pitch-plastered o'er and o'er ;
It, and the lateen yard that crossed its way,
    Of hard dry Couplets, to the view did bring
    Their wooden substance with a clear display :
The parrels, prattling with the vessel's swing,
    Were Redondillas, and in rows arrayed
    To tinkle forth an easy rattling ring ;
The cordage was of Seguidillas made,
    Bright with a thousand fooleries and more,
    That titillate the soul in serenade ;
The prow-ribs, Stanzas honest to the core,
    Formed tablets large, and ponderous as could be,
    With this and t'other poem garnished o'er ;
The flags and streamers were a sight to see,
    That waved and fluttered with the moving air,
    Of varied rhymes, a trifle loose and free ;
The sailor boys, that flitted here and there,
    Seemed to me coupled verses in one stave,
    Though each did work with free and jaunty air;
The bulwarks were composed of Sextains grave,
    Or verses blank, and to the galley bright
    A stouter and more firm appearance gave !

En fin, con modos blandos y süaves,
    Viendo Mercurio que yo visto habia
    El bajel, que es razon, letor, que alabes,
Junto á si me sentó, y su voz envía
    A mis oídos en razones claras,
    Y llenas de suavisima armonia,
Diciendo:—Entre las cosas que son raras
    Y nuevas en el mundo y peregrinas,
    Verás, si en ello adviertes y reparas,
Que es una este bajel de las mas dinas
    De admiracion, que llegue á ser espanto
    A naciones remotas y vecinas.
No le formaron máquinas de encanto,
    Sino el ingenio del divino Apolo,
    Que puede, quiere, y llega y sube á tanto.
Formóle, ¡oh nuevo caso! para solo
    Que yo llevase en él cuantos poetas
    Hay desde el claro Tajo hasta Pactolo.
De Malta el gran maestre, á quien secretas
    Espías dan aviso que en Oriente
    Se aperciben las bárbaras saetas,
Teme, y envia á convocar la gente
    Que sella con la blanca cruz el pecho,
    Porque en su fuerza su valor se aumente.
A cuya imitacion Apolo ha hecho
    Que los famosos vates al Parnaso
    Acudan, que está puesto en duro estrecho.

Journey to Parnassus. 31

At length, with manners gentle and polite,
   Mercurius, seeing my inspection end,
   (Herewith thy praise, O reader, I invite,)
Took seat by me, and to my ears did send
   His voice with reasons forcible and fair,
   Wherewith the sweetest harmony did blend,
And said to me : " 'Mong matters that are rare
   And novel in this world, and strange to hear,
   Thou'lt see, if thou dost note and mark with care,
That such a barque, as thou beholdest here,
   Hath highest claims the reverence to command
   Of all the wondering nations far and near.
It sprang to being by no wizard's hand,
   But by divine Apollo's wit supreme,
   Whose will and power achieved a work so grand:
He fashioned it that I, though strange it seem,
   Should bear therein as many poets great
   As dwell 'twixt Tagus and Pactolus' stream.
Malta's grand master, who hath heard of late,
   From secret spies, that hordes of Eastern bands
   Sharpen their barbarous shafts for onslaught great,
In fear hath summoned from the neighbouring lands
   The Knights that bear the white cross on the breast,
   To gain the confidence such force commands ;
Like him, Apollo now hath given behest,
   All famous seers shall to Parnassus hie,
   Which stands this day beleaguered and distressed.

Yo, condolido del doliente caso,
    En el lijero casco, ya instruido
    De lo que he de hacer, aguijo el paso.
De Italia las riberas he barrido,
    He visto las de Francia y no tocado,
    Por venir solo á España dirigido.
Aquí con dulce y con felice agrado
    Hará fin mi camino, á lo que creo,
    Y seré fácilmente despachado.
Tú, aunque en tus canas tu pereza veo,
    Serás el paraninfo de mi asunto,
    Y el solicitador de mi deseo.
Parte, y no te detengas solo un punto,
    Y á los que en esta lista van escritos
    Dirás de Apolo cuanto aquí yo apunto.—
Sacó un papel, y en él casi infinitos
    Nombres vi de poetas, en que habia
    Yangüeses, vizcaínos y coritos.
Allí famosos ví de Andalucía,
    Y entre los castellanos vi unos hombres,
    En quien vive de asiento la poesía.
Dijo Mercurio:—Quiero que me nombres
    Desta turba gentil, pues tú lo sabes,
    La alteza de su ingenio, con los nombres.—
Yo respondí:—De los que son mas graves
    Diré lo que supiere, por moverte
    A que ante Apolo su valor alabes.—
    Él escuchó. Yo dije desta suerte.

I, looking on the case with pitying eye,
  Put on my wingèd cap, and learning plain
  What should be done, with quickened pace did fly;
I coasted all along the Italian main,
  The shores of France I saw, but did not land,
  My mission having sole respect to Spain;
But with this meeting, fortunate and bland,
  I'll bring to happy issue my affairs,
  And straight dispatch them with an easy hand.
Thou, though I see scant power in thy grey hairs,
  Shalt be the paranymph of my design,
  And rid me of the burden of my cares;
Set out, nor let delay be fault of thine,
  And to those written on this list convey
  The message of Apollo, line for line!"
He shewed the list; and 'mong the vast array
  Of poet's names I saw Yanguesians there,
  Coritos[10] too, and dwellers in Biscay;
Of Andalusians many a name and rare,
  And of Castilians saw I not a few
  Whose dwelling poesy delights to share.
Mercurius said: "This most distinguished crew,
  Since thou dost know them, pray, describe the same,
  And with their names their height of genius too."
I made response: "Of those of loftiest name
  I'll tell thee what I know, that thou may'st deign
  Before Apollo to exalt their fame."
He listened: and I answered in this strain.

CAPITULO II.

Colgado estaba de mí antigua boca
    El dios hablante, pero entónces mudo;
    Que al que escucha, el guardar silencio toca.
Cuando dí de improviso un estornudo,
    Y haciendo cruces por el mal agüero,
    Del gran Mercurio al mandamiento acudo.
Miré la lista, y vi que era el primero
    El LICENCIADO JUAN DE OCHOA, amigo
    Por poeta, y cristiano verdadero.
Deste varon en su alabanza digo
    Que puede acelerar y dar la muerte
    Con su claro discurso al enemigo,
Y que si no se aparta y se divierte
    Su ingenio en la gramática española,
    Será de Apolo sin igual la suerte;
Pues de su poesía al mundo sola
    Puede esperar poner el pié en la cumbre
    De la inconstante rueda, ó varia bola.

CHAPTER II.

Upon mine ancient lips all eager hung
   The speaking god, now mute and at his ease,
   For he who listens may not use his tongue;
When all at once I gave a potent sneeze,
   And, crossing me for that ill-omened feat,
   I set myself great Mercury to please.
I scanned the list;[11] and first upon the leet
   Came JUAN DE OCHOA the Licentiate,
   My friend as poet, Christian most complete;
In praise of such a man I can but state
   That from his clear discourse, a blade of might,
   The foe must meet a sure and speedy fate;
And should his genius well direct its flight,
   Now curbed by Spanish grammar, as I fear,
   Then would Apollo's fortune reach its height;
For with his poesy, that hath no peer,
   He well might gain the top of Fortune's wheel,
   And plant his foot upon its whirling sphere.

Este que de los cómicos es lumbre,
    Que el LICENCIADO POYO es su apellido,
    No hay nube que á su sol claro deslumbre.
Pero como está siempre entretenido
    En trazas, en quimeras é invenciones,
    No ha de acudir á este marcial ruido.
Este, que en lista por tercero pones,
    Que HIPÓLITO se llama DE VERGARA,
    Si llevarle al Parnaso te dispones,
Haz cuenta que en él llevas una jara,
    Una saeta, un arcabuz, un rayo,
    Que contra la ignorancia se dispara.
Este, que tiene como mes de mayo
    Florido ingenio, y que comienza ahora
    A hacer de sus comedias nuevo ensayo,
GODINEZ es. Y estotro que enamora
    Las almas con sus versos regalados,
    Cuando de amor ternezas canta ó llora,
Es uno, que valdrá por mil soldados,
    Cuando á la extraña y nunca vista empresa
    Fueren los escogidos y llamados:
Digo que es DON FRANCISCO, el que profesa
    Las armas y las letras con tal nombre,
    Que por su igual Apolo le confiesa:
Es DE CALATAYUD su sobrenombre.
    Con esto queda dicho todo cuanto
    Puedo decir con que á la invidia asombre.

With POYA, the Licentiate, now we deal,
    Who of all comic writers is the star
    Whose brilliant light no clouds can e'er conceal;
But as his mind is ever borne afar
    By quips, and quirks, and whimsies of the brain,
    He hath no stomach for the din of war.
Here DE VERGARA'S name is written plain,
    Third on the list; and if thou should'st decree
    To bear him to Parnassus in thy train,
He'll be a shaft, a javelin to thee,
    An arquebuse, a bolt, to cause dismay
    And force the hosts of ignorance to flee.
GODINEZ this; whose wit like month of May
    Is crowned with flowers, and who in novel style
    Brings forth new comedies to suit the day.
This other here, whose verses sweet beguile
    The souls of men, and from Love's flowing fount
    Draw tender thoughts that cause to weep or smile,
Is one, who'll for a thousand soldiers count
    When, summoned to the strange assault and rude,
    The called and chosen stand before the mount;
'Tis DON FRANCISCO DE CALATAYUD,
    Who both in arms and letters takes a pride,
    And holds them with such equal claim and good,
That great Apollo ranks him by his side;
    I've said enough, and all that I desire,
    That envy now her sombre head may hide.

Este que sigue es un poeta sánto,
   Digo famoso: MIGUEL CID se llama,
   Que al coro de las musas pone espanto.
Estotro que sus versos encarama
   Sobre los mismos hombros de Calisto,
   Tan celebrado siempre de la fama,
Es aquel agradable, aquel bienquisto,
   Aquel agudo, aquel sonoro y grave
   Sobre cuantos poetas Febo ha visto:
Aquel que tiene de escribir la llave
   Con gracia y agudeza en tanto extremo,
   Que su igual en el orbe no se sabe,
Es DON LUIS DE GONGORA, á quien temo
   Agraviar en mis cortas alabanzas,
   Aunque las suba al grado mas supremo.
O tú, divino espíritu, que alcanzas
   Ya el premio merecido á tus deseos,
   Y á tus bien colocadas esperanzas:
Ya en nuevos y justísimos empleos,
   Divino HERRERA, tu caudal se aplica,
   Aspirando del cielo á los trofeos.
Ya de tu hermosa luz clara y rica
   El bello resplandor miras seguro
   En la que la alma tuya beatifica:
Y arrimada tu hiedra al fuerte muro
   De la immortalidad, no estimas cuanto
   Mora en las sombras deste mundo escuro.

Next comes a poet of the sacred lyre,
 Known wide as MIGUEL CID,[12] whose holy rhyme
 Strikes terror into all the Muses' quire.
This other here, whose soaring verse doth climb
 The very shoulders of the greater Bear,
 So eulogized by fame, in this our time,
The best beloved, and eke most debonnair,
 Most pungent, most sonorous, most refined,
 Of all the poets Phœbus hath in care,
Who holds the key of writing, that rare kind,
 Wherein such mingled grace and wit appear
 That on this orb its like we cannot find,
Is DON LUIS DE GONGORA,[13] whom I fear
 By such brief praise of mine to have disgraced,
 Although I raise it to the highest sphere.
O soul divine! who art already graced
 With honours high that to thy worth are due,
 And to thy hopes so well and wisely placed!
E'en now, in fitting offices and new,
 Thy powers, divine HERRERA,[14] move aright,
 With heavenly glories ever in thy view;
Upon the splendours of thy beauteous Light,
 So rich and clear, thine eyes with rapture fall,
 As seen in her who is thy soul's delight;
And, clinging like the ivy to the wall
 Of Immortality, it boots not thee
 What matters in our darkened world befall.

Y tú, DON JUAN DE JAUREGUI, que á tanto
  El sabio curso de tu pluma aspira,
  Que sobre las esferas le levanto:
Aunque Lucano por tu voz respira,
  Déjale un rato, y con piadosos ojos
  A la necesidad de Apolo mira;
Que te están esperando mil despojos
  De otros mil atrevidos, que procuran
  Fértiles campos ser, siendo rastrojos.
Y tú, por quien las musas aseguran
  Su partido, DON FELIX ARIAS, siente,
  Que por su gentileza te conjuran,
Y ruegan que defiendas desta gente
  Non sancta su hermosura, y de Aganipe
  Y de Hipocrene la inmortal corriente.
¿Consentirás tú á dicha participe
  Del licor suavísimo un poeta,
  Que al hacer de sus versos sude y hipe?
No lo consentirás, pues tu discreta
  Vena, abundante y rica, no permite
  Cosa que sombra tenga de imperfeta.
Señor, este que aquí viene se quite,
  Dije á Mercurio, que es un chacho necio,
  Que juega, y es de sátiras su envite.
Este si que podrás tener en precio,
  Que es ALONSO DE SALAS BARBADILLO,
  A quien me inclino y sin medida aprecio.

And thou as well, DON JUAN DE JAUREGUI,[15]
 Whose pen with subtle course doth upward speed,
 And fain would soar above all spheres that be ;
Though Lucan through thy voice doth breathe indeed,
 One moment leave him, and with pitying eye
 Regard Apollo in his time of need ;
For now to thee a thousand spoils are nigh
 Of thousand shameless daring ones, who fain
 Would rank as fruitful fields, though stubble dry.
And thou, whose cause the Muses all maintain,
 DON FELIX ARIAS, wilt give ear, I ween,
 While they entreat thee, in most melting strain,
To save their beauty from that rabble mean,
 And guard the immortal streams that gushing go
 From Aganippe and from Hippocrene ;
Wilt thou consent to share the sparkling glow
 Of that rich liquor with some poet vile,
 Who sweats and belches while his numbers flow ?
Thou wilt not ; for thy chastely classic style,
 So precious and so rare, will not permit
 The veriest trace of aught that can defile !
My lord, I said, let him be forced to quit
 Who next appears ; he's but a brainless wight
 Who gambles, and with satire makes a hit.
But let the next find favour in thy sight,
 DE SALAS BARBADILLO is his name,
 Him I regard, and with supreme delight.

Este que viene aquí, si he de decillo,
   No hay para qué le embarques, y asi puedes
   Borrarle.   Dijo el dios: gusto de oíllo.
Es un cierto rapaz, que á Ganimédes
   Quiere imitar, vistiéndose á lo godo,
   Y así aconsejo que sin él te quedes.
No lo harás con este dese modo,
   Que es el gran LUIS CABRERA, que pequeño
   Todo lo alcanza, pues lo sabe todo:
Es de la historia conocido dueño,
   Y en discursos discretos tan discreto,
   Que á Tácito verás, si te le enseño.
Este que viene es un galan, sujeto
   De la varia fortuna á los vaivenes,
   Y del mudable tiempo al duro aprieto.
Un tiempo rico de caducos bienes,
   Y ahora de los firmes é inmudables
   Mas rico, á tu mandar firme le tienes:
Pueden los altos riscos siempre estables
   Ser tocados del mar, mas no movidos
   De sus ondas en cursos variables.
Ni ménos á la tierra trae rendidos
   Los altos cedros Bóreas, cuando airado
   Quiere humillar los mas fortalecidos.
Y este que vivo ejemplo nos ha dado
   Desta verdad con tal filosofía
   DON LORENZO RAMIREZ es DE PRADO.

Who hither comes, if I be not to blame,
   Hath no right to embark, and strike him out
   Thou mayst; quoth Mercury: "I think the same."
A certain urchin he, who loves to flout
   In Gothic dress, a would-be Ganymede,
   'Twere best to turn him to the right about.
The next in turn deserves a better meed,
   The great LUIS CABRERA, who, though small,
   Achieveth much, for much he knows indeed;
A master he of history, prized by all,
   And in discreet discourses so discreet,
   That Tacitus himself seems at thy call.
Now comes to view a man of grace complete,
   Across whose life hath changing Fortune passed,
   And on whose head the storms of Time have beat;
Once was he rich in goods that would not last,
   Now richer still in goods that last for aye,
   He stands at thy command both firm and fast;
Around the beetling rocks in fierce array
   The sea may rage, and all its billows bound,
   Nor move them from their solid base away;
And Boreas, too, may howl and rave around
   The lofty cedars, but he strives in vain
   To make their giant trunks bestrew the ground;
A living instance of this truth we gain
   In DON LORENZO, he DE PRADO hight,
   With sweet philosophy that makes it plain.

Deste que se le sigue aquí, diria
  Que es DON ANTONIO DE MONROY, que veo
  En él lo que es ingenio y cortesía.
Satisfacion al mas alto deseo
  Puede dar de valor heroico y ciencia,
  Pues mil descubro en él y otras mil creo.
Este es un caballero de presencia
  Agradable, y que tiene de Torcato
  El alma sin alguna diferencia.
De DON ANTONIO DE PAREDES trato,
  A quien dieron las musas sus amigas
  En tierna edad anciano ingenio y trato.
Este que por llevarle te fatigas,
  Es DON ANTONIO DE MENDOZA, y veo
  Cuánto en llevarle al sacro Apolo obligas.
Este que de las musas es recreo,
  La gracia, y el donaire, y la cordura,
  Que de la discrecion lleva el trofeo:
Es PEDRO DE MORALES, propia hechura
  Del gusto cortesano, y es asilo
  Adonde se repara mi ventura.
Este, aunque tiene parte de Zoílo,
  Es el grande ESPINEL, que en la guitarra
  Tiene la prima, y en el raro estilo.
Este, que tanto alli tira la barra,
  Que las cumbres se deja atras de Pindo,
  Que jura, que vocea y que desgarra,

I'll say of him who cometh now in sight,
    ANTONIO DE MONROY, a very store
    Of wit and courtesy in him unite ;
The proofs of his heroic might and lore
    May satisfy the loftiest desire,
    Thousands I've seen, I've faith in thousands more.
Here comes a cavalier whom all admire,
    Of presence fine, and one who holds, I ween,
    Torquato's soul with unabated fire ;
I DON ANTONIO DE PAREDES mean,
    Whose tender years his friends the Muses crowned
    With antique genius, and a brow serene.
The next to carry with thee thou art bound,
    ANTONIO DE MENDOZA, and with right
    Apollo is thy debtor on this ground.
The next, who is the Muses' chief delight,
    Their grace, their charm, their wisdom, all in one,
    Who bears the palm for goodly wit at sight,
Is PEDRO DE MORALES,[16] true-born son
    Of courtly taste, the sure retreat always
    My poor luck finds that else might be undone.
This, though the part of Zoilus he plays,
    Is ESPINEL[17] the grand, whose gay guitar,
    And style so rare, are worthy of all praise.
He, who with such a flight can fling the bar
    As leaves the heights of Pindus far behind,
    Who swears, and bursts, and sends his voice afar,

Tiene mas de poeta que de lindo,
   Y es JUSEPE DE VARGAS, cuyo astuto
   Ingenio y rara condicion deslindo.
Este, á quien pueden dar justo tributo
   La gala y el ingenio, que mas pueda
   Ofrecer á las musas flor y fruto,
Es el famoso ANDRES DE BALMASEDA,
   De cuyo grave y dulce entendimiento
   El magno Apolo satisfecho queda.
Este es ENCISO, gloria y ornamento
   Del Tajo, y claro honor de Manzanares,
   Que con tal hijo aumenta su contento.
Este, que es escogido entre millares
   DE GUEVARA LUIS VELEZ es el bravo,
   Que se puede llamar quitapesares.
Es poeta gigante, en quien alabo
   El verso numeroso, el peregrino
   Ingenio, si un Gnaton nos pinta, o un Davo.
Este es DON JUAN DE ESPAÑA, que es mas dino
   De alabanzas divinas que de humanas,
   Pues en todos sus versos es divino.
Este, por quien de Lugo están ufanas
   Las musas, es SILVEIRA, aquel famoso,
   Que por llevarle con razon te afanas.
Este, que se le sigue, es el curioso
   Gran DON PEDRO DE HERRERA, conocido
   Por de ingenio elevado en punto honroso.

With more of poet's fire, than grace refined,
　Is JUSEPE DE VARGAS, whose astute
　And strangely-ordered wit I've thus defined.
He, who from lustre and great wit to boot
　Receives fit tribute, and with homage true
　Can offer to the Muses flower and fruit,
Is famed ANDRÈS DE BALMASEDA, who
　With solid judgment, and most pure intent,
　Will great Apollo please, and charm him too.
ENCISO this; the pride and ornament
　Of Tagus and of Manzanares fair,
　Who well with such a son may live content.
Here comes a man, amongst a thousand there,
　The valiant LUIS DE GUEVARA he,
　Who might in truth be better styled Kill-care;
A giant poet whom to praise I'm free
　For sounding verse, and wit that can outline
　A Gnatho or a Davus as they be.
DON JUAN DE ESPAÑA this, a poet fine,
　More worthy of divine than human fame,
　For in his verses he is all divine.
Comes famed SILVEIRA, through whom Lugo's name
　Is vaunted by the Muses, reason more
　Why thou shouldst strive to bear with thee the same.
Who follows is that man of curious lore,
　Great PEDRO DE HERRERA, who doth shine
　Through lofty wit, with honour at the core.

Este que de la cárcel del olvido
   Sacó otra vez á Proserpina hermosa,
   Con que á España y al Dauro ha enriquecido,
Verásle en la contienda rigurosa,
   Que se teme y se espera en nuestros dias,
   Culpa de nuestra edad poco dichosa,
Mostrar de su valor las lozanías.
   Pero ¿qué mucho, si es aqueste el doto
   Y grave DON FRANCISCO DE FARÍAS?
Este de quien yo fui siempre devoto,
   Oráculo y Apolo de Granada,
   Y aun deste clima nuestro y del remoto,
PEDRO RODRIGUEZ es. Este es TEJADA,
   De altitonantes versos y sonoros
   Con majestad en todo levantada.
Este, que brota versos por los poros,
   Y halla patria y amigos donde quiera,
   Y tiene en los ajenos sus tesoros,
Es MEDINILLA, el que la vez primera
   Cantó el romance de la tumba escura,
   Entre cipreses puestos en hilera.
Este, que en verdes años se apresura
   Y corre al sacro lauro, es DON FERNANDO
   BERMUDEZ, donde vive la cordura.
Este es aquel poeta memorando,
   Que mostró de su ingenio la agudeza
   En las selvas de Erífile cantando.

The bard who snatched the lovely Proserpine
   A second time from dark oblivion's cage,
   And gave to Spain and Daurus wealth divine,
Thou'lt find him in the strife where rigours rage,
   (So feared and dreaded in our day, I ween,
   Fault of our pinched and not too happy age,)
Shewing his lusty powers and courage keen;
   But what of that? It is the grave and wise
   FRANCISCO DE FARÍAS whom we mean.
PEDRO RODRIGUEZ this; whose worth I prize,
   The oracle of fair Granada's shrine,
   The Apollo of our own and distant skies.
TEJADA follows next, as I divine,
   Who on his lofty-sounding verse doth soar,
   And travels upward with majestic line.
The next, whose verses burst from every pore,
   Who finds his home and friends where'er he goes,
   And culls from every source his wealthy store,
Is MEDINILLA, who did first propose
   To sing the ballad of the sombre tomb
   Amongst the cypress-trees, arranged in rows.
Next comes BERMUDEZ, who, with life in bloom
   The sacred laurel seeks with eager smile,
   To cull fresh wisdom ere his years consume.
This is the poet, noted for his style,
   Who well displayed the sharpness of his wit
   By chanting in the woods of Erifile.

Este, que la coluna nueva empieza,
　Con estos dos que con su sér convienen,
　Nombrarlos, aun lo tengo por bajeza.
MIGUEL CEJUDO, y MIGUEL SANCHEZ vienen
　Juntos aquí, ¡oh par sin par! En estos
　Las sacras musas fuerte amparo tienen.
Que en los piés de sus versos bien compuestos,
　Llenos de erudicion rara y dotrina,
　Al ir al grave caso serán prestos.
Este gran caballero, que se inclina
　A la leccion de los poetas buenos,
　Y al sacro monte con su luz camina,
DON FRANCISCO DE SILVA es por lo ménos:
　¿Que será por lo mas? ¡Oh edad madura,
　En verdes años de cordura llenos!
DON GABRIEL GOMEZ viene aquí, segura
　Tiene con él Apolo la vitoria,
　De la canalla siempre necia y dura,
Para honor de su ingenio, para gloria
　De su florida edad, para que admire
　Siempre de siglo en siglo su memoria.
En este gran sugeto se retire
　Y abrevie la esperanza deste hecho,
　Y Febo al gran VALDES atento mire;
Verá en él un gallardo y sabio pecho,
　Un ingenio sutil y levantado,
　Con que le deje en todo satisfecho.

To name the one, who at the head doth sit
    Of this new column, and the other two
    Of kindred soul, I hardly think it fit.
Now comes MIGUEL CEJUDO into view
    With MIGUEL SANCHEZ, pair without a peer,
    A bulwark of the Muses, stout and true ;
Who, on the feet of their strong verse and clear,
    So full of doctrine rare and erudite,
    May march to face the combat without fear.
This cavalier, who reads with great delight
    And with the grand old poets doth consort,
    To reach the sacred mountain by their light,
DON FRANCISCO DE SILVA is in short,
    What will he be in full ? O age mature,
    So green in years, yet full of wise retort !
DON GABRIEL GOMEZ hither comes, who's sure
    To gift Apollo with no triumph mean
    Over the rabble witless and impure ;
To crown his genius and his brow serene
    With fitting fame ; that so from age to age,
    And ever on, his memory may be green.
In VALDES, that great personage and sage,
    The hope of such a deed is at its best,
    And well may great Apollo's doubts assuage ;
In him he'll find a wise and gallant breast
    A lofty genius, full of subtlety,
    Whereon his confidence may safely rest.

FIGUEROA es estotro, el dotorado,
  Que cantó de Amarili la constancia
  En dulce prosa y verso regalado.
Cuatro vienen aquí en poca distancia
  Con mayúsculas letras de oro escritos,
  Que son del alto asunto la importancia.
De tales cuatro, siglos infinitos
  Durará la memoria, sustentada
  En la alta gravedad de sus escritos.
Del claro Apolo la real morada
  Si viniere á caer de su grandeza,
  Será por estos cuatro levantada;
En ellos nos cifró naturaleza
  El todo de las partes, que son dinas
  De gozar celsitud, que es mas que alteza.
Esta verdad, gran CONDE DE SALINAS,
  Bien la acreditas con tus raras obras,
  Que en los términos tocan de divinas.
Tú, el de ESQUILACHE PRÍNCIPE, que cobras
  De dia en dia crédito tamaño,
  Que te adelantas á tí mismo y sobras:
Serás escudo fuerte al grave daño,
  Que teme Apolo con ventajas tantas,
  Que no te espere el escuadron tacaño.
Tú, CONDE DE SALDAÑA, que con plantas
  Tiernas pisas de Pindo la alta cumbre,
  Y en alas de tu ingenio te levantas;

Journey to Parnassus. 53

Comes FIGUEROA, Doctor by degree,
   Who sung in dulcet prose and dainty verse
   Of Amaryllis and her constancy.
Now four[15] appear, whose names we must rehearse,
   Writ full and large in characters of gold,
   All doubts of their importance to disperse.
Of such quartette the glory shall be told
   Through countless ages, for their works remain
   With massive weight their memory to uphold;
Should the grand throne, where Phœbus holds his reign,
   Be seen to topple from its lofty place,
   These four alone would raise it up again;
In them doth nature bounteously embrace
   The whole of all the parts, held justly now
   To merit Highness which is more than Grace.
This truth, great CONDE DE SALINAS, thou
   Dost well accredit with thy works so rare,
   Which touch the limits of divine, I trow.
Thou, prince of ESQUILACHE, biddest fair,
   From day to day, to rise to such a place
   That thou thyself wilt pass and overbear;
Thou'lt be a buckler strong in that dire case
   Which Phœbus dreads; arrayed in power complete,
   The scurvy squadron will not brook thy face.
Thou, CONDE DE SALDAÑA, who, with feet
   So tender, climb'st up Pindus' lofty height,
   And soarest with thy wit on pinions fleet,

Hacha has de ser de inextinguible lumbre,
  Que guie al sacro monte, al deseoso
  De verse en él, sin que la luz deslumbre.
Tú, el de VILLAMEDIANA, el mas famoso
  De cuantos entre griegos y latinos
  Alcanzaron el lauro venturoso;
Cruzarás por las sendas y caminos
  Que al monte guian, porque mas seguros
  Lleguen á él los simples peregrinos.
A cuya vista destos cuatro muros
  Del Parnaso caerán las arrogancias
  De los mancebos sobre necios duros.
¡Oh cuántas, y cuán graves circunstancias
  Dijera destos cuatro, que felices
  Aseguran de Apolo las ganancias!
Y mas si se les llega el de ALCAÑICES
  MARQUES insigne, harán (puesto que hay una
  En el mundo no mas) cinco fenices.
Cada cual de por si sera coluna,
  Que sustente y levante el edificio
  De Febo sobre el cerco de la luna.
Este (puesto que acude al grave oficio
  En que se ocupa) el lauro y palma lleva,
  Que Apolo da por honra y beneficio.
En esta ciencia es maravilla nueva,
  Y en la jurispericia único y raro,
  Su nombre es DON FRANCISCO DE LA CUEVA.

Journey to Parnassus.

Thou hast to be a torch of quenchless light,
  To guide the pilgrims who would pay their vow
  Upon the sacred hill, nor dread the night.
Most famous, VILLAMEDIANA,[19] thou
  Of all, amongst the Greeks and Latins, who
  Have pressed the happy laurel on their brow;
Thou must patrol the road and sideways too
  Which to the mountain lead; that safely all
  The simple strangers may their path pursue:
Before the sight of which quadruple wall,
  That girds Parnassus, shall the brainless throng
  Of these rude striplings totter down and fall.
What wondrous stories might I tell, and long,
  Of this quartette; what gains they have in store
  For great Apollo in the realms of song!
But lo! if ALCAÑICES join the corps,
  Marquess renowned, five Phœnixes will rise,
  Though in the world there be but one—no more!
Each one shall be a column of such size
  As Phœbus' mansion singly to sustain,
  And bear its fabric far above the skies.
The next, although his weighty duties strain
  His utmost powers, still bears the palm of fame
  Apollo grants for honour and for gain;
Strange gifts in such a science hath the same,
  In jurisprudence, too, unique and rare,
  FRANCISCO DE LA CUEVA is his name.

Este, que con Homero le comparo,
　Es el gran DON RODRIGO DE HERRERA,
　Insigne en letras, y en virtudes claro.
Este, que se le sigue, es el DE VERA
　DON JUAN, que por su espada y por su pluma
　Le honran en la quinta y cuarta esfera.
Este, que el cuerpo y aun el alma bruma
　De mil, aunque no muestra ser cristiano,
　Sus escritos el tiempo no consuma.
Cayóseme la lista de la mano
　En este punto, y dijo el dios:—Con estos
　Que has referido está el negocio llano.
Haz que con piés y pensamientos prestos
　Vengan aquí, donde aguardando quedo
　La fuerza de tan válidos supuestos.
—Mal podrá DON FRANCISCO DE QUEVEDO
　Venir, dije yo entónces; y él me dijo:
　—Pues partirme sin él de aqui non puedo.
Ese es hijo de Apolo, ese es hijo
　De Caliope musa, no podemos
　Irnos sin él, y en esto estaré fijo.
Es el flagelo de poetas memos,
　Y echará á puntillazos del Parnaso
　Los malos que esperamos y tememos.
—Oh señor, repliqué, que tiene el paso
　Corto, y no llegará en un siglo entero.
　—Deso, dijo Mercurio, no hago caso.

He, whom with Homer I may well compare,
  Is DON RODRIGO DE HERRERA: he
  Who holds in letters as in worth the chair.
Now comes DON JUAN DE VERA, brave and free,
  Who, for his martial sword and lettered plume,
  Hath in the fifth and fourth sphere high degree.
This, who in soul and body casts a gloom
  O'er thousands, though he be no Christian sure,
  Still may his works survive till crack of doom!
On this I dropped the list: in accents pure
  The god exclaimed: "With numbers such and great
  As thou hast named our business is secure;
See that, with ready feet and hearts elate,
  They hither come, while I shall keep me free
  To welcome allies of such sterling weight!"
"Scarce can FRANCISCO DE QUEVEDO[20] be
  In time," I said: "Nay," quoth he, "on this cruise
  I do not go, unless he go with me;
He is Apollo's son, son of the Muse
  Calliope; we cannot, it is clear,
  Go hence without him, and I do not chuse;
He is the scourge of all the poets drear,
  And from Parnassus, at the point of wit,
  Will chase the miscreants we expect and fear!"
"My lord," I said, "his pace is most unfit,
  He'll be a century upon the route!"
  Quoth Mercury: "It matters not a whit;

Que el poeta que fuere caballero,
  Sobre una nube entre pardilla y clara
  Vendrá muy á su gusto caballero.
—Y el que no, pregunté, ¿qué le prepara
  Apolo? ¿que carrozas, ó que nubes?
  ¿Qué dromedario, ó alfana en paso rara?
—Mucho, me respondió, mucho te subes
  En tus preguntas; calla y obedece.
  —Sí haré, pues no es infando lo que jubes.—
Esto le respondí, y él me parece
  Que se turbó algun tanto; y en un punto
  El mar se turba, el viento sopla y crece.
Mi rostro entónces, como el de un difunto
  Se debió de poner, y si haria,
  Que soy medroso á lo que yo barrunto.
Vi la noche mezclarse con el dia,
  Las arenas del hondo mar alzarse
  A la region del aire, entónces fría.
Todos los elementos vi turbarse,
  La tierra, el agua, el aire, y aun el fuego
  Vi entre rompidas nubes azorarse.
Y en medio deste gran desasosiego
  Llovian nubes de poetas llenas
  Sobre el bajel, que se anegara luego,
Si no acudieran mas de mil sirenas
  A dar de azotes á la gran borrasca,
  Que hacia el saltarel por las entenas.

For be the poet gentleman to boot,
  Upon a dappled cloud, and through the air,
  He shall be borne, his courtly taste to suit!"
"For him who's none what is Apollo's care?"
  I asked, "what clouds, what carriages at hand?
  What dromedary? Brute of action rare?"
"Thy questions savour much," he said offhand,
  "Of hardihood; be silent and resigned!"
  "Since not ineffable is thy command,
I yield!" So answered I, and to my mind
  He seemed somewhat irate, and straight ahead
  Rough rose the sea, and blew the gusty wind.
Then grew my face, like visage of one dead,
  Bedewed with pallor, for, if truth be told,
  I'm somewhat fearful of the thing I dread;
I saw the night and day together rolled,
  The sands of ocean deep began to dash
  Up to the realms of air, that froze with cold;
Now seemed the elements in rage to clash,
  Earth, water, air, and lambent fire, whose light
  Pierced the rent clouds with intermittent flash.
In midst of this confusion and affright,
  Clouds full of poets sent a pouring rain   [quite,
  Down on the barque, and would have swamped it
Had not some thousand Sirens come amain,
  And with their whips, from yard to yard, did make
  That hurly-burly take to flight again;

Una, que ser pensé Juana la Chasca,
    De dilatado vientre y luengo cuello,
    Pintiparado á aquel de la tarasca,
Se llegó á mi, y me dijo:—De un cabello
    Deste bajel estaba la esperanza
    Colgada, á no venir á socorrello.
Traemos, y no es burla, á la bonanza,
    Que estaba descuidada oyendo atenta
    Los discursos de un cierto Sancho Panza.—
En esto sosegóse la tormenta,
    Volvió tranquilo el mar, serenó el cielo,
    Que al regañon el céfiro le ahuyenta.
Volví la vista, y ví en lijero vuelo
    Una nube romper el aire claro
    De la color del condensado hielo.
¡Oh maravilla nueva! Oh caso raro!
    Vilo, y he de decillo, aunque se dude
    Del hecho que por brújula declaro.
Lo que yo pude ver, lo que yo pude
    Notar fué, que la nube dividida
    En dos mitades á llover acude.
Quien ha visto la tierra prevenida
    Con tal disposicion, que cuando llueve,
    Cosa ya averiguada y conocida,
De cada gota en un instante breve
    Del polvo se levanta ó sapo, ó rana,
    Que á saltos, ó despacio el paso mueve;

One, whom for Joan la Chasca I did take,
  With paunch extensive, and long neck and bare,
  In fashion like to that of curling snake,
Accosted me and said: " 'Twas by a hair
  That hung the hope of coming, as designed,
  Our timely succour to the barque to bear;
We tarried, 'tis no jest, on the fair wind
  That listless stood, in rapt attention, while
  A certain Sancho Panza told his mind!"
On this began to abate that tempest vile,
  The sea grew calm, the sky serene and bright,
  And Boreas fled before the Zephyr's smile.
I turned to look, and lo! on pinions light,
  A cloud came bursting through the upper air,
  Like unto virgin ice as purely white:
O marvel without peer! O wonder rare!
  I saw it, and must tell it, though I strain
  The faith of men in what I now declare!
What I could see, and what I will maintain,
  Is that the cloud, careering on its way,
  Split into halves, and then began to rain.
Whoe'er has seen the earth with such array
  Of power prepared, that when it rains apace,
  (A patent fact that none can well gainsay)
From every drop, and in the briefest space,
  A frog or toad from out the dust takes birth,
  That upward jumps, or creeps with sluggish pace;

Tal se imagine ver (¡Oh soberana
    Virtud!) de cada gota de la nube
    Saltar un bulto, aunque con forma humana.
Por no creer esta verdad estuve
    Mil veces, pero vila con la vista,
    Que entónces clara y sin legañas tuve.
Eran aquestos bultos de la lista
    Pasada los poetas referidos,
    A cuya fuerza no hay quien la resista.
Unos por hombres buenos conocidos,
    Otros de rumbo y hampo, y Dios es Cristo,
    Poquitos bien, y muchos mal vestidos.
Entre ellos pareciéme de haber visto
    A DON ANTONIO DE GALARZA el bravo,
    Gentilhombre de Apolo, y muy bienquisto.
El bajel se llenó de cabo á cabo,
    Y su capacidad á nadie niega
    Copioso asiento, que es lo mas que alabo.
Llovió otra nube al gran LOPE DE VEGA,
    Poeta insigne, á cuyo verso ó prosa
    Ninguno le aventaja, ni aun le llega.
Era cosa de ver maravillosa
    De los poetas la apretada enjambre,
    En recitar sus versos muy melosa.
Este muerto de sed, aquel de hambre;
    Yo dije, viendo tantos, con voz alta:
    —¡Cuerpo de mi con tanta poetambre!—

Such may conceive (O power of sovereign worth!)
  How from the cloud, and from each drop, he sees
  A bulging shape, though human-like, leap forth;
To credit such a fact, with thousand pleas
  I did resist in vain; for, void of mist
  And rheum, mine eyes beheld it with great ease.
These bulging forms were poets of the list,
  Which we have just recited with great care,
  Whose energy none living can resist;
Some, honest men and honoured everywhere,
  Others, mere swaggerers with flaunting crest,
  A few well-robed, and many more threadbare.
One man of might I saw among the rest,
  ANTONIO DE GALARZA, as I trow,
  Apollo's chamberlain, in high request.
The barque was filled outright from poop to prow,
  So great its bulk that each one could command
  A spacious seat; such praise I must allow.
Another cloud rained down that poet grand,
  LOPE DE VEGA,[1] whom in prose or verse
  None can surpass, nor one beside him stand.
'Twas fine to see, to speak in language terse,
  The needy swarm of poetasters try
  With honied voice their poems to rehearse,
This wild with thirst, and that with hungry eye;
  At such a sight I loudly made remark:
  "Good God! to sail with such a scurvy fry!"

Por tantas sobras conoció una falta
  Mercurio, y acudiendo á remedialla,
  Lijero en la mitad del bajel salta.
Y con una zaranda que allí halla,
  No sé si antigua, ó si de nuevo hecha,
  Zarandó mil poetas de gramalla.
Los de capa y espada no desecha,
  Y destos zarandó dos mil y tantos;
  Que fué neguilla entónces la cosecha.
Colábanse los buenos y los santos,
  Y quedábanse arriba los granzones,
  Mas duros en sus versos que los cantos.
Y sin que les valiesen las razones
  Que en su disculpa daban, daba luego
  Mercurio al mar con ellos á montones.
Entre los arrojados se oyó un ciego,
  Que murmurando entre las ondas iba
  De Apolo con un pésete y reniego.
Un sastre (aunque en sus piés flojos estriba,
  Abriendo con los brazos el camino)
  Dijo:—Sucio es Apolo, asi yo viva.—
Otro (que al parecer iba mohino,
  Con ser un zapatero de obra prima)
  Dijo dos mil, no un solo desatino.
Trabaja un tundidor, suda, y se anima
  Por verse á la ribera conducido,
  Que mas la vida que la honra estima.

As Mercury this needless swarm did mark,
  He sought his remedy, and with a shout
  He leapt into the middle of the barque;
And with a large sieve, lying there about—
  Whether antique or new I'm not aware—
  Riddled a thousand slipshod poets out;
Those of the cloak and sword he fain would spare,
  He sifted out two thousand souls or more,
  Yet sooth, 'twas but a cockle harvest there!
This crucial test the good and holy bore,
  The gritty, husky ones remained behind,
  Whose verse was hard as millstone at the core;
To all the clamant pleadings they could find,
  In their defence, Mercurius gave no ear,
  But to the sea the shouting mob consigned.
Of the expelled a blind man I did hear,   [cry:
  Who, floundering, grumbling, 'mid the waves did
  "Shame on Apollo, I renounce him here!"
A taylor[22] there, of weak legs and awry,
  Who with his arms made sturdy strokes and great,
  Bawled out: "Apollo's naught, so long live I!"
Another one, a cobbler and first-rate,
  And yet a moody being all the same,
  With twice a thousand follies cursed his fate;
There toils a shearer, sweats, and doth inflame
  His soul, to cleave the waves and gain the beach,
  For life to him is dearer far than fame!

El escuadron nadante reducido
  A la marina, vuelve á la galera
  El rostro con señales de ofendido.
Y uno por todos dijo :—Bien pudiera
  Ese chocante embajador de Febo
  Tratarnos bien, y no desta manera.
Mas oigan lo que dijo :—Yo me atrevo
  A profanar del monte la grandeza
  Con libros nuevos, y en estilo nuevo.
Calló Mercurio, y á poner empieza
  Con gran curiosidad seis camarines,
  Dando á la gracia ilustre rancho y pieza.
De nuevo resonaron los clarines,
  Y asi Mercurio lleno de contento,
  Sin darle mal agüero los delfines,
Remos al agua dió, velas al viento.

Soon as the swimming shoals the shore did reach
    They turned them to the galley, and gave vent
    To their disgust, with gestures and with speech !
One said for all : " Thou brutal Envoy, sent
    By Phœbus, it was surely worth thy while
    To treat us well, not rouse our discontent !
But list ye : 'tis my purpose to defile
    The sacred mountain's height, from top to base,
    With novel books, and in a novel style ! "
Dumb was Mercurius ; and commenced with grace
    To raise six stately cabins wondrous rare,
    To give the better folk a worthy place ;
Anew the sounding clarions smote the air ;
    Mercurius stood with calm, contented mind,
    And while the dolphins leapt with omen fair,
They dipped their oars, and sailed before the wind.

CAPITULO III.

Eran los remos de la real galera
    De esdrújulos, y dellos compelida
    Se deslizaba por el mar lijera.
Hasta el tope la vela iba tendida,
    Hecha de muy delgados pensamientos,
    De varios lizos por amor tejida.
Soplaban dulces y amorosos vientos,
    Todos en popa, y todos se mostraban
    Al gran viaje solamente atentos.
Las sirenas en torno navegaban,
    Dando empellones al bajel lozano,
    Con cuya ayuda en vuelo le llevaban.
Semejaban las aguas del mar cano
    Colchas encarrujadas, y hacian
    Azules visos por el verde llano.
Todos los del bajel se entretenian,
    Unos glosando piés dificultosos,
    Otros cantaban, otros componian.

CHAPTER III.

The royal galley's oars appeared to be
   Of lines dactyllic, and impelled by these
   It glided forth, and bounded o'er the sea;
The main-sail, bellying out to catch the breeze,
   Was formed of fancies, culled from every land,
   Whose varied threads were wove by Love at ease;
Now softly blew the amorous winds and bland
   Fair on the stern, and all combined to cheer
   And speed the vessel on its voyage grand;
The Sirens gambolled round it far and near,
   And to the lusty barque gave impulse keen,
   That sent it bounding on in full career;
The waters of the hoary main, I ween,
   Seemed sheets of wavy silk that made display
   Of azure colour through a field of green.
Thus whiled the voyagers the time away:
   Some took to gloss some hard and crabbed phrase,
   This chanted forth, and that composed a lay;

Otros de los tenidos por curiosos
   Referian sonetos, muchos hechos
   A diferentes casos amorosos.
Otros alfeñicados y deshechos
   En puro azúcar, con la voz süave,
   De su melifluidad muy satisfechos,
En tono blando, sosegado y grave,
   Eglogas pastorales recitaban,
   En quien la gala y la agudeza cabe.
Otros de sus señoras celebraban
   En dulces versos de la amada boca
   Los excrementos que por ella echaban.
Tal hubo á quien amor así le toca,
   Que alabó los riñones de su dama,
   Con gusto grande, y no elegancia poca.
Uno cantó, que la amorosa llama
   En mitad de las aguas le encendia,
   Y como toro agarrochado brama.
Desta manera andaba la poesía
   De uno en otro, haciendo que hablase
   Este latin, aquel algarabia.
En esto sesga la galera vase
   Rompiendo el mar con tanta lijereza,
   Que el viento aun no consiente que la pase.
Y en esto descubrióse la grandeza
   De la escombrada playa de Valencia
   Por arte hermosa y por naturaleza.

Some, who as dilettanti earned high praise,
  Recited sonnets, which behoved to toy
  With Love's grand passion, every mood and phase;
Others, with palates they were wont to cloy
  With sugared sweets, in voice of sweetest sound
  Whose honied accent filled their hearts with joy,
And in a tone that lulled the listeners round,
  Recited Eclogues, of the country sprung,
  A medley of the simple and profound.
A certain one in sweetest verses sung
  The dulcet mouth[23] that decked his lady's face,
  And eke the moisture dropping from her tongue;
A second gave to Love yet daintier place,
  And praised the fair one's haunches to the full
  With highest gusto, and no little grace;
A third bemoaned Love's flame, so hard to cool,
  That even in mid-water it would blaze,
  And make him bellow like a goaded bull!
And so from one to t'other in a maze
  Went poesy, and this and that would try
  To chant in Latin or with Moorish phrase.
In such a fashion did the galley fly,
  And with such speed went cleaving thro' the sea,
  That not the wind itself could pass it by.
In course of time came looming on the lee
  Valencia's plain,[21] that vast and fertile floor,
  Through art and nature wondrous fair to see.

Hizo luego de si grata presencia
 El gran DON LUIS FERRER, marcado el pecho
 De honor, y el alma de divina ciencia.
Desembarcóse el dios, y fué derecho
 A darle cuatro mil y mas abrazos,
 De su vista y su ayuda satisfecho.
Volvió la vista, y reiteró los lazos
 En DON GUILLEN DE CASTRO, que venía
 Deseoso de verse en tales brazos.
CRISTÓBAL DE VIRUES se le seguia,
 Con PEDRO DE AGUILAR, junta famosa
 De las que Turia en sus riberas cria.
No le pudo llegar mas valerosa
 Escuadra al gran Mercurio, ni él pudiera
 Desearla mejor, ni mas honrosa.
Luego se descubrió por la ribera
 Un tropel de gallardos valencianos,
 Que á ver venían la sin par galera.
Todos con instrumentos en las manos
 De estilos y librillos de memoria,
 Por bizarria y por ingenio ufanos,
Codiciosos de hallarse en la vitoria,
 Que ya tenian por segura y cierta,
 De las heces del mundo y de la escoria.
Pero Mercurio les cerró la puerta:
 Digo, no consintió que se embarcasen,
 Y el por qué no lo dijo, aunque se acierta.

Journey to Parnassus. 73

To our delight we spied upon the shore
  Great DON LUIS FERRER, his breast inlaid
  With honour, and his soul with sacred lore;
Mercurius landed, and with nothing said
  He hugged him thousand times, and kissed his face,
  Right glad to see him, and receive his aid.
He turned him round; and gave an equal grace
  To DON GUILLEN DE CASTRO, who was cheered,
  And proud to find himself in such embrace.
Then CHRISTOBAL DE VIRUES appeared
  With PEDRO DE AGUILAR; both chiefs of fame,
  Whom Thuria on her teeming banks had reared;
To great Mercurius surely never came,
  Nor could he ever hope to find, a corps
  Of men more honoured, or of higher name.
Now presently came trooping to the shore
  Of stout Valencians a sturdy band,
  In haste the peerless galley to explore;
With quaint old instruments they came to hand,—
  Their styles and memorandum-books, I ween—
  Exulting in their wit and bearing grand;
On victory bent, and all alert and keen,
  To trample under foot earth's vermin base,
  And gain such triumph as was never seen;
But Mercury withstood them to the face,
  In sooth, he would not let them leave the land,
  He said not why, but such was e'en the case;

Y fué, porque temió que no se alzasen,
　Siendo tantos y tales, con Parnaso,
　Y nuevo imperio y mando en él fundasen.
En esto vióse con brioso paso
　Venir al magno ANDRES REY DE ARTIEDA,
　No por la edad descaecido ó laso.
Hicieron todos espaciosa rueda,
　Y cogiéndole en medio, le embarcaron,
　Mas rico de valor que de moneda.
Al momento las ancoras alzaron,
　Y las velas ligadas á la entena
　Los grumetes apriesa desataron.
De nuevo por el aire claro suena
　El son de los clarines, y de nuevo
　Vuelve á su oficio cada cual sirena.
Miró el bajel por entre nubes Febo,
　Y dijo en voz que pudo ser oida:
　—Aqui mi gusto y mi esperanza llevo.—
De remos y sirenas impelida
　La galera se deja atras el viento,
　Con milagrosa y próspera corrida.
Leíase en los rostros el contento
　Que llevaban los sabios pasajeros,
　Durable, por no ser nada violento.
Unos por el calor iban en cueros,
　Otros por no tener godescas galas
　En traje se vistieron de romeros.

He feared lest such a mighty troop and grand
  Should storm Parnassus, and possess its height,
  And found thereon new empire and command.
On this there came, with gallant step and light,
  Great ANDRES REY DE ARTIEDA[25] near,
  Whom age could not enfeeble nor affright;
They of the barque came swooping from the rear,
  And him, a willing captive, they conveyed
  On board, more rich in valour than in gear.
The anchors then with sudden haste they weighed,
  The yards the main-top sailors gaily manned,
  And let the sails go free with grand parade;
Anew the clarions sound on every hand,
  Awakening echoes in the azure skies,
  While to their work the eager Sirens stand.
Apollo from the clouds, with beaming eyes,
  Beholds the barque, and calls that all may hear:
  "Here sail my hopes, and all the power I prize!"
By oars and Sirens driven, with good cheer
  The bounding galley left the breeze behind,
  To seek its strange and prosperous career.
Upon their faces shone the easy mind
  Which all the learnèd voyagers possessed,
  A calm content, but of a lasting kind;
Some doffed their garments, by the heat oppressed,
  While those, who had no Gothic dress to wear,
  In pilgrims' weeds were fain to look their best.

Hendia en tanto las neptúneas salas
   La galera, del modo como hiende
   La grulla el aire con tendidas alas.
En fin, llegamos donde el mar se extiende,
   Y ensancha y forma el golfo de Narbona,
   Que de ningunos vientos se defiende.
Del gran Mercurio la cabal persona
   Sobre seis resmas de papel sentada
   Iba con cetro y con real corona:
Cuando una nube, al parecer preñada,
   Parió cuatro poetas en crujía,
   O los llovió, razon mas concertada.
Fué el uno aquel, de quien Apolo fia
   Su honra, JUAN LUIS DE CASANATE,
   Poeta insigne de mayor cuantia.
El mismo Apolo de su ingenio trate,
   Él le alabe, él le premie y recompense;
   Que el alabarle yo seria dislate.
Al segundo llovido, el uticense
   Caton no no le igualó, ni tiene Febo
   Quien tanto por él mire, ni en él piense.
Del contador GASPAR DE BARRIONUEVO
   Mal podrá el corto flaco ingenio mio
   Loar el suyo asi como yo debo.
Llenó del gran bajel el gran vacío
   El gran FRANCISCO DE RIOJA al punto
   Que saltó de la nube en el navío.

Through Neptune's halls the ship went gliding fair,
  As sails the crane with motion fine and free,
  When with its pinions spread it cleaves the air.
At length we reached that wide expanse of sea
  Which forms Narbona's gulf: a watery sheet
  That lies exposed to all the winds that be.
Great Mercury, in form and grace complete,
  Decked fine with sceptre and with royal crown,
  On six good reams of paper took his seat;
When lo! a pregnant cloud, big with renown,
  Produced four poets from its teeming womb,
  To speak more properly, it rained them down.
The first, LUIS DE CASANATE, whom
  Apollo holds the guardian of his fame,
  To fill a loftier post may none presume;
So highly doth Apollo rate his name,
  Exalt his wit, and crown him with high grace,
  That praise from me would sound exceeding tame.
Not Cato, he of Utica, holds place
  Beside the second poet who came down,
  Nor Phœbus' self has friend of nobler race:
GASPAR DE BARRIONUEVO'S high renown,
  As Treasurer, above my mark hath soared,
  My scanty wit adds little to his crown.
The vessel's vacant room was fully stored
  When great FRANCISCO DE RIOJA came,
  And from the cloudlet lightly leapt on board.

A Cristóbal de Mesa ví allí junto
   A los piés de Mercurio, dando fama
   A Apolo, siendo dél propio trasunto.
A la gavia un grumete se encarama,
   Y dijo á voces:—La ciudad se muestra,
   Que Jénova, del dios Jano se llama.
—Déjesele la ciudad á la siniestra
   Mano, dijo Mercurio, el bajel vaya,
   Y siga su derrota por la diestra.
Hacer al Tíber vimos blanca raya
   Dentro del mar, habiendo ya pasado
   La ancha romana y peligrosa playa.
De léjos vióse el aire condensado
   Del humo que el estrómbalo vomita,
   De azufre, y llamas, y de horror formado.
Huyen la isla infame, y solicita
   El suave poniente, así el viaje
   Que lo acorta, lo allana y facilita.
Vímonos en un punto en el paraje,
   Do la nutriz de Enéas píadoso
   Hizo el forzoso y último pasaje.
Vimos desde allí á poco el mas famoso
   Monte que encierra en sí nuestro hemisfero,
   Mas gallardo á la vista y mas hermoso.
Las cenizas de Titiro y Sincero
   Están en él, y puede ser por esto
   Nombrado entre los montes por primero.

At Mercury's feet, to give Apollo fame,
  Sat CHRISTOBAL DE MESA, who in truth
  Was but a living transcript of the same.
Up to the main-top climbed a gallant youth
  Who holloed out : " Lo ! Genoa comes in sight,
  To which god Janus gave his name, in sooth!"
" Leave it upon the left, that town of might,"
  Cried Mercury, " and turn the vessel's head,
  To take its course with bearing to the right!"
Anon we saw the stream of Tiber's bed,
  Fresh from the wide and perilous Roman plain,
  Glide on into the sea like silvery thread ;
Far off, dark clouds seemed rising from the main,
  Of densest smoke that Stromboli could vent,
  Where sulphur, flames, and dismal demons reign.
They flee the cursèd isle ; with sweet intent
  The western breeze begins to woo the barque,
  Which glides along light-hearted and content.
We coasted onward and the spot did mark,
  Where great Æneas' nurse the passage took,
  The last, the unavoidable, the dark.
A little distance off we spied the nook
  Where stands the famed hill of our hemisphere,
  On statelier and on fairer none may look ;
The first of mountains ; where the ashes dear
  Of Tityrus[26] and eke Sincerus lie,
  For this it bears the palm both far and near.

Luego se descubrió, donde echó el resto
    De su poder naturaleza amiga,
    De formar de otros muchos un compuesto.
Vióse la pesadumbre sin fatiga
    De la bella Parténope, sentada
    A la orilla del mar, que sus piés liga,
De castillos y torres coronada,
    Por fuerte y por hermosa en igual grado
    Tenida, conocida y estimada.
Mandóme el del alíjero calzado,
    Que me aprestase y fuese luego á tierra
    A dar á los LUPERCIOS un recado,
En que les diese cuenta de la guerra
    Temida, y que á venir les persuadiese
    Al duro y fiero asalto, al cierra, cierra.
—Señor, le respondí, si acaso hubiese
    Otro que la embajada les llevase,
    Que mas grato á los dos hermanos fuese,
Que yo no soy, sé bien que negociase
    Mejor.—Dijo Mercurio:—No te entiendo,
    Y has de ir ántes que el tiempo mas se pase.
—Que no me han de escuchar estoy temiendo,
    Le repliqué, ya si el ir yo no importa,
    Puesto que en todo obedecer pretendo.
Que no sé quién me dice, y quién me exhorta,
    Que tienen para mi, á lo que imagino,
    La voluntad, como la vista corta.

Beyond, a range of peaks we could descry,
  Where the remains of Nature's grandeur meet
  To form a composite of vast and high :
Now burst upon our view the unrest sweet
  Of fair Parthenope, who sits as queen
  Beside the sea, that laves and links her feet ;
Fair towers and castles crown her brow serene,
  And she is held by all a gem complete,
  Whose like for strength and beauty ne'er was seen ;
Now gave command, he of the wingèd feet,
  That I should haste on shore without delay,
  And in his stead the two LUPERCIOS[27] greet ;
And tidings of the dreaded war convey,
  And bid them with us to the combat hie,
  To join our serried ranks, and face the fray ! "
" My lord," I said, " if there be other nigh
  Upon this embassy of thine to go,
  More grateful to the brothers twain than I,
Thy business will be better done, I know ! "
  Quoth Mercury : " Thy words are strange indeed,
  For go thou must, and quickly too, I trow ; "
" I fear," cried I, " they'll give me little heed !
  Although thy bidding I would gladly do,
  My visit there would have but sorry speed ;
Some have assured me, though I know not who,
  That their good will for me has grown as weak
  As is their eyesight, and it seemeth true ;

G

Que si esto así no fuera, este camino
　　Con tan pobre recámara no hiciera,
　　Ni diera en un tan hondo desatino.
Pues si alguna promesa se cumpliera
　　De aquellas muchas, que al partir me hicieron,
　　Lléveme Dios si entrara en tu galera.
Mucho esperé, si mucho prometieron,
　　Mas podrá ser que ocupaciones nuevas
　　Les obligue á olvidar lo que dijeron.
Muchos, señor, en la galera llevas,
　　Que te podran sacar el pié del lodo,
　　Parte, y excusa de hacer mas pruebas.
— Ninguno, dijo, me hable dese modo,
　　Que si me desembarco y los embisto,
　　Voto á Dios, que me traiga al Conde, y todo.
Con estos dos famosos me enemisto,
　　Que habiendo levantado á la poesía
　　Al buen punto en que está, como se ha visto,
Quieren con perezosa tirania
　　Alzarse, como dicen, á su mano
　　Con la ciencia que á ser divinos guia.
Por el solio de Apolo soberano
　　Juro... y no digo mas; y ardiendo en ira
　　Se echó á las barbas una y otra mano.
Y prosiguió diciendo: El DOTOR MIRA,
　　Apostaré, si no lo manda el Conde,
　　Que tambien en sus puntos se retira.

Were this not so, I had no cause to seek
  A passage here in such a beggar's suit,
  Nor bear a part in such a foolish freak:
Had one of all the promises ta'en root
  They gave on parting, never God me aid
  If in thy galley I had e'er set foot;
I hoped for much, when much protest they made,
  But it may be, that strange affairs and new
  Have caused them to forget the thing they said!
My lord, within this galley thou canst view
  Enow to draw thy foot from out the hole;
  Set out, and make of this no more ado!"
"Speak not so pertly!" said the god in dole,
  " For if I land me, then by Jove I swear
  I'll seize the Count and carry off the whole;
Of these two famous men I have a fear,
  That, having raised to such a lofty line
  The art of poesy, as doth appear,
They now with lazy tyranny incline
  To hold, forsooth, within their sole command,
  The lofty science that makes men divine.
Now by Apollo's throne, the great and grand,
  I swear .... and say no more!" and, much irate,
  He plucked his beard with this and t'other hand.
"The DOCTOR MIRA," he went on to state,
  " I'll wager now, without the Count's behest,
  Is also pricked with scruples delicate;

Señor galan, parezca; ¿á que se esconde?
　　Pues á fe por llevarle, si él no gusta,
　　Que ni le busque, aseche, ni le ronde.
¿Es esta empresa acaso tan injusta,
　　Que se esquiven de hallar en ella cuantos
　　Tienen conciencia limitada y justa?
¿Carece el cielo de poetas santos?
　　¿Puesto que brote á cada paso el suelo
　　Poetas, que lo son tantos y tantos?
¿No se oyen sacros himnos en el cielo?
　　¿La arpa de David allá no suena,
　　Causando nuevo accidental consuelo?
Fuera melindres, y cese la entena,
　　Que llegue al tope;—y luego obedeciendo
　　Fué de la chusma sobre buenas buena.
Poco tiempo pasó, cuando un ruïdo
　　Se oyó, que los oídos atronaba,
　　Y era de perros áspero ladrido.
Mercurio se turbó, la gente estaba
　　Suspensa al triste son, y en cada pecho
　　El corazon mas válido temblaba.
En esto descubrióse el corto estrecho
　　Que Escila y que Caríbdis espantosas
　　Tan temeroso con su furia han hecho.
—Estas olas que veis presuntüosas
　　En visitar las nubes de contino,
　　Y aun de tocar el cielo codiciosas,

Sir gallant, shew thy face! where hast thy nest?
Yet if, i'faith, he hath no heart to go,
I'll neither woo nor wile him, let him rest!
Is this emprise, forsooth, so very low
  That they, who have a nice and narrow creed,
  Should cast disdainful looks, and spurn it so?
Of holy Bards doth Heaven stand in need,
  When sprouting from the soil at every pace
  Spring up as good, and better far indeed?
Have sacred hymns in Heaven now no place?
  Is not the harp of David sounding there,
  Diffusing comfort round and sweet solace?
A curse on scruples: let the yards go fair,
  And set the sails!" And, hurrying at his call,
  The eager crew obeyed, and did not spare.
Short time elapsed when on our ears did fall
  A horrid noise, like to the barking drear
  Of furious dogs,[21] most fitted to appal.
Mercurius paled: the folk grew dumb with fear
  Before the dismal sound; the stoutest breast
  Beat quicker as the thunder-growl came near;
On this we spied that narrow strait compressed,
  The same which Scylla, and Charybdis fell,
  Have made so dreaded by their wild unrest;
" These waves ye see that in presumption swell,
  To claim acquaintance with the clouds of light,
  And e'en to kiss the very heavens as well—

Venciólas el prudente peregrino
  Amante de Calipso, al tiempo cuándo
  Hizo, dijo Mercurio, este camino.
Su prudencia nosotros imitando,
  Echarémos al mar en que se ocupen,
  En tanto que el bajel pasa volando.
Que en tanto que ellas tasquen, roan, chupen,
  Al mísero que al mar ha de entregarse,
  Seguro estoy que al paso desocupen.
Miren si puede en la galera hallarse
  Algun poeta desdichado acaso,
  Que á las fieras gargantas pueda darse.—
Buscáronle, y halláron á LOFRASO,
  Poeta militar, sardo, que estaba
  Desmayado á un rincon marchito y laso:
Que á sus diez libros de Fortuna andaba
  Añadiendo otros diez, y el tiempo escoge,
  Que mas desocupado se mostraba.
Gritó la chusma toda:—Al mar se arroje,
  Vaya LOFRASO al mar sin resistencia.
  —Por Dios, dijo Mercurio, que me enoje.
¿Cómo? ¿y no será cargo de conciencia,
  Y grande, echar al mar tanta poesía,
  Puesto que aqui nos hunda su inclemencia?
Viva LOFRASO, en tanto que dé al dia
  Apolo luz, y en tanto que los hombres
  Tengan discreta alegre fantasía.

These waves," quoth Mercury, "were vanqu'shed
　By fair Calypso's lover, worldly wise,　　[quite
　What time he took this passage in his flight;
Let us prepare for them a like surprise,
　And cast into the sea some tempting bait,
　To keep them busy while the good ship flies;
For while they rive, and rend, and masticate
　The writhing wretch that wriggles in the sea,
　I'm sure they'll leave us free to pass the strait!
Look now if in the galley ye can see
　Some wretched bard, who may perchance by right
　A fitting victim for the monsters be!"
They found him in that man, LOFRASO[20] hight,
　Sardinian martial poet, who now lay
　Curled in a corner, and in dismal plight;
In his 'Ten books of Fortune' all the day
　Immersed; to add yet other ten to these
　He strove, to while the idle hours away;
Cried all the crew as one: "LOFRASO seize!
　Down with him to the deep, and leave him there!"
"Perdy," cried Mercury, "I do not please!
What? Can my soul the heavy burden bear
　Of casting to the sea such poesy,
　Although its foaming wrath demands our care?
Long live LOFRASO, while the day we see
　Spring from Apollo's light, and men can smile
　And hold as wisdom sprightly fantasy!

Tocante á tí, oh LOFRASO, los renombres,
  Y epítetos de agudo y de sincero,
  Y gusto que mi cómitre te nombres.—
Esto dijo Mercurio al caballero,
  El cual en la crujía en pié se puso
  Con un rebenque despiadado y fiero.
Creo que de sus versos le compuso,
  Y no sé cómo fué, que en un momento
  (O ya el cielo, ó LOFRASO lo dispuso)
Salimos del estrecho á salvamento,
  Sin arrojar al mar poeta alguno:
  Tanto del sardo fué el merecimiento.
Mas luego otro peligro, otro importuno
  Temor amenazó, si no gritara
  Mercurio, cual jamas gritó ninguno,
Diciendo al timonero:—A orza, para,
  Amáinese de golpe;—y todo á un punto
  Se hizo, y el peligro se repara.
Estos montes que veis que están tan juntos,
  Son los que Acroceraunos son llamados,
  De infame nombre, como yo barrunto.
Asieron de los remos los honrados,
  Los tiernos, los melífluos, los godescos,
  Y los de á cantimplora[31] acostumbrados.
Los frios los asieron y los frescos,
  Asiéronlos tambien los calurosos,
  Y los de calzas largas y gregüescos.

To thee belong, LOFRASO without guile,
  The epithets of subtle and sincere,
  My 'boatswain' henceforth be thy name and style!"
Thus said Mercurius to our cavalier,
  Who in the gangway quick assumed his grade,
  Armed with a rattan, cutting and severe;
Of his own verse, I fancy, it was made,
  And in a twinkling, how I do not know,
  Whether by Heaven's or LOFRASO'S aid,
On through the strait we safe and sound did go,
  Without immersing any poet there;
  Such strength lay in the good Sardinian's blow.
But presently there loomed another scare,
  Had not Mercurius shouted with avail,
  And with a roar that rent the very air:
"Helmsman, to windward! Easy, shorten sail
  At once!" And in a trice the whole was done;
  And danger fled, though fiercely blew the gale.
"These hills ye see, that seem to join in one,
  Are styled th' Acroceraunian,[30] fatal name;
  A worse repute, I trow, than these have none."
Took to the oars the honoured men of fame,
  The tender, gothic, they of honied song,
  And those who cool their drinks to damp their flame;
The bards cold-blooded, and the frisky throng,
  The hot-brained also to the work did warm,
  And those with hosen short, and hosen long.

Del sopraestante daño temerosos,
   Todos á una la galera empujan,
   Con flacos y con brazos poderosos.
Debajo del bajel se somurmujan
   Las sirenas que dél no se apartaron,
   Y á si mismas en fuerzas sobrepujan.
Y en un pequeño espacio la llevaron
   A vista de Corfú, y á mano diestra
   La isla inexpugnable se dejaron.
Y dando la galera á la siniestra
   Discurria de Grecia las riberas,
   Adonde el cielo su hermosura muestra.
Mostrábanse las olas lisonjeras,
   Impeliendo el bajel süavemente,
   Como burlando con alegres véras.
Y luego al parecer por el oriente,
   Rayando el rubio sol nuestro horizonte
   Con rayas rojas, hebras de su frente,
Gritó un grumete y dijo: El monte, el monte,
   El monte se descubre, donde tiene
   Su buen rocin el gran Belorofonte.
Por el monte se arroja, y á pié viene
   Apolo á recebirnos.—Yo lo creo,
   Dijo LOFRASO, ya llega á la Hipocrene.
Yo desde aquí columbro, miro y veo
   Que se andan solazando entre unas matas
   Las musas con dulcisimo recreo.

The gloom o'erhanging filled them with alarm,
   And all, as one, did make the galley go,
   With flaccid muscle, or with brawny arm.
The Sirens in their turn dived down below
   The barque, from which to part they had no mind,
   And each with unaccustomed strength did glow;
And in brief space they bore it with the wind
   In sight of Corfu; and upon the right
   They left the isle impregnable behind;
And to the left they turned the galley quite,
   And coasted all along the shores of Greece,
   Where beams the sky, with beauty wondrous bright.
The light waves wooed the barque, and would not cease
   With flattering touch and soft to kiss its prow,
   Like wits that trifle with some stately piece.
And as the Sun 'bove our horizon now
   Began to show his glorious head, bedight
   With ruby rays, the tresses of his brow,
"The hill, the hill!" sang out a watch-boy bright,
   "I spy the hill, where that great man, I ween,
   Bellorophon doth stall his steed of might!
Apollo down the hill with eager mien
   Doth haste to welcome us." "Zounds! I believe,"
   LOFRASO cried, "He's got to Hippocrene!
From here I almost, yea, I do perceive
   The Muses walking on the verdant floors,
   And 'neath the bushes taking sweet reprieve;

Unas antiguas son, otras novatas,
    Y todas con lijero paso y tardo
    Andan las cinco en pié, las cuatro á gatas.
—Si tú tal ves, dijo Mercurio, oh sardo
    Poeta, que me corten las orejas,
    O me tengan los hombres por bastardo,
Dime, ¿por qué algun tanto no te alejas
    De la ignorancia, pobreton, y adviertes
    Lo que cantan tus rimas en tus quejas?
¿Por qué con tus mentiras nos diviertes
    De recebir á Apolo cual se debe,
    Por haber mejorado vuestras suertes?—
En esto mucho mas que el viento leve
    Bajó el lucido Apolo á la marina,
    A pié, porque en su carro no se atreve.
Quitó los rayos de la faz divina,
    Mostróse en calzas y en jubon vistoso,
    Porque dar gusto á todos determina.
Seguiale detras un numeroso
    Escuadron de doncellas bailadoras,
    Aunque pequeñas, de ademan brioso.
Supe poco despues, que estas señoras,
    Sanas las mas, las ménos mal paradas,
    Las del tiempo y del sol eran las Horas.
Las medio rotas eran las menguadas,
    Las sanas las felices, y con esto
    Eran todas en todo apresuradas.

Some are of old aspect, and some with stores
    Of youth : and with a slow or lithesome gait
    Five walk on foot, and four upon all fours!"
" Sardinian Bard!" cried Mercury irate,
    " If such thou seest, may villains slit my ears,
    And brand the name of bastard on my pate!
Say, scurvy one, why dost not with thy years
    Leave off thy folly, and with wisdom scan
    What thine own rhymes are chanting thro' thy tears?
Why with thy lies dost thou disturb our plan,
    Of giving Phœbus a reception rare
    For having turned thee out a better man?"
On this, more quickly than the wind could bear,
    The bright Apollo hied him to the shore
    On foot, for with his car he would not dare:
The beams from off his face divine he tore,
    In hose and comely doublet was he seen,
    That simply dressed he all might please the more.
Behind him came a bevy, o'er the green,
    Of damsels gaily tripping one by one,
    Of middling stature, yet of sprightly mien;
I knew these maidens, dancing as they run,—
    Most of them blooming, and ill-fared the rest—
    To be the Hours of Time and of the Sun:
The half-dishevelled were the Hours unblest,
    The blooming were the lucky; and withal
    They tripped along with measureless unrest.

Apolo luego con alegre gesto
　　Abrazó á los soldados, que esperaba
　　Para la alta ocasion que se ha propuesto.
Y no de un mismo modo acariciaba
　　A todos, porque alguna diferencia
　　Hacia con los que él mas se alegraba.
Que á los de señoria y excelencia
　　Nuevos abrazos dió, razones dijo,
　　En que guardó decoro y preeminencia.
Entre ellos abrazó á DON JUAN DE ARGUIJO,
　　Que no sé en qué, ó cómo, ó cuándo hizo
　　Tan áspero viaje y tan prolijo.
Con él á su deseo satisfizo
　　Apolo y confirmó su pensamiento,
　　Mandó, vedó, quitó, hizo y deshizo.
Hecho pues el sin par recebimiento,
　　Do se halló DON LUIS DE BARAHONA,
　　Llevado allí por su merecimiento,
Del siempre verde lauro una corona
　　Le ofrece Apolo en su intencion, y un vaso
　　Del agua de Castalia y de Helicona.
Y luego vuelve el majestoso paso,
　　Y el escuadron pensado y de repente
　　Le sigue por las faldas del Parnaso.
Llegóse en fin á la Castalia fuente,
　　Y en viéndola, infinitos se arrojaron
　　Sedientos al cristal de su corriente.

Apollo now, with joy that was not small,
 Embraced the soldiers, whose embattled host
 Had come for lofty service at his call;
But not with equal warmth did he accost
 Each one; a certain shade of difference
 Was shewn to such as he affected most:
He gave to those of lordly excellence
 A fresh embrace; and from his mouth there thronged
 Words full of dignity and lofty sense.
DON JUAN DE ARGUIJO[32] to this class belonged;
 I know not when, nor by what means conveyed,
 He made the voyage, toilsome and prolonged;
With him Apollo in the highest grade
 Was satisfied, whose thoughts confirmed his own:
 He bade, forbade, unbound, made and unmade.
Like matchless favour to that man was shown,
 LUIS DE BARAHONA of renown,
 Who hither came by good desert alone;
Apollo offered him a laurel crown
 Unfading, and a jar of water clear
 Drawn from Castalia and from Helicon.
With stately step he turned; and in his rear
 The squadron marched, the eager and the grave,
 And by Parnassus' skirts their course did steer;
At length he reached Castalia's bubbling wave,
 And at its sight the crowds, with compact will,
 Rushed to its crystal stream, and 'gan to lave;

Unos no solamente se hartaron,
　Sino que piés y manos, y otras cosas
　Algo mas indecentes se lavaron.
Otros mas advertidos, las sabrosas
　Aguas gustaron poco á poco, dando
　Espacio al gusto, á pausas melindrosas.
El brindez y el caraos se puso en bando,
　Porque los mas de bruces, y no á sorbos,
　El suave licor fueran gustando.
De ambas manos hacian vasos corvos
　Otros, y algunos de la boca al agua
　Temian de hallar cien mil estorbos.
Poco á poco la fuente se desagua,
　Y pasa en los estómagos bebientes,
　Y aun no se apaga de su sed la fragua.
Mas díjoles Apolo:—Otras dos fuentes
　Aun quedan, Aganipe é Hipocrene,
　Ambas sabrosas, ambas excelentes;
Cada cual de licor dulce y perene,
　Todas de calidad aumentativa
　Del alto ingenio que á gustarlas viene.—
Beben, y suben por el monte arriba,
　Por entre palmas, y entre cedros altos,
　Y entre árboles pacíficos de oliva.
De gusto llenos y de angustia faltos,
　Siguiendo á Apolo el escuadron camina,
　Unos á pedicoj, otros á saltos.

Some, not content their thirsty mouths to fill,
  Made eager haste to bathe their hands and feet,
  And sundry matters more uncomely still;
Others, with higher wisdom and discreet,
  Imbibed the savoury waters drop by drop,
  And paused and lingered to enjoy the treat;
For social toast the many would not stop,
  Nor quaffed the wholesome liquor with their lips,
  But bending earthward lapped it like a sop:
Others from hollowed hands took gulping sips,
  Whilst some, 'twixt mouth and water, on the spot,
  Trembled to meet a hundred thousand slips;
The fountain's water less and lesser got
  As down the drinkers' gullets it did pour;
  But still their thirst was like a furnace hot.
Apollo cried: "We have two fountains more,
  Fair Aganippe and bright Hippocrene,
  Both good to drink, and both with ample store;
Sweet and perennial are their streams, I ween,
  And each with qualities designed to make
  The lofty genius loftier and serene!"
They drink; and up the mountain's slope they take
  Their way, amid the palms and cedars high,
  And at their tramp the peaceful olives quake;
Filled to the full with good they onward hie
  Behind Apollo in a lengthened line—
  Some jog along, some leaping seem to fly.

Al pié sentado de una antigua encina
  Ví á ALONSO DE LEDESMA, componiendo
  Una cancion angélica y divina.
Conocile, y á él me fui corriendo
  Con los brazos abiertos como amigo,
  Pero no se movió con el estruendo.
—¿No ves, me dijo Apolo, que consigo
  No está LEDESMA ahora? No ves claro
  Que está fuera de si, y está conmigo?—
A la sombra de un mirto, al verde amparo
  JERÓNIMO DE CASTRO sesteaba.
  Varon de ingenio peregrino y raro.
Un motete imagino que cantaba
  Con voz süave; yo que dé admirado
  De verle alli, porque en Madrid quedaba.
Apolo me entendió, y dijo:—Un soldado
  Como este no era bien que se quedara
  Entre el ocio y el sueño sepultado.
Yo le truje, y sé cómo; que á mi rara
  Potencia no la impide otra ninguna,
  Ni inconveniente alguno la repara.—
En esto se llegaba la oportuna
  Hora á mi parecer de dar sustento
  Al estómago pobre, y mas si ayuna;
Pero no le pasó por pensamiento
  A Delio, que el ejército conduce,
  Satisfacer al misero hambriento.

Beneath an ancient oak I saw recline
  ALONSO DE LEDESMA, deep in thought,
  Anent some lay angelic and divine ;
I knew him well ; and running up I sought
  To clasp my friend, with open arms and free,
  But though I called he moved not as he ought ;
Apollo said to me : " And dost not see
  LEDESMA is not with himself to-day,
  He is beyond himself, he is with me ! "
Beneath a myrtle's shade, with grand array
  Of green, JERÓNIMO DE CASTRO sate,
  A man of wit uncommon in our day ;
I fancy he was chanting a motet
  With dulcet voice ; since in Madrid he stayed,
  I marvelled much to see him here in state.
Apollo answered to my thoughts and said :
  " It was not well, that soldier such as he
  Should buried lie in dreams and slothful shade ;
I brought him and know how ; no powers that be
  Can turn my rare power from its purpose fast,
  Nor aught malign can hinder my decree ! "
It seemed to me the hour had come at last,
  For giving fresh supply and nutriment
  To my poor stomach, wearied of its fast ;
But Delius' thoughts on higher things were bent,
  And, at his army's head, he would not stay
  A hungry wretch's cravings to content !

Primero á un jardin rico nos reduce,
   Donde el poder de la naturaleza,
   Y el de la industria mas campea y luce.
Tuvieron los Hespérides belleza
   Menor, no le igualaron los Pensiles
   En sitio, en hermosura y en grandeza.
En su comparacion se muestran viles
   Los de Alcinoo, en cuyas alabanzas
   Se han ocupado ingenios bien sotiles:
No sujeto del tiempo á las mudanzas,
   Que todo el año primavera ofrece
   Frutos en posesion, no en esperanzas.
Naturaleza y arte alli parece
   Andar en competencia, y está en duda
   Cuál vence de las dos, cuál mas merece.
Muéstrase balbuciente y casi muda,
   Si le alaba la lengua mas experta,
   De adulacion y de mentir desnuda.
Junto con ser jardin, era una huerta,
   Un soto, un bosque, un prado, un valle ameno,
   Que en todos estos titulos concierta,
De tanta gracia y hermosura lleno,
   Que una parte del cielo parecia
   El todo del bellisimo terreno.
Alto en el sitio alegre Apolo hacia,
   Y allí mandó que todos se sentasen
   A tres horas despues de mediodia.

First to a garden rich he led the way,
  Where Nature's power the palm did fully share
  With Labour's skill to make a grand array;
The famed Hesperides were not so fair;
  The Hanging gardens held a lower scale
  For site, and loveliness, and grandeur rare;
Those of Alcinoüs[33] were coldly pale
  Compared with it; though many wits sublime
  Have of their beauty told a wondrous tale;
It changeth not at all with changing Time,
  For all the year Spring offers, in her glee,
  Not hopeful blooms, but fruits in all their prime.
Here Art and Nature strive for mastery,
  And still the doubt remains, which of the two
  Is master yet, and which deserves to be;
The tongue most practised, and most apt to woo,
  Begins to stutter, crying in the dark
  For words to praise it, adequate and true.
More than a garden, 'tis a pleasure park,
  A grove, an orchard, vale, and meadow sweet,
  For all these titles aptly hit the mark;
With such superb delights is it replete,
  That everywhere, throughout that wonder-land,
  A part of Heaven itself we seem to meet.
On this fair site Apollo took his stand,
  And here, that each one should himself install
  At three hours after noon, he gave command;

Y porque los asientos señalasen
El ingenio y valor de cada uno,
Y unos con otros no se embarazasen,
A despecho y pesar del importuno
Ambicioso deseo, les dió asiento
En el sitio y lugar mas oportuno.
Llegaban los laureles casi á ciento,
A cuya sombra y troncos se sentaron
Algunos de aquel número contento.
Otros los de las palmas ocuparon,
De los mirtos y hiedras, y los robles
Tambien varios poetas albergaron.
Puesto que humildes, eran de los nobles
Los asientos cual tronos levantados,
Porque tú, oh envidia, aqui tu rabia dobles.
En fin, primero fuéron ocupados
Los troncos de aquel ancho circuito,
Para honrar á poetas dedicados,
Antes que yo, en el número infinito,
Hallase asiento: y así en pié quedéme
Despechado, colérico y marchito.
Dije entre mi: ¿Es posible que se extreme
En perseguirme la fortuna airada,
Que ofende á muchos y á ninguno teme?
Y volviéndome á Apolo, con turbada
Lengua le dije lo que oirá el que gusta
Saber, pues la tercera es acabada,
La cuarta parte desta empresa justa.

And that each special seat might well recall
　The sitters' genius and peculiar grace,
　And give no cause for strife, nor inward gall,
The god himself apportioned each his place,
　Upon the spot most fitting to his fame,
　And left Ambition nowhere in the race.
To full a hundred there the laurels came,
　Beneath whose leafy trunks and shades profound
　A certain number sat, in happy frame;
Others among the palms a refuge found,
　While sundry poets sought for harbourage
　Beneath the myrtles, oaks, and ivy round;
The noblest seats were on a lofty stage,
　Humble, I ween, but high as thrones in pride,
　For this, O Envy, fume with double rage!
And so, throughout that circuit large and wide,
　The shady trunks were occupied at last,
　Which for the poets' use were set aside,
Before that I, among that number vast,
　Could find a seat; and so I stood alone
　On foot, with wonder and with rage aghast;
I inly said: "Is't possible that one
　To such extremes by Fortune can be stung,
　Who injures many, and hath fear of none?"
And turning to Apollo, with a tongue
　Somewhat confused, I said what may be heard
　By him who lists, while part the fourth is sung
Of this grand work; for here ends part the third.

CAPITULO IV.

Suele la indignacion componer versos;
  Pero si el indignado es algun tonto,
  Ellos tendrán su todo de perversos.
De mi yo no sé mas, sino que pronto
  Me hallé para decir en tercia rima
  Lo que no dijo el desterrado al Ponto.
Y asi le dije á Delio:—No se estima,
  Señor, del vulgo vano el que te sigue
  Y al árbol sacro del laurel se arrima.
La envidia y la ignorancia le persigue,
  Y asi envidiado siempre y perseguido,
  El bien que espera por jamas consigue.
Yo corté con mi ingenio aquel vestido,
  Con que al mundo la hermosa *Galatea*
  Salió para librarse del olvido.
Soy por quien *la Confusa* nada fea
  Pareció en los teatros admirable,
  Si esto á su fama es justo se le crea.

CHAPTER IV.

Anger at times will issue forth in verse,
    But, if the angry one be light of head,
    His rhymes are apt to take a turn perverse;
For me I know but this: by passion led,
    I found me chanting forth, in tercets free,
    Things which the Pontine exile never said:
" Not by the mob," quoth I, " esteemed is he
    Who follows you, my lord, and leans his back
    For rest agaiust the laurel's sacred tree;
Envy and folly ever dog his track,
    And, envied thus and driven to distress,
    The good he hopes for he must ever lack.
I cut and fashioned by my wit the dress,
    With which fair *Galatea*[34] sought the light,
    And left the region of forgetfulness;
I'm he whose *La Confusa*, handsome quite,
    Made in the theatres a grand display,
    If common fame hath told the matter right;

Yo con estilo en parte razonable
   He compuesto *Comedias*, que en su tiempo
   Tuvieron de lo grave y de lo afable.
Y he dado en *Don Quijote* pasatiempo
   Al pecho melancólico y mohino
   En cualquiera sazon, en todo tiempo.
Yo he abierto en mis *Novelas* un camino,
   Por do la lengua castellana puede
   Mostrar con propiedad un desatino.
Yo soy aquel que en la invencion excede
   A muchos, y al que falta en esta parte,
   Es fuerza que su fama falta quede.
Desde mis tiernos años amé el arte
   Dulce de la agradable poësia,
   Y en ella procuré siempre agradarte.
Nunca voló la pluma humilde mia
   Por la region satirica, bajeza
   Que á infames premios y desgracias guia.
Yo el soneto compuse que asi empieza,
   Por honra principal de mis escritos:
   Voto á Dios, que me espanta esta grandeza.
Yo he compuesto *Romances* infinitos,
   Y el de los *Celos* es aquel que estimo,
   Entre otros que los tengo por malditos.
Por esto me congojo y me lastimo
   De verme solo en pié, sin que se aplique
   Arbol que me conceda algun arrimo.

I've *Comedies* composed whose style of play
 To reason so conformed, that on the stage
 They showed fair mingling of the grave and gay;
I've given in *Don Quixote*,[35] to assuage
 The melancholy and the moping breast,
 Pastime for every mood, in every age;
I've in my *Novels* opened, for the rest,
 A way whereby the language of Castile
 May season fiction with becoming zest;
I'm he who soareth in creative skill
 'Bove many men; who lacks a goodly share
 Of this, his fame at last will fare but ill;
From tender years I've loved, with passion rare,
 The winsome art of Poesy the gay,
 In this to please thee hath been all my care;
My humble pen hath never winged its way
 Athwart the field satiric, that low plain
 Which leads to foul rewards, and quick decay;
I penned the *Sonnet*[36] with this opening strain,
 (To crown my writings with their chiefest grace,)
 I vow to God, such grandeur stuns my brain!
I've of *Romances*[37] penned a countless race—
 The one of Jealousy I prize the best—
 The rest, I trow, are in a parlous case;
And so I'm very wroth, and much distressed
 To see me here on foot, alone to gaze,
 No tree to give me but a little rest;

Yo estoy, cual decir suelen, puesto á pique
  Para dar á la estampa al gran *Persiles*,
  Con que mi nombre y obras multiplique.
Yo en pensamientos castos y sotiles,
  Dispuestos en soneto de á docena,
  He honrado tres sugetos fregoniles.
Tambien al par de *Filis* mi *Filena*
  Resonó por las selvas, que escucharon
  Mas de una y otra alegre cantilena.
Y en dulces varias rimas se llevaron
  Mis esperanzas los lijeros vientos,
  Que en ellos y en la arena se sembraron.
Tuve, tengo y tendré los pensamientos,
  Merced al cielo que á tal bien me inclina,
  De toda adulacion libres y exentos.
Nunca pongo los piés por do camina
  La mentira, la fraude y el engaño,
  De la santa virtud total ruina.
Con mi corta fortuna no me ensaño,
  Aunque por verme en pié, como me veo,
  Y en tal lugar, pondero asi mi daño.
Con poco me contento, aunque deseo
  Mucho.—A cuyas razones enojadas,
  Con estas blandas respondió Timbreo:
—Vienen las malas suertes atrasadas,
  Y toman tan de léjos la corriente,
  Que son temidas, pero no excusadas.

I'm on the point—to use a common phrase—
  Of giving great *Persiles* to the press,
  Which shall my name and works still higher raise;
I, with chaste thoughts and full of subtleness,
  In sonnets by the dozen did array
  Three scullion beings in a comely dress;
To rival *Phyllis,* my *Phylena* gay
  Hath carolled through the woods, whose leafy land
  Gave back the sound of many a merry lay;
In sweet and varied rhymes the zephyrs bland
  Have borne my dreamy hopes away from me,
  Which sowed their seed on these, and on the sand.
My thoughts were ever, are, and still shall be—
  Thanks be to Heaven that so hath bent my mind—
  From every form of flattery safe and free.
Whate'er betide, my steps are ne'er inclined
  Where travel falsehood, fraud, and base deceit,
  The total wreck of honour in mankind.
My narrow fortune doth not stir my heat,
  Although to stand on foot, and in this throng,
  As now I see me, makes my loss complete;
With little I'm content, although I long
  For much." To such proofs of disordered mind
Thymbræus answered, with the blandest tongue:
" Men's evil fortunes swell up from behind,
  Bringing their current with them from afar,
  And so are feared, but cannot be declined;

El bien les viene á algunos de repente,
  A otros poco á poco y sin pensallo,
  Y el mal no guarda estilo diferente.
El bien que está adquirido, conservallo
  Con maña, diligencia y con cordura,
  Es no menor virtud que el granjeallo.
Tú mismo te has forjado tu ventura,
  Y yo te he visto alguna vez con ella,
  Pero en el imprudente poco dura.
Mas si quieres salir de tu querella,
  Alegre, y no confuso, y consolado,
  Dobla tu capa, y siéntate sobre ella.
Que tal vez suele un venturoso estado,
  Cuando le niega sin razon la suerte,
  Honrar mas merecido, que alcanzado.
—Bien parece, señor, que no se advierte,
  Le respondí, que yo no tengo capa.—
  Él dijo:—Aunque sea así, gusto de verte.
La virtud es un manto con que tapa
  Y cubre su indecencia la estrecheza,
  Que exenta y libre de la envidia escapa.—
Incliné al gran consejo la cabeza,
  Quedéme en pié; que no hay asiento bueno,
  Si el favor no le labra, ó la riqueza.
Alguno murmuró, viéndome ajeno
  Del honor que pensó se me debia,
  Del planeta de luz y virtud lleno.

To some, good comes at once with sudden jar,
   To others, bit by bit without a strain,
   The steps of evil no wise different are ;
The good, that hath been wrested, to maintain
   With shrewd, firm grasp that cannot be undone,
   Is no less virtue than the good to gain ;
Thyself hast fickle Fortune wooed and won,
   Oft have I seen thee with her times agone,
   But from the imprudent she is fain to run.
Yet would'st thou shew thyself, all quarrel gone,
   Gay, gladsome, not put out in any wise,
   Double thy cloak, and seat thyself thereon !
For he, who merits luck which fate denies
   Without good reason, and in mood severe,
   Is honoured more than if he won the prize ! "
" My lord, it hath escaped you quite, I fear,
   That I possess no cloak ! " was my reply ;
   " No less," quoth he, " I'm glad to see thee here,
For virtue is the cloak which poverty
   Wraps round her form, to clothe withal her shame,
   And so the shafts of envy pass her by ! "
I bowed my head before the court of Fame,
   And stood on foot ; good seat hath none by right,
   If wealth or favour do not urge the claim.
One near me murmured, pitying my plight,
   Deprived of honour which he thought my due,
   Fresh from the orb of potence and of light.

En esto pareció que cobró el dia
　Un nuevo resplandor, y el aire oyóse
　Herir de una dulcisima armonía.
Y en esto por un lado descubrióse
　Del sitio un escuadron de ninfas bellas,
　Con que infinito el rubio dios holgóse.
Venia en fin, y por remate dellas
　Una resplandeciendo, como hace
　El sol ante la luz de las estrellas.
La mayor hermosura se deshace
　Ante ella, y ella sola resplandece
　Sobre todas, y alegra y satisface.
Bien asi semejaba, cual se ofrece
　Entre liquidas perlas y entre rosas
　La aurora que despunta y amanece.
La rica vestidura, las preciosas
　Joyas que la adornaban, competian
　Con las que suelen ser maravillosas.
Las ninfas que al querer suyo asistian,
　En el gallardo brio y bello aspecto,
　Las artes liberales parecian.
Todas con amoroso y tierno afecto,
　Con las ciencias mas claras y escogidas,
　Le guardaban santisimo respeto.
Mostraban que en servirla eran servidas,
　Y que por su ocasion de todas gentes
　En mas veneracion eran tenidas.

Methought at once a strange resplendent hue
O'erspread the sky, and lo ! the smitten air
Was pierced with sweetest music through and
And at one side I spied a squadron fair   [through;
Of beauteous nymphs come dancing to the song,
With whom the ruddy god made sporting rare.
In rear of these there came at length along
A wondrous being,³⁰ radiant as the light
The Sun emits amid the starry throng;
The highest beauty pales before her sight
And she remains alone in her array,
Diffusing round contentment and delight.
She looked the likeness of Aurora gay,
When, mid the roses and the pearly dew,
She wakes to life and ushers in the day ;
The garments rich, and jewels bright of hue
Which gemmed her person, might hold rivalry
With all the world of wonders ever knew.
The nymphs that did her bidding faithfully,
In brilliant bearing and in sprightly case,
Seemed to me all the liberal arts should be ;
They all with tender love, and joined to these
The Sciences, most clear and most reserved,
Did pay her reverence as on bended knees ;
Showed that in serving her themselves were served,
And that through her they, mid the nations all,
A higher honour and respect preserved.

Su influjo y su reflujo las corrientes
　Del mar y su profundo le mostraban,
　Y el ser padre de rios y de fuentes.
Las yerbas su virtud la presentaban,
　Los árboles sus frutos y sus flores,
　Las piedras el valor que en si encerraban.
El santo amor, castisimos amores,
　La dulce paz, su quietud sabrosa,
　La guerra amarga todos sus rigores.
Mostrábasele clara la espaciosa
　Via, por donde el sol hace contino
　Su natural carrera y la forzosa.
La inclinacion, ó fuerza del destino,
　Y de qué estrellas consta y se compone,
　Y cómo influye este planeta ó sino,
Todo lo sabe, todo lo dispone
　La santa hermosisima doncella,
　Que admiracion como alegria pone.
Preguntéle al parlero, si en la bella
　Ninfa alguna deidad se disfrazaba,
　Que fuese justo el adorar en ella.
Porque en el rico adorno que mostraba
　Y en el gallardo sér que descubria,
　Del cielo y no del suelo semejaba.
—Descubres, respondió, tu bobería,
　Que há que la tratas infinitos años,
　Y no conoces que es la Poësia.

The Ocean's currents at her simple call
   Their ebb and flow displayed; the abyss revealed
   The parent source of waters great and small;
The herbs their virtues at her touch did yield,
   The trees their fruits, its sweetest flowers the vale,
   The stones their inward worth which lay concealed;
To her did love its chastest joys unveil,
   Benignant peace its quietude and cheer,
   Terrific war its horrors and its wail;
The spacious path was to her vision clear,
   Through which the Sun, in never-ending line,
   Pursues his natural and constrained career;
The force of fate which makes our wills incline,
   The elements that form the starry light,
   The influence of this planet or that sign—
All this she knows, all this she wields aright,
   That holy maid of loveliness complete,
   Who claims at once our wonder and delight.
I asked the spokesman, if beneath that sweet
   And radiant form no god lay in disguise,
   Whom to adore in her were worship meet;
Since by the rich adornment of her guise,
   And by her gallant mien and bravery,
   She seemed no child of earth but of the skies:
" Thou shew'st," quoth he, " thy crass stupidity,
   Since thou hast wooed her now for many a year,
   And knowest not that she is Poesy!"

—Siempre la he visto envuelta en pobres paños,
   Le repliqué; jamas la vi compuesta
   Con adornos tan ricos y tamaños:
Parece que la he visto descompuesta,
   Vestida de color de primavera
   En los dias de cutio y los de fiesta.
—Esta, que es la poesia verdadera,
   La grave, la discreta, la elegante,
   Dijo Mercurio, la alta y la sincera,
Siempre con vestidura rozagante
   Se muestra en cualquier acto que se halla,
   Cuando á su profesion es importante.
Nunca se inclina, ó sirve á la canalla
   Trovadora, maligna y trafalmeja,
   Que en lo que mas ignora, ménos calla.
Hay otra falsa, ansiosa, torpe y vieja,
   Amiga de sonaja y morteruelo,
   Que ni tabanco, ni taberna deja.
No se alza dos, ni aun un coto del suelo,
   Grande amiga de bodas y bautismos,
   Larga de manos, corta de cerbelo.
Tómanla por momentos parasismos,
   No acierta á pronunciar, y si pronuncia,
   Absurdos hace, y forma solecismos.
Baco donde ella está, su gusto anuncia,
   Y ella derrama en coplas el polco,
   Campo y vereda, y el mastranzo, y juncia.

"To me," I said, " she ever did appear
  In homely clothes, but never met my gaze
  Arrayed in robes so rich and grand as here ;
Seems 'tis her undress I have seen always,
  Picked out with colours of the spring demure,
  Alike on working as on holidays!"
Mercurius answered : " 'Tis but reason sure
  That Poesy the true, the grave, discreet,
  The elegant, the lofty, and the pure,
Should robe herself in vesture that is meet
  For all the actions which her rank become,
  For each in turn appropriate and complete ;
She never stoops to serve the common scum
  Of ballad mongers, impudent and mean,
  Who bawl the loudest when they should be dumb.
There is a false, a base, old, haggard quean,
  Friend of the drum and timbrel mummery,
  Seldom from bench or tavern to be seen ;
Hardly two hand-breadths from the floor springs she,
  At weddings and at baptisms she sits,
  Though huge her fists, her brains but scanty be ;
At times she falleth into sudden fits,
  Cannot articulate, or if she can,
  Her blundering grammar proves her muddled wits ;
Her tastes are those of Bacchus and his clan,
  And in her couplets, over mead and wold,
  She scatters thyme and mint and gentian.

Pero aquesta que ves es el asco,
    La gala de los cielos y la tierra,
    Con quien tienen las musas su burco;
Ella abre los secretos y los cierra,
    Toca y apunta de cualquiera ciencia
    La superficie y lo mejor que encierra.
Mira con mas ahinco su presencia,
    Verás cifrada en ella la abundancia
    De lo que en bueno tiene la excelencia.
Moran con ella en una misma estancia
    La divina y moral filosofía,
    El estilo mas puro y la elegancia.
Puede pintar en la mitad del dia
    La noche, y en la noche mas escura
    El alba bella que las perlas cria.
El curso de los rios apresura,
    Y le detiene; el pecho á furia incita,
    Y le reduce luego á mas blandura.
Por mitad del rigor se precipita
    De las lucientes armas contrapuestas,
    Y da vitorias, y vitorias quita.
Verás cómo le prestan las florestas
    Sus sombras, y sus cantos los pastores,
    El mal sus lutos y el placer sus fiestas,
Perlas el Sur, Sabea sus olores,
    El oro Tiber, Hibla su dulzura,
    Galas Milan, y Lusitania amores.

But she whom thou dost see is, as of old,
　　The charm and glory of the heavens and earth,
　　With whom the Muses secret counsel hold;
She seals up secrets and she lets them forth,
　　And of each science scans, in graver mood,
　　At once its surface and its inner worth.
Survey her person with an eye more shrewd,
　　Thou'lt see enshrined, and in abundance great,
　　The very sum and quintessence of good;
There lodge with her, within the self-same gate,
　　Philosophies both moral and divine,
　　A style the purest and the most ornate.
At mid-day she can paint in sombrest line
　　The night, and in the depth of deepest night
　　The rosy dawn that makes the pearls to shine.
The river's course she quickens into might,
　　Then curbs; she makes the breast with fury rise,
　　Then soothes to blandness with her touch so light.
Into the midst of clashing arms she flies,
　　Where ranks opposing meet with dire intent,
　　She victory gives and victory denies.
Mark how the forests at her sight present
　　Their shades, their songs the shepherds of the dale,
　　Sorrow its weeds, and pleasure its content;
Pearls from the south, odours from Saba's vale,
　　Gold from the Tiber, sweets from Hybla's mount,
　　Galas from Milan, loves from Portingale,

En fin, ella es la cifra, do se apura
  Lo provechoso, honesto y deleitable,
  Partes con quien se aumenta la ventura.
Es de ingenio tan vivo y admirable,
  Que á veces toca en punto que suspenden,
  Por tener no sé qué de inexcrutable.
Alábanse los buenos, y se ofenden
  Los malos con su voz, y destos tales
  Unos la adoran, otros no la entienden.
Son sus obras heróicas immortales,
  Las liricas süaves, de manera
  Que vuelven en divinas las mortales.
Si alguna vez se muestra lisonjera,
  Es con tanta elegancia y artificio,
  Que no castigo, sino premio espera.
Gloria de la virtud, pena del vicio
  Son sus acciones, dando al mundo en ellas
  De su alto ingenio y su bondad indicio—
En esto estaba, cuando por las bellas
  Ventanas de jazmines y de rosas,
  Que amor estaba á lo que entiendo en ellas,
Divisé seis personas religiosas,
  Al parecer de honroso y grave aspeto,
  De luengas togas, limpias y pomposas.
Preguntéle á Mercurio:—¿Por qué efeto
  Aquellos no parecen y se encubren,
  Y muestran ser personas de respeto?—

Fall at her feet. In fine, she is the fount
  Where blend the sweet, the useful, and the sound,
  Whence human bliss doth swell its rich account.
She is of wit so lively and profound,
  That oft she touches points, whose tangled knot
  By mortal fingers cannot be unbound.
Her voice exalts the good; an evil lot
  She gives the bad; and at her holy shrine
  The former kneel, the last regard her not.
Her works heroic shall immortal shine:
  Her lyrics sweet obey such sovereign laws,
  That mortal things they change into divine;
If she at times with flattery urge her cause,
  It is with skill so rare and so refined,
  As deadens censure and demands applause;
The scourge of vice and virtue's crown combined,
  Her deeds proclaim to all the world aright
  Her lofty genius and her gentle mind."
I stood entranced, when thro' some loop-holes bright
  With jasmines, and with roses sweet entwined,
  Where Love, methinks, might harbour with delight,
I spied six persons[11] of a clerkly kind,
  Who seemed of reverend and grave aspect,
  With long white togas stately and refined.
I asked Mercurius: "Why do such affect
  To hide and burrow in this lurking-place,
  Who yet appear most worthy of respect?"

A lo que él respondió:—No se descubren
   Por guardar el decoro al alto estado
   Que tienen, y asi el rostro todos cubren.
—¿Quién son, le repliqué, si es que te es dado
   Decirlo?—Respondióme:—No por cierto,
   Porque Apolo lo tiene asi mandado.
—¿No son poetas?—Si.—Pues yo no acierto
   A pensar por qué causa se desprecian
   De salir con su ingenio á campo abierto.
¿Para qué se embobecen y se aneciam,
   Escondiendo el talento que da el cielo
   A los que mas de ser suyos se precian?
Aquí del rey: ¿qué es esto? ¿qué recelo,
   O celo les impide á no mostrarse
   Sin miedo ante la turba vil del suelo?
¿Puede ninguna ciencia compararse
   Con esta universal de la poesia,
   Que límites no tiene do encerrarse?
Pues siendo esto verdad, saber querria
   Entre los de la carda, ¿cómo se usa
   Este miedo, ó melindre, ó hipocresia?
Hace monseñor versos, y rehusa
   Que no se sepan, y él los comunica
   Con muchos, y á la lengua ajena acusa.
Y mas que siendo buenos, multiplica
   La fama su valor, y al dueño canta
   Con voz de gloria y de alabanza rica.

He answered : "Fain would they preserve the grace
  And chaste reserve, that fit the high degree
  They occupy, and so they veil the face!"
"Who are they," cried I, "if 'tis given thee
  To tell the same?" "Nay," quoth he, "by my fay,
  Such is Apollo's mandate and decree!"
"Are they not poets?" "Yea!" "Then sooth to say,
  It puzzles me to guess why they should fear
  To bring their genius to the light of day;
Why do they play the fool and ninny here,
  Wrapping their talent up, great Heaven's gift
  To all her sons who hold the favour dear?
Ho! in the King's name! what may be their drift?
  What dread or shame forbids them now to face
  Earth's scurvy groundlings and their veils uplift?
Can any science claim to hold a place
  Beside the science vast of Poesy,
  That brooks no limit to its wide embrace?
If this be truth, then prithee tell to me,
  To such fraternity what end doth serve
  This fear, this niceness, this hypocrisy?
Monsignor maketh verses, with reserve
  That none shall know it, and he shares the same
  With friends; yet will incognito preserve!
But be they good, it is the work of Fame
  To spread their worth, and to their master sing
  With voice of glory, blazoning his name!

¿ Qué mucho pues, si no se le levanta
    Testimonio á un pontifice poeta,
    Que digan que lo es ? por Dios que espanta.
Por vida de Lanfusa la discreta,
    Que si no se me dice quién son estos
    Togados de bonete y de muceta;
Que con trazas y modos descompuestos
    Tengo de reducir á behetria
    Estos tan sosegados y compuestos.
—Por Dios, dijo Mercurio, y á fe mia,
    Que no puedo decirlo, y si lo digo,
    Tengo de dar la culpa á tu porfia.
—Dilo, señor, que desde aqui me obligo
    De no decir que tú me lo dijiste,
    Le dije, por la fe de buen amigo.—
El dijo :—No nos cayan en el chiste,
    Llégate á mi, dirételo al oido,
    Pero creo que hay mas de los que viste.
Aquel que has visto alli del cuello erguido,
    Lozano, rozagante y de buen talle,
    De honestidad y de valor vestido,
Es el DOTOR FRANCISCO SANCHEZ : dalle
    Puede cual debe Apolo la alabanza,
    Que pueda sobre el cielo levantalle.
Y aun mas su famoso ingenio alcanza,
    Pues en las verdes hojas de sus dias
    Nos da de santos frutos esperanza.

Why this ado then ? Is't a treasonous thing
    To call a pontiff poet, and repeat
    The name aloud ? By heaven, 'tis maddening!
Now, by Lanfusa's life, the fair discreet,
    If I be told not who these gentry are,
    With rochet and biretta robed complete,
In boisterous fashion will I levy war,
    And bring confusion on this brotherhood,
    Who seem too quiet and composed by far!"
"By God," cried Mercury, " and all that's good!
    I may not tell thee, but an' if I do,
    I'll lay the blame upon thy hardihood!"
" My lord, I bind me now and henceforth too
    To tell to none what thou shalt tell to me,
    'Pon honour," quoth I, "of good friend and true!"
He answered : "They may think our jesting free,
    Come closer, I will whisper in thine ear;
    Faith, there be more of them than thou didst see.
He, whom thou saw'st with stiff neck and austere,
    Lusty, resplendent, stately to the view,
    In worth arrayed and modesty severe,
Is DOCTOR DON FRANCISCO SANCHEZ, who
    Will soar in praises far above the skies,
    If now Apollo gives him but his due ;
And higher yet his famous wit shall rise,
    Since in the green leaves of his tender prime
    The pregnant hope of holy fruitage lies.

Aquel que en elevadas fantasias,
　　Y en éxtasis sabrosos se regala,
　　Y tanto imita las acciones mias,
Es el MAESTRO ORENSE, que la gala
　　Se lleva de la mas rara elocuencia
　　Que en las aulas de Aténas se señala.
Su natural ingenio con la ciencia
　　Y ciencias aprendidas le levanta
　　Al grado que le nombra la excelencia.
Aquel de amarillez marchita y santa,
　　Que le encubre de lauro aquella rama,
　　Y aquella hojosa y acopada planta,
FRAY JUAN BAPTISTA CAPATAZ se llama,
　　Descalzo y pobre, pero bien vestido
　　Con el adorno que le da la fama.
Aquel que del rigor fiero de olvido
　　Libra su nombre con eterno gozo,
　　Y es de Apolo y las musas bien querido,
Anciano en el ingenio, y nunca mozo,
　　Humanista divino, es segun pienso,
　　El insigne DOTOR ANDRES DEL POZO.
Un licenciado de un ingenio immenso
　　Es aquel, y aunque en traje mercenario,
　　Como á señor le dan las musas censo:
RAMON se llama, auxilio necesario
　　Con que Delio se esfuerza y ve rendidas
　　Las obstinadas fuerzas del contrario.

His neighbour, who on fantasies sublime
  And savoury ecstasies doth feast withal,
  And with my actions makes his own to chime,
El MAESTRO ORENSE is, with claim not small
  To plume himself on higher eloquence
  Than ever sounded in Athenian hall;
His native wit, joined to the sober sense
  Which science lends, exalts him to the grade
  Which stamps him with the name of Excellence.
Whose face with saintly pallor is o'erlaid,
  Of whom that laurel branch conceals the sight,
  To whom that leafy cup-like plant gives shade,
FRAY JUAN BAPTISTA CAPATAZ is hight;
  Barefooted, poor, but well arrayed withal,
  For fame enrobes him with her vesture bright.
He, who from dark oblivion's tyrant thrall
  Hath snatched his name, and endless rapture found,
  Loved by Apollo and the Muses all,
In wit an ancient, in his youth profound,
  A humanist divine, is, let me say,
  DOCTOR ANDRES DE POZO the renowned.
The next, a graduate with mighty play
  Of wit, although in Mercy's garb he go,
  To him as lord the Muses tribute pay;
By name RAMÓN; whose strength will deal a blow,
  Whereby Apollo shall to every wind
  Scatter the stolid forces of the foe.

El otro, cuyas sienes ves ceñidas
    Con los brazos de Dafne en triunfo honroso,
    Sus glorias tiene en Alcalá esculpidas.
En su ilustre teatro vitorioso
    Le nombra el cisne en canto no funesto,
    Siempre el primero como á mas famoso.
A los donaires suyos echo el resto
    Con propiedades al gorron debidas,
    Por haberlos compuesto ó descompuesto.
Aquestas seis personas referidas,
    Como están en divinos puestos puestas,
    Y en sacra religion constituidas,
Tienen las alabanzas por molestas,
    Que les dan por poetas, y holgarian
    Llevar la loa sin el nombre á cuestas.
—¿Por qué, le pregunté, señor, porfian
    Los tales á escribir y dar noticia
    De los versos que paren y que crian?
Tambien tiene el ingenio su codicia,
    Y nunca la alabanza se desprecia;
    Que al bueno se le debe de justicia.
Aquel que de poeta no se precia,
    ¿Para qué escribe versos, y los dice?
    ¿Por qué desdeña lo que mas aprecia?
Jamas me contenté, ni satisfice
    De hipócritas melindres.   Llanamente
    Quise alabanzas de lo que bien hice.

Of him, whose temples thou dost see entwined
  With Daphne's arms, and triumph in his face,
  The glories are in Alcalá enshrined;
Within the theatre of that famed place,
  The Swan, with song auspicious, doth proclaim
  And hail him first and foremost in the race;
Upon his piquant jests he staked his fame,
  With sallies that the college youth befit,
  Whose wit composed or decomposed the same.
These six, whose characters we now have hit,
  Who proudly are installed in posts divine,
  And on the high chairs of religion sit,
Esteem as irksome all the praises fine
  That would proclaim them poets, yet delight
  To have the honour and the name decline."
"Why then, my lord," I cried, "do such men write,
  And notify the verses to mankind
  It suits them to conceive and bring to light?
For genius too is greedily inclined,
  And will not brook that any praise be lost
  Which justly falls to merit of high kind;
Who of the name of poet will not boast,
  Why doth he scribble and the matter tell,
  Why doth he scorn the thing he covets most?
I never sat content beneath the spell
  Of prim mock-modesty; without pretence
  I courted praise for that which I did well!"

K

—Con todo quiere Apolo, que esta gente
   Religiosa se tenga aquí secreta,
   Dijo el dios que presume de elocuente.
Oyóse en esto el son de una corneta,
   Y un trapa, trapa, aparta, afuera, afuera,
   Que viene un gallardísimo poeta.
Volví la vista y ví por la ladera
   Del monte un postillon y un caballero
   Correr, como se dice, á la lijera.
Servia el postillon de pregonero,
   Mucho mas que de guia, á cuyas voces
   En pié se puso el escuadron entero.
Preguntóme Mercurio:—¿No conoces
   Quién es este gallardo, este brioso?
   Imagino que ya le reconoces.
   Bien, yo le respondí; que es el famoso
   Gran DON SANCHO DE LEIVA, cuya espada
   Y pluma harán á Delio venturoso.
Venceráse sin duda esta jornada
   Con tal socorro;—y en el mismo instante,
   Cosa que parecia imaginada,
Otro favor no ménos importante
   Para el caso temido se nos muestra;
   De ingenio y fuerzas, y valor bastante.
Una tropa gentil por la siniestra
   Parte del monte descubrióse: ¡oh cielos,
   Que dais de vuestra providencia muestra!

"It is Apollo's wish, take no offence,
  That these religious folk keep secret here!"
Quoth he, the god who vaunts his eloquence.
On this a cornet's sound struck on mine ear, [way!
  With tramp, tramp! stand aside! ho, clear the
  For lo! a stalwart poet draweth near!
I turned mine eyes, and up the mountain way
  They fell on a postilion and a knight
  Posting at tip-top speed, as people say;
He served as herald, that postilion wight,
  More than as guide, and at his shouts and cries
  The assembled squadron rose and stood upright;
Mercurius asked me: "Dost thou recognize
  This gallant one, so lordly in his state,
  I fancy he's familiar to thine eyes?
"I know him well, he is the famed and great
  DON SANCHO DE LEIVA, he whose blade
  And pen shall make Apollo fortunate;
Beyond a doubt with such distinguished aid
  He'll win the day!" And presently in sight
  There came unlooked for, and with grand parade,
A band of allies as important quite,
  To try conclusions with the dreaded foe,
  Equipped with genius, solid worth, and might.
A gallant troop it was, and from below
  It up the left side of the hill did prance;
  Ye heavens! what proofs of providence ye show!

Aquel discreto JUAN DE VASCONCELOS
   Venia delante en un caballo bayo,
   Dando á las musas lusitanas celos.
Tras él el CAPITAN PEDRO TAMAYO
   Venia, y aunque enfermo de la gota,
   Fué al enemigo asombro, fué desmayo.
Que por él se vió en fuga, y puesto en rota;
   Que en los dudosos trances de la guerra
   Su ingenio admira y su valor se nota.
Tambien llegaron á la rica tierra,
   Puestos debajo de una blanca seña,
   Por la parte derecha de la sierra,
Otros, de quien tomó luego reseña
   Apolo; y era dellos el primero
   El jóven DON FERNANDO DE LODEÑA,
Poeta primerizo, insigne, empero
   En cuyo ingenio Apolo deposita
   Sus glorias para el tiempo venidero.
Con majestad real, con inaudita
   Pompa llegó, y al pié del monte pára
   Quien los bienes del monte solicita:
El LICENCIADO fué JUAN DE VERGARA
   El que llégo, con quien la turba ilustre
   En sus vecinos medios se repara.
De Esculapio y de Apolo gloria y lustre,
   Si no, dígalo el santo bien partido,
   Y su fama la misma envidia ilustre.

On a bay charger, riding in advance,
   Came JUAN DE VASCONCELOS, shrewd and gay,
   On whom the Lusian Muses look askance;
Behind him rode TAMAYO on the way,
   That Captain bold who, crippled with the gout,
   Yet struck the foe with terror and dismay;
At sight of him fled all the rabble rout,
   For in a doubtful strife, and hand to hand,
   Flame forth his genius and his valour stout.
Then by the right side of the mountain grand,
   Beneath the shadow of a banner white,
   Came others marching to the wealthy land,
Whose ranks Apollo mustered with delight;
   And first and foremost came upon the stage
   That youth, FERNANDO DE LODEÑA hight,
A budding poet, and withal a sage,
   Within whose wit Apollo graciously
   Doth hoard his glories for the coming age.
With rarest pomp, and regal majesty,
   A new arrival prancèd up in state
   To claim the mountain's hospitality;
JUAN DE VERGARA he, Licentiate,
   Whom all the squadron welcomed with delight,
   Of all their dearest rights a champion great;
Apollo's glory, Esculapius' light,
   In him a man of double fame we hail,
   And Envy's self proclaims his honour bright.

Con él fué con aplauso recebido
   El docto JUAN ANTONIO DE HERRERA,
   Que puso en fil el desigual partido.
¡Oh, quién con lengua en nada lisonjera,
   Sino con puro afecto en grande exceso,
   Dos que llegaron alabar pudiera!
Pero no es de mis hombros este peso.
   Fuéron los que llegaron los famosos,
   Los dos maestros CALVO Y VALDIVIESO.
Luego se descubrió por los undosos
   Llanos del mar una pequeña barca
   Impelida de remos presurosos:
Llegó, y al punto della desembarca
   El gran DON JUAN DE ARGOTE Y DE GAMBOA
   En compañia de DON DIEGO ABARCA,
Sugetos dinos de incesable loa;
   Y DON DIEGO JIMENEZ Y DE ENCISO
   Dió un salto á tierra desde la alta proa.
En estos tres la gala y el aviso
   Cifró cuanto de gusto en sí contienen,
   Como su ingenio y obras dan aviso.
Con JUAN LOPEZ DEL VALLE otros dos vienen
   Juntos allí, y es PAMONES el uno,
   Con quien las musas ojeriza tienen,
Porque pone sus piés por do ninguno
   Los puso, y con sus nuevas fantasías
   Mucho mas que agradable es importuno.

Now welcomed we, with shouts that rent the vale,
  JUAN DE HERRERA, learned man and strong,
  Whose weight alone might turn the unequal scale.
O who, with fitting and unflattering tongue
  But with a truthful accent, pure and plain,
  Shall praise aright these two who march along?
But on my shoulders doth not rest this strain,
  For these be men renowned for learned stores,
  CALVO and VALDIVIESO, masters twain!
Anon we saw, impelled by lusty oars,
  A little barque skim o'er the ocean wide,
  Which sought a refuge on the sacred shores;
We spied therein, as nearer it did glide,
  DON JUAN DE ARGOTE, and a man no less
  Than DON DIEGO ABARCA at his side;
And with them DON DIEGO XIMENES
  Y DE ENCISO; from the lofty prow
  He gave one leap the sacred land to press;
To these great three the praise we must allow
  Of matchless taste, combined with wisdom's glance
  Their genius and their works proclaim it now.
With JUAN LOPEZ DEL VALLE two advance,
  And in their midst may PAMONES be seen,
  On whom the Muses look somewhat askance:
For why, he treads where foot hath never been,
  And with new fantasies, not void of blame,
  He wearies more than he delights, I ween.

De lejas tierras por incultas vías
   Llegó el bravo irlandes DON JUAN BATEO,
   Jerjes nuevo en memoria en nuestros dias.
Vuelvo la vista, á MANTUANO veo,
   Que tiene al gran Velasco por Mecénas,
   Y ha sido acertadísimo su empleo.
Dejarán estos dos en las ajenas
   Tierras, como en las propias, dilatados
   Sus nombres, que tú, Apolo, así lo ordenas.
Por entre dos fructíferos collados
   (¿ Habrá quien esto crea, aunque lo entienda?
   De palmas y laureles coronados,
El grave aspecto del ABAD MALUENDA
   Pareció, dando al monte luz y gloria,
   Y esperanzas de triunfo en la contienda.
¿ Pero de qué enemigos la vitoria
   No alcanzará un ingenio tan florido,
   Y una bondad tan digna de memoria?
DON ANTONIO GENTIL DE VARGAS, pido
   Espacio para verte, que llegaste
   De gala y arte y de valor vestido:
Y aunque de patria jinoves, mostraste
   Ser en las musas castellanas doto,
   Tanto que al escuadron todo admiraste.
Desde el indio apartado del remoto
   Mundo llegó mi amigo MONTESDOCA,
   Y el que anudó de Arauco el nudo roto.

By trackless paths DON JUAN BATEO came,
  That sturdy Irishman, across the sea,
  In this our day a Xerxes new to fame!
I turn me round and MANTUANO see,
  Whose patron is VELASCO the renowned,
  No worthier Mæcenas could there be;
The names of these two worthies yet shall sound
  Throughout their own, and foreign lands to boot,
  Phœbus hath willed it, so it shall be found.
Between two hillocks bearing wealth of fruit,
  (Can one believe so strange a thing hath been?)
  With palms and laurels crowned from brow to foot,
The Abbot MALUENDA'S form was seen,
  Gilding the mount with light and lustre sage,
  With hope of triumph in the struggle keen;
For say, what chance hath any foeman's rage
  Against that kindly heart, that genius bright,
  So worthy of a place in Memory's page?
GENTIL DE VARGAS, DON ANTONIO hight,
  I crave fit space thy manly form to greet,
  With art, and elegance, and worth bedight!
A Genoese by birth, yet at the feet
  Of our Castilian Muses wert thou bred,
  And so the squadron gives thee honour meet.
From India's furthest confines, travel-sped,
  Came MONTESDOCA to the front, my friend,
  And he who knit Arauco's broken thread;

Dijo Apolo á los dos :—A entrambos toca
   Defender esta vuestra rica estancia
   De la canalla de vergüenza poca.
La cual de error armada y de arrogancia
   Quiere canonizar y dar renombre
   Inmortal y divino a la ignorancia;
Que tanto puede la aficion que un hombre
   Tiene á sí mismo, que ignorante siendo,
   De buen poeta quiere alcanzar nombre.—
En esto otro milagro, otro estupendo
   Prodigio se descubre en la marina,
   Que en pocos versos declarar pretendo.
Una nave á la tierra tan vecina
   Llegó, que desde el sitio donde estaba,
   Se ve cuanto hay en ella y determina.
De mas de cuatro mil salmas pasaba,
   Que otros suelen llamarlas toneladas,
   Ancha de vientre y de estatura brava:
Así como las naves que cargadas
   Llegan de la oriental India á Lisboa,
   Que son por las mayores estimadas;
Esta llegó desde la popa á proa
   Cubierta de poetas, mercancía
   De quien hay saca en Calicut y en Goa.
Tomóle al rojo dios alferecía
   Por ver la muchedumbre impertinente,
   Que en socorro del monte le venia.

"Ye twain!" Apollo cried, "must now defend
  This wealthy land of yours, from the advance
  Of that most shameless crew who hither wend!
For, armed with error and with arrogance,
  They fain would canonize and give acclaim,
  Immortal and divine, to ignorance;
For such conceit in human breast doth flame,
  That ignorance itself will make men bold
  To deck them with the poet's worthy name!"
On this another prodigy, untold
  And monstrous, met our vision on the strand,
  Which in few stanzas I will now unfold:
For lo! a ship sailed up so close to land,
  That I could see, from my commanding site,
  Its whole contents and wherewith it was manned;
Four thousand lasts, I ween, it measured quite,
  Or tons, the common word used by the mass,
  With spacious beam, and spars of towering height;
Like to the ships that with their cargoes pass
  From Eastern India to Lisboa's shore,
  Which are esteemed the grandest of their class;
It came, from poop to prow, crammed o'er and o'er
  With poets, goodly merchandise they sell
  In Calicut's and Goa's ample store;
The ruddy god into convulsions fell
  At sight of such a vile presumptuous crew,
  Who came to grace, and save the hill as well;

Y en silencio rogó devotamente
   Que el vaso naufragase en un momento
   Al que gobierna el húmido tridente.
Uno de los del número hambriento
   Se puso en esto al borde de la nave,
   Al parecer mohino y mal contento:
Y en voz que ni de tierna ni süave
   Tenia un solo adarme, gritando
   (Dijo tal vez colérico, y tal grave)
Lo que impaciente estuve yo escuchando,
   Porque vi sus razones ser sactas,
   Que iban mi alma y corazon clavando.
—O tú, dijo, traidor, que los poetas
   Canonizaste de la larga lista,
   Por causas y por vias indirectas:
¿Dónde tenias, Magances, la vista
   Aguda de tu ingenio, que asi ciego
   Fuiste tan mentiroso coronista?
Yo te confieso, ó barbaro, y no niego
   Que algunos de los muchos que escogiste
   Sin que el respeto te forzase ó el ruego,
En el debido punto los pusiste;
   Pero con los demas sin duda alguna
   Pródigo de alabanzas anduviste.
Has alzado á los cielos la fortuna,
   De muchos que en el centro del olvido
   Sin ver la luz del sol ni de la luna,

And silently he prayed a prayer or two
  That he, who holds the trident in his hand,
  Would sink the ship and in an instant too.
One of the number of that hungry band,
  Who seemed a moping and a peevish knave,
  Upon the vessel's bulwarks took his stand,
And with a croaking voice, that never gave
  One note or soft or sweet, his words did roll
  Right out, now choleric, now grave :
Whereat my temper I could scarce control,
  For, like to barbs, his words were all devised
  To go right whizzing through my heart and soul :
"Thou traitor," cried he, "who hast canonized
  The poets on thy list of wondrous size,
  By crooked methods and most ill-advised !
O Magancés, where didst thou keep the eyes
  Of thy sharp wit, that, being stricken blind,
  Thou mad'st thyself the chronicler of lies?
I give thee credit, man of barbarous mind,
  That, of the many thou hast gathered here,
  Without request or force of any kind,
Thou hast put some within their proper sphere ;
  But with the rest thou hast been out of sight
  Too prodigal of praises, it is clear !
For many hast thou raised to Fortune's height,
  Who still in dark Oblivion's den should be,
  Without or Sun or Moon to give them light ;

Yacian: ni llamado, ni escogido
  Fué el gran pastor de Iberia, el gran BERNARDO
  Que DE LA VEGA tiene el apellido.
Fuiste envidioso, descuidado y tardo,
  Y á las ninfas de Henáres y pastores
  Como á enemigo les tiraste un dardo.
Y tienes tú poetas tan peores
  Que estos en tu rebaño, que imagino
  Que han de sudar si quieren ser mejores.
Que si este agravio no me turba el tino,
  Siete trovistas desde aqui diviso,
  A quien suelen llamar de torbellino,
Con quien la gala, discrecion y aviso
  Tienen poco que ver, y tú los pones
  Dos leguas mas allá del paraíso.
Estas quimeras, estas invenciones
  Tuyas, te han de salir al rostro un dia,
  Si mas no te mesuras y compones.—
Esta amenaza y gran descortesia
  Mi blando corazon llenó de miedo
  Y dió al traves con la paciencia mia.
Y volviéndome á Apolo con denuedo
  Mayor del que esperaba de mis años,
  Con voz turbada y con semblante acedo,
Le dije:—Con bien claros desengaños
  Descubro, que el servirte me granjea
  Presentes miedos de futuros daños.

Iberia's shepherd, grand BERNARDO he,
   Had in thy mission neither lot nor part,
   Who bears LA VEGA'S surname and degree;
Thou hadst an envious, careless, sluggish heart,
   And at Henares' nymphs and shepherds fine,
   As if they were thy foes, didst hurl thy dart;
And yet, within that great sheepfold of thine,
   Worse poets hast thou, who must sweat and strain,
   If they would better be, as I opine!
If such an outrage hath not turned my brain,
   Seven rhymesters there I see before mine eyes
   Of the Spasmodic order, it is plain;
In whom the witty, elegant, and wise
   Are at their lowest, yet thou giv'st them place
   Two leagues within the bounds of Paradise;
These quirks of thine, these whimsies void of grace,
   If so thou act not more composedly,
   Will rise one day and shame thee to thy face!"
This threat, and eke this great discourtesy,
   Did in my tender heart much dread inspire,
   And made the remnants of my patience flee;
And turning to Apollo, with more ire
   Than might be thought befitting my grave years,
   With quivering voice, and eke a spark of fire,
I said: "By such plain proofs it now appears,
   That serving thee makes worse my sorry plight,
   My future loss I read in present fears;

Haz, ó señor, que en público se lea
    La lista que Cilenio llevó á España,
    Porque mi culpa poca aqui se vea.
Si tu deidad en escoger se engaña,
    Y yo solo aprobé lo que él me dijo,
    ¿Por qué este simple contra mi se ensaña?
Con justa causa y con razon me affijo,
    De ver cómo estos bárbaros se inclinan
    A tenerme en temor duro y prolijo.
Unos, porque los puse, me abominan,
    Otros, porque he dejado de ponellos,
    De darme pesadumbre determinan.
Yo no sé cómo me avendré con ellos:
    Los puestos se lamentan, los no puestos
    Gritan, yo tiemblo destos y de aquellos.
Tú, señor, que eres dios, dales los puestos
    Que piden sus ingenios: llama y nombra
    Los que fueren mas hábiles y prestos.
Y porque el turbio miedo que me asombra,
    No me acabe, acabada esta contienda,
    Cúbreme con tu manto y con tu sombra.
O ponme una señal por do se entienda
    Que soy hechura tuya y de tu casa:
    Y así no habrá ninguno que me ofenda.
—Vuelve la vista y mira lo que pasa,—
    Fué de Apolo enojado la respuesta,
    Que ardiendo en ira el corazon le abrasa.

Let them, my lord, in public now recite
    The list Mercurius brought with him to Spain,
    Then shall my slender blame be brought to light;
If that your godship made wrong choice and vain,
    And I but echoed what Mercurius said,
    Why rails this fool at me with words insane?
With cause and reason do I vex my head,
    To see how men like these, with barbarous din,
    Conspire to keep me in perpetual dread:
Some scowl on me because I put them in,
    Others resolve, because I left them out,
    To make me feel the burden of my sin;
How to make peace with all I am in doubt,
    The chosen groan, the left-out cry apace,
    By both together am I put to rout.
Thou who art god, my lord, give each the place
    That fits his worth; name, summon to thine aid
    The ablest and the readiest in the race;
And lest this turmoil, which keeps me afraid,
    Should kill me quite, I would be let alone,
    Cast over me thy mantle and thy shade:
Grant me a sign, whereby it may be known
    That I'm thine offspring, of thy house and name,
    And henceforth none at me will cast a stone!"
" Turn thee to see a sight, and mark the same!"
    Apollo cried, with accents nowise sweet,
    While burning fury wrapped his heart in flame.

Volvíla, y vi la mas alegre fiesta,
 Y la mas desdichada y compasiva,
 Que el mundo vió, ni aun la verá cual esta.
Mas no se espere que yo aquí la escriba,
 Sino en la parte quinta, en quien espero
 Cantar con voz tan entonada y viva,
 Que piensen que soy cisne, y que me muero.

I turned me, and beheld the sweetest treat,
    The most distressful too, most worth a tear,
    The world e'er met with, or again shall meet ;
But do not think that I will tell it here,
    But in the fifth part ; where I hope and plan
    To sing with such a living voice and clear,
    That men will take me for a dying swan!

CAPITULO V.

Oyó el señor del húmido tridente
   Las plegarias de Apolo, y escuchólas
   Con alma tierna y corazon clemente.
Hizo de ojo, y dió del pié á las olas,
   Y sin que lo entendiesen los poetas
   En un punto hasta el cielo levantólas.
Y él por ocultas vías y secretas
   Se agazapó debajo del navío,
   Y usó con él de sus traidoras tretas.
Hirió con el tridente en lo vacio
   Del buco, y el estómago le llena
   De un copioso corriente amargo rio.
Advertido el peligro, al aire suena
   Una confusa voz, la cual resulta
   De otras mil que el temor forma y la pena.
Poco á poco el bajel pobre se oculta
   En las entrañas del cerúleo y cano
   Vientre, que tantas ánimas sepulta.

CHAPTER V.

The lord, that wields the humid trident, heard
   Apollo's prayers, and listened to his cries,
   With tender bosom and a kind regard.
He slyly winked, and made the waves to rise
   By dint of foot, and ere the poets knew,
   They reared their curling crests to kiss the skies;
And then, by secret paths and out of view,
   He burrowed 'neath the ship, where, uncontrolled,
   He better might his wicked plans pursue.
He struck his trident right into its hold,
   And, through the wound, into its vacant womb
   A rushing, roaring, briny current rolled.
A panic rose : and through the air did boom
   Of fear and pain a multitudinous cry,   [doom.
   Which sprung from thousand lips that wailed their
The luckless barque sinks slowly from the eye,
   Into the bosom of the hoary main,
   Wherein so many souls sepulchred lie ;

Suben los llantos por el aire vano
  De aquellos miserables, que suspiran
  Por ver su irreparable fin cercano.
Trepan y suben por las jarcias, miran
  Cuál del navío es el lugar mas alto,
  Y en él muchos se apiñan y retiran.
La confusion, el miedo, el sobresalto
  Les turba los sentidos, que imaginan
  Que desta á la otra vida es grande el salto.
Con ningun medio ni remedio atinan;
  Pero creyendo dilatar su muerte,
  Algun tanto á nadar se determinan.
Saltan muchos al mar de aquella suerte;
  Que al charco de la orilla saltan ranas
  Cuando el miedo ó el ruido las advierte.
Hienden las olas del romperse canas,
  Menudean las piernas y los brazos,
  Aunque enfermos están, y ellas no sanas.
Y en medio de tan grandes embarazos
  La vista ponen en la amada orilla,
  Deseosos de darla mil abrazos.
Y sé yo bien, que la fatal cuadrilla
  Antes que allí, holgara de hallarse
  En el Compas famoso de Sevilla.
Que no tienen por gusto el ahogarse,
  Discreta gente al parecer en esto;
  Pero valióles poco el esforzarse;

Up to the heavens rise the moanings vain
   Of these poor wretches as they shriek aloud,
   To see their end so certain and so plain ;
They clamber up by rigging and by shroud,
   They seek the top-most point with desperate strife,
   And cling together in a seething crowd ;
The flutter and the fear with horror rife
   Confound their senses, as they vent the whim :
   " How great the leap from this to t'other life!",
But close and closer comes the peril grim ;
   And some, determined further out to spin
   Their dying, make a bold resolve to swim ;
Into the sea they jump, to frogs akin,
   Which make from bank to pond a jerking bound,
   When fear assails them or some horrid din ;
They cleave the waves and cast the foam around,
   They ply their legs and arms with effort sore,
   Though feeble these, and those in no wise sound ;
And as they toil, on to the wished-for shore
   Their straining eyes with eager longing pass,
   Fain would they give it thousand hugs and more.
Full well I know that this doomed crew, alas!
   Had they the chance, with bounding joy would haste
   To tread again Sevilla's famed Compas !
For drowning, certes, doth not suit their taste,
   In this their great discretion may be seen,
   But all in vain their waning strength they waste.

Que el padre de las aguas echó el resto
  De su rigor, mostrándose en su carro
  Con rostro airado y ademan funesto.
Cuatro delfines, cada cual bizarro,
  Con cuerdas hechas de tejidas ovas
  Le tiraban con furia y con desgarro.
Las ninfas en sus húmidas alcobas
  Sienten tu rabia, ó vengativo nume,
  Y de sus rostros la color les robas.
El nadante poeta que presume
  Llegar á la ribera defendida,
  Sus ayes pierde y su teson consume;
Que su corta carrera es impedida
  De las agudas puntas del tridente,
  Entónces fiero y áspero homicida.
Quien ha visto muchacho diligente
  Que en goloso á sí mesmo sobrepuja,
  Que no hay comparacion mas conveniente,
Picar en el sombrero la granuja,
  Que el hallazgo le puso allí ó la sisa,
  Con punta alfileresca, ó ya de aguja;
Pues no con menor gana, ó menor prisa
  Poetas ensartaba el nume airado
  Con gusto infame, y con dudosa risa.
En carro de cristal venía sentado,
  La barba luenga y llena de marisco,
  Con dos gruesas lampreas coronado.

For now the briny Sire his rigour keen
    Will show, and in his car, in state arrayed,
    He shows his fiery face, and threatening mien ;
Four Dolphins, each the lustiest of their grade,
    With cords of sea-weed spun with cunning art,
    Drag it along with fierce fanfarronade ;
The nymphs within their humid alcoves start,
    O vengeful Sea-god, when they feel thine ire,
    Pale grow their ruddy cheeks beneath thy smart !
The swimming poet, who with keen desire
    Would plant his foot on the forbidden shore,
    Pants all in vain, and spends his flickering fire ;
For on the trident's points, full sharp and sore—
    A homicidal weapon then, I ween—
    He ends his short career, and swims no more.
Hast ever watched an urchin, brisk and keen,
    Himself o'ertopping in his greedy glow—
    More apt comparison hath never been—
Spike in his cap the grape-pips all a-row,
    Which honest find or filching placed therein,
    With point of needle, or hair-pin, or so ?
With no less pleasure, no less lusty din,
    Did Neptune spit the poets in his hate,
    With shameless gusto, and a dubious grin.
Upon a crystal car he sat in state,
    With flowing beard, all crisp with shells marine,
    While two fat lampreys crowned his ample pate :

Hacian de sus barbas firme aprisco
  La almeja, el morsillon, pulpo y cangrejo,
  Cual le suelen hacer en peña ó risco.
Era de aspecto venerable y viejo;
  De verde, azul y plata era el vestido,
  Robusto al parecer y de buen rejo;
Aunque como enojado, denegrido
  Se mostraba en el rostro; que la saña
  Así turba el color como el sentido.
Airado contra aquellos mas se ensaña
  Que nadan mas, y sáleles al paso,
  Juzgando á gloria tan cobarde hazaña.
En esto, ¡oh nuevo y milagroso caso,
  Dino de que se cuente poco á poco,
  Y con los versos de Torcato Taso!
Hasta aquí no he invocado, ahora invoco
  Vuestro favor, ó musas, necessario
  Para los altos puntos en que toco.
Descerrajad vuestro mas rico almario,
  Y el aliento me dad que el caso pide,
  No humilde, no ratero ni ordinario.
Las nubes hiende, el aire pisa y mide
  La hermosa Vénus Acidalia, y baja
  Del cielo, que ninguno se lo impide.
Traia vestida de pardilla raja
  Una gran saya entera, hecha al uso,
  Que le dice muy bien, cuadra y encaja.

Amongst his locks there nestled all serene
    The muscle, limpet, crab and polypus,
    Just as on reef or rock they may be seen ;
He was of old aspect and ponderous,
    With robes of green, and blue, and silvery white,
    And seemed robust withal, and vigorous ;
Being irate, his visage to the sight
    Appeared a swarthy black, for rage indeed,
    That fires the reason, turns the colour quite.
Against the stoutest swimmers doth he speed,
    And, as he passes, ploughs them down in ire,
    And counts as glory such a coward deed.
Now doth a new and wondrous thing transpire,
    Most worthy to be sung with great parade,
    And to the music of Torquato's lyre !
Till now have I no invocation made,
    But here, O Muses, I invoke your grace,
    The lofty theme I touch demands your aid ;
Unlock and ope your richest treasure-case,
    Clothe me with strength for this event so rare,
    Not mean, nor vulgar, nay, nor common-place.
The clouds are rent, and, poising in the air,
    From heaven descends, unhindered on the way,
    The Venus Acidalia, wondrous fair !
She comes arrayed in dress of sack-cloth grey,
    A goodly gown that wrapped her o'er and o'er,
    And fair and square, as people quaintly say ;

Luto que por su Adónis se le puso,
  Luego que el gran colmillo del berraco
  A atravesar sus ingles se dispuso.
A fe que si el mocito fuera Maco,
  Que él guardara la cara al colmilludo,
  Que dió á su vida y su belleza saco.
O valiente garzon, mas que sesudo,
  ¿Cómo estando avisado, tu mal tomas,
  Entrando en trance tan horrendo y crudo?
En esto las mansísimas palomas
  Que el carro de la diosa conducian
  Por el llano del mar, y por las lomas,
Por unas y otras partes discurrian,
  Hasta que con Neptuno se encontraron,
  Que era lo que buscaban y querian.
Los dioses que se ven, se respetaron,
  Y haciendo sus zalemas á lo moro,
  De verse juntos en extremo holgaron.
Guardáronse real grave decoro,
  Y procuró Ciprinia en aquel punto
  Mostrar de su belleza el gran tesoro.
Ensanchó el verdugado, y dióle el punto
  Con ciertos puntapiés que fuéron coces
  Para el dios que las vió y quedó difunto.
Un poeta llamado DON QUINCOCES
  Andaba semivivo en las saladas
  Ondas, dando gemidos y no voces.

Mourning which she for her Adonis wore,
  What time his groin received the slanting blow
  From the huge tusk of that most savage boar:
Had but the stripling bearded been, I know,
  That tusky one had thrust at him in vain,
  Nor ta'en his life, nor laid his beauty low!
O youth, of greater hardihood than brain,
  Why, shunning counsel, didst thy fate pursue,
  Courting a risk so monstrous and insane?
Now came the softest doves that ever flew,
  Guiding the chariot of that goddess blest,
  By plain and steep across the ocean blue;
They hurried hither, thither, without rest,
  Until they met with Neptune on the main,
  The wished-for object of their eager quest.
The immortals, as they met, to greet were fain,
  And making their salaams in Moorish way,
  Expressed their joy at meeting once again;
With royal gravity their part they play,
  And at this point the Cyprian had a mind
  The cream of all her beauty to display;
She spread her ample skirts before, behind,
  And with her twinkling toes gave kicks outright
  At the rapt god, who saw them and grew blind.
A certain poet, DON QUINCOCES hight,
  Was swimming half-alive amid the brine,
  Sputtering out groans, not words, with all his might;

Con todo dijo en mal articuladas
    Palabras:—O señora, la de Pafo,
    Y de las otras dos islas nombradas,
Muévate á compasion el verme gafo
    De piés y manos, y que ya me ahogo,
    En otras linfas que las del Garrafo.
Aquí será mi pira, aquí mi rogo,
    Aquí será QUINCOCES sepultado,
    Que tuvo en su crianza pedagogo.—
Esto dijo el mezquino, esto escuchado
    Fué de la diosa con ternura tanta,
    Que volvió á componer el verdugado.
Y luego en pié y piadosa se levanta,
    Y poniendo los ojos en el viejo,
    Desembudó la voz de la garganta.
Y con cierto desden y sobrecejo,
    Entre enojada y grave y dulce, dijo
    Lo que al húmido dios tuvo perplejo.
Y aunque no fué su razonar prolijo,
    Todavía le trujo á la memoria
    Hermano de quién era y de quién hijo.
Representóle cuán pequeña gloria
    Era llevar de aquellos miserables
    El triunfo infausto y la crüel vitoria.
El dijo:—Si los hados imnudables
    No hubieran dado la fatal sentencia
    Destos en su ignorancia siempre estables,

At length he said with stuttering speech and whine:
"O lady, thou of Paphos, and of two
More islands still, becrowned with fame divine !
My cramped condition now with pity view
 In hand and foot, for see I sink forlorn
 And drown in floods the Karaaf never knew ;
Here shall my pyre be lit ; here, to my scorn,
 QUINCOCES shall lie buried in the main,
 Who had a pedagogue when he was born !"
So said the hapless one ; and not in vain
 The goddess listened to his tale complete,
 As she arranged her much disordered train ;
And presently she started to her feet,
 And, glancing at the victim of the rod,
 She cleared her throat to make her voice more sweet;
And with a certain supercilious nod,
 Irate, and grave, and gracious all in one,
 She said what much perplexed the humid god :
And though her arguments were not long-spun,
 She yet contrived to bring before his mind
 What god he was, whose brother and whose son !
"What glory," quoth she, "dost thou hope to find
 In cruel triumphs, of so little weight,
 Over these wretches, feeblest of their kind !"
"Had not the Fates," he said, "with changeless hate
 Pronounced a fatal sentence on this band,
 Whose ignorance is fixed and obstinate,

Una brizna no mas de tu presencia
    Que viera yo, bellísima señora,
    Fuera de mi rigor la resistencia.
Mas ya no puede ser, que ya la hora
    Llegó donde mi blanda y mansa mano
    Ha de mostrar que es dura y vencedora.
Que estos de proceder siempre inhumano,
    En sus versos han dicho cien mil veces:
    Azotando las aguas del mar cano.
—Ni azotado, ni viejo me pareces,
    Replicó Vénus,—y él le dijo á ella:
    —Puesto que me enamoras, no enterneces;
Que de tal modo la fatal estrella
    Influye destos tristes, que no puedo
    Dar felice despacho á tu querella.
Del querer de los hados solo un dedo
    No me puedo apartar, ya tú lo sabes,
    Ellos han de acabar, y ha de ser cedo.
—Primero acabarás que los acabes,
    Le respondió madama, la que tiene
    De tantas voluntades puerta y llaves;
Que aunque el hado feroz su muerte ordene,
    El modo no ha de ser á tu contento,
    Que muchas muertes el morir contiene,—
Turbóse en esto el líquido elemento,
    De nuevo renovóse la tormenta,
    Sopló mas vivo y mas apriesa el viento.

A single thread held by thy gentle hand,
  Linking me, fairest lady, unto thee,
  Might curb my ruthlessness and make it bland!
But now it cannot; for the hour I see,
  When this soft hand of mine must show again
  How masterful and cruel it can be!
For hundred thousand times, in savage strain,
  Have these bold rhymesters sang most spitefully:
  Lashing the waters of the hoary main!
" Nor lashed, nor hoary, dost thou seem to me!"
  Responded Venus, and to her he said:
  " Though deep in love, yet bland I must not be;
For with such menace doth the star of dread
  Hang o'er these wretches, that I cannot do
  Thy bidding now, nor please thee on this head;
What the Fates will thou know'st I must pursue,
  Nor swerve one jot, so, please thee or displease,
  They must succumb and that right quickly too!"
"Thou shalt succumb thyself, ere thou make these!"
  Rejoined milady with no small disdain,
  Who of so many hearts holds gate and keys,
" For though ferocious Fate their death ordain,
  The manner of it doth not rest with you,
  For Death itself doth many deaths contain!"
On this the sullen waters restless grew,
  Afresh the tempest gathered in the sky,
  And wild and wilder still the strong winds blew;

La hambrienta mesnada, y no sedienta,
    Se rinde al huracan recien venido,
    Y por mas no penar muere contenta.
¡Oh raro caso y por jamas oido,
    Ni visto! Oh nuevas y admirables trazas
    De la gran reina obedecida en Gnido!
En un instante el mar, de calabazas
    Se vió cuajado, algunas tan potentes,
    Que pasaban de dos y aun de tres brazas.
Tambien hinchados odres y valientes,
    Sin deshacer del mar la blanca espuma,
    Nadaban de mil talles diferentes.
Esta trasmutacion fué hecha en suma
    Por Vénus de los lánguidos poetas,
    Porque Neptuno hundirlos no presuma.
El cual le pidió a Febo sus saetas,
    Cuya arma arrojadiza desde aparte
    A Vénus defraudara de sus tretas.
Negóselas Apolo; y veis do parte
    Enojado el vejon con su tridente,
    Pensándolos pasar de parte á parte;
Mas este se resbala, aquel no siente
    La herida, y dando esguince se desliza,
    Y él queda de la cólera impaciente.
En esto Bóreas su furor atiza,
    Y lleva antecogida la manada,
    Que con la de los cerdos simboliza.

The hungry crew, not thirsty then, trow I,
  Cowered as the hurricane came o'er the scene,
  And to be rid of pain were glad to die.
O rare event, till now nor heard nor seen!
  O new invention, dreamed not of before,
  The work of her whom Gnidus hails as queen!
For in a trice the sea seemed curdled o'er
  With pumpkins, some as stout as stout could be,
  That had a girth of twenty feet or more;
And bladders too went floating jauntily
  About, of every fancied form and size,
  Breasting the white foam of the curling sea;
These were the poor weak poets in disguise,
  Transmuted then by Venus, in such phase
  That Neptune might not drown them by surprise.
In wrath to Phœbus for his shafts he prays,
  That he, with cunning shots and stealthy too,
  Might frustrate Venus and her tricksome ways.
Phœbus declines; and now the old one view,
  How with his trident, sailing round and round,
  He tries to prick and pierce them through and
But this recoiled, and that felt not the wound, [through;
  But with a sidling motion sought the shore;
  Gods! how the wrathful ancient fumed and frowned!
Now woke up Boreas with a furious roar,
  And drove before his blast that rabble rough,
  That seemed like squeaking brood of bristly boar.

Pidiósclo la diosa aficionada
 A que vivan poetas zarabandos,
 De aquellos de la seta almidonada :
De aquellos blancos, tiernos, dulces, blandos,
 De los que por momentos se dividen
 En varias setas y en contrarios bandos.
Los contrapuestos vientos se comiden
 A complacer la bella rogadora,
 Y con un solo aliento la mar miden :
Llevando la piara gruñidora,
 En calabazas y odres convertida,
 A los reinos contrarios del aurora.
Desta dulce semilla referida,
 España, verdad cierta, tanto abunda,
 Que es por ella estimada y conocida.
Que aunque en armas y en letras es fecunda
 Mas que cuantas provincias tiene el suelo,
 Su gusto en parte en tal semilla funda.
Despues desta mudanza que hizo el cielo,
 O Vénus, ó quien fuese, que no importa
 Guardar puntualidad como yo suelo,
No veo calabaza, ó luenga ó corta,
 Que no imagine que es algun poeta
 Que allí se estrecha, encubre, encoge, acorta.
Pues que cuando veo un cuero (¡ oh mal discreta
 Y vana fantasía, así engañada,
 Que á tanta liviandad estas sujeta !)

The art-devoted goddess cried : Enough !
  Begged he would spare the poets zaraband,
  The jaunty ones, those of the starch and ruff,
The gay, the tender, honied and the bland,
  Those who, because they cannot well agree,
  Split up at times, and combat band with band !
The winds of every quarter join with glee
  To grant the lovely plaintiff her request,
  And with a single breath calm down the sea ;
Which bears the grunting herd upon its breast,
  In shape of pumpkins and of bladders light,
  On to the distant kingdoms of the west.
Of this sweet seed, whose fortunes I recite,
  Spain, of a truth, hath such an ample store
  That she thereby is known and gives delight ;
For though in arms and letters fertile more
  Than any other province of the earth,
  To this in part she owes her tuneful lore.
Since that great transformation which had birth
  In Heaven, or Venus, or some source akin—
  A nice exactness here has little worth—
I never see a pumpkin, stout or thin,
  But I imagine some poetic wight
  Lies curled up, cabined, cribbed, confined within ;
Then when I see a bladder, to what height,
  O fancy, dost thou soar, how dost thou flout,
  Becoming, sooth to say, a wanton light !

Pienso que el piezgo de la boca atada
   Es la faz del poeta, transformado
   En aquella figura mal hinchada.
Y cuando encuentro algun poeta honrado,
   Digo, poeta firme y valedero,
   Hombre vestido bien y bien calzado,
Luego se me figura ver un cuero,
   O alguna calabaza, y desta suerte
   Entre contrarios pensamientos muero;
Y no sé si lo yerre, ó si lo acierte,
   En que á las calabazas y á los cueros,
   Y á los poetas trate de una suerte.
Cernícalos que son lagartijeros
   No esperen de gozar las preeminencias
   Que gozan gavilanes no pecheros.
Puestas en paz ya las diferencias
   De Delio, y los poetas transformados
   En tan vanas y huecas apariencias,
Los mares y los vientos sosegados,
   Sumergióse Neptuno mal contento
   En sus palacios de cristal labrados.
Las mansísimas aves por el viento
   Volaron, y á la bella Cipriana
   Pusieron en su reino á salvamento.
Y en señal que del triunfo quedó ufana,
   Lo que hasta allí nadie acabó con ella,
   Del luto se quitó la saboyana,

For in its mouthlet, puckered all about,
  I seem to see loom out some poet's face,
  Transformed into that figure ill-blown out!
And when I meet some poet of the place,
  A so-called honoured, solid one, say I,
  A rhymester trimly clad, and shod with grace,
It seems to me a bladder I espy,
  Or else a pumpkin, and I feel inclined
  'Mid these conflicting thoughts, to faint and die!
Say am I too acute, or am I blind,
  These pumpkins, bladders, poets to array
  As natural products of the self-same kind?
The low-bred kites, that on the lizards prey,
  Must not expect to share the lofty prize
  With the free falcons, soaring as they may!
Apollo's griefs now settled in this wise,
  The weakly poets, saved from watery graves,
  Changed into vain and hollow mockeries,
The winds now hushed, and peaceful all the waves,
  Neptune plunged down, with discontented mind,
  And sought a refuge in his crystal caves.
The soft sweet doves took wing before the wind,
  And o'er the silvery sea did Venus glide,
  And reached her kingdom, leaving care behind.
And as a proof her triumph gave her pride,—
  What up till now she had declined to do—
  She straightway put her mourning gown aside;

Quedando en cueros tan briosa y bella,
   Que se supo despues que Marte anduvo
   Todo aquel dia y otros dos tras ella.
Todo el cual tiempo el escuadron estuvo
   Mirando atento la fatal ruina,
   Que la canalla transformada tuvo.
Y viendo despejada la marina,
   Apolo, del socorro mal venido,
   De dar fin al gran caso determina.
Pero en aquel instante un gran ruido
   Se oyó, con que la turba se alboroza,
   Y pone vista alerta y presto oído.
Y era quien le formaba una carroza
   Rica, sobre la cual venía sentado
   El grave DON LORENZO DE MENDOZA,
De su felice ingenio acompañado,
   De su mucho valor y cortesia,
   Joyas inestimables, adornado.
PEDRO JUAN DE REJAULE le seguia
   En otro coche, insigne valenciano
   Y grande defensor de la poesia.
Sentado viene á su derecha mano
   JUAN DE SOLIS, mancebo generoso,
   De raro ingenio, en verdes años cano.
Y JUAN DE CARVAJAL, dotor famoso,
   Les hace tercio, y no por ser pesado
   Dejan de hacer su curso presuroso.

And shone in Nature's garb so bright of hue,
   That Mars, as afterwards it came to light,
   Pursued her all that day, and other two.
All of which time the squadron stood in sight,
   Gazing upon the fatal wreckage there,
   Which left that vulgar mob transmuted quite;
And when Apollo saw the sea was bare
   Of these unwelcome allies, far and near,
   He made resolve to end the grand affair.
But hark! a rumbling sound strikes on the ear,
   Whereat the crowd is moved like troubled wave,
   And keep their ears erect, and vision clear!
It was a splendid chariot that gave
   Such clattering noise, wherein there sat in state
   LORENZO DE MENDOZA, wise and grave;
Attended by his happy wit and great,
   Adorned with worth and courtesy refined,
   Most precious jewels, and of sterling weight.
Within another coach there rode behind
   JUAN DE REJAULE, that Valencian brig
   A poet he, and bulwark of his kind;
JUAN DE SOLIS was seated at his right,
   A generous youth with rare wit at his call,
   And in his tender years a shining light;
That famous Doctor, JUAN DE CARVAJAL,
   Made up the third; though ponderous his weight
   They lessened not their eager speed at all;

Porque el divino ingenio al levantado
   Valor de aquestos tres que el coche encierra,
   No hay impedirle monte ni collado.
Pasan volando la empinada sierra,
   Las nubes tocan, llegan casi al cielo,
   Y alegres pisan la famosa tierra.
Con este mismo honroso y grave celo,
   BARTOLOMÉ DE MOLA Y GABRIEL LASO
   Llegaron a tocar del monte el suelo.
Honra las altas cimas de Parnaso
   DON DIEGO, que de SILVA tiene el nombre,
   Y por ellas alegre tiende el paso.
A cuyo ingenio y sin igual renombre
   Toda ciencia se inclina y le obedece,
   Y le levanta á sér mas que de hombre.
Dilátanse las sombras, y descrece
   El dia, y de la noche el negro manto
   Guarnecido de estrellas aparece.
Y el escuadron que habia esperado tanto
   En pié, se rinde al sueño perezoso
   De hambre y sed, y de mortal quebranto.
Apolo entónces poco luminoso,
   Dando hasta los antipodas un brinco,
   Siguió su accidental curso forzoso.
Pero primero licenció á los cinco
   Poetas titulados á su ruego,
   Que lo pidieron con extraño ahinco,

For neither hillock small nor mountain great
  Could check the wit divine or valour spoil
  Of those brave three who in the carriage sate;
They pass the topmost ridge with wingèd toil,
  They cleave the clouds, they almost touch the sky,
  And press with joyful feet the famous soil.
With like distinguished zeal, and earnest eye,
  BARTOLOMÉ DE MOLA climbs the height,
  While GABRIEL LASO with his friend doth vie.
Then DON DIEGO, he DE SILVA hight,
  Upon Parnassus' summit lighteth down,
  And pays it honour with supreme delight;
Before whose wit and unsurpassed renown
  Each science bends, and gives him homage fine,
  And decks his brow with more than mortal crown.
The shadows lengthen as the hours decline,
  And, peeping through the sable cloak of night,
  The twinkling stars with heightened lustre shine;
The squadron, that had been on foot since light,
  Sunk on the ground to sleep, as best they knew,
  Hungry and thirsty and exhausted quite.
Apollo then, whose light to nothing grew,
  To realms Antipodean gave a bound,
  To follow there his fated course anew;
But ere he parted he took leave profound
  Of the five titled poets who were there,
  And begged dismissal on most urgent ground;

Por parecerles risa, burla y juego
  Empresas semejantes; y asi Apolo
  Condescendió con sus deseos luego;
Que es el galan de Dafne único y solo
  En usar cortesia sobre cuantos
  Descubre el nuestro y el contrario polo.
Del lóbrego lugar de los espantos
  Sacó su hisopo el lánguido Morfeo,
  Con que ha rendido y embocado á tantos.
Y del licor que dicen que es Leteo,
  Que mana de la fuente del Olvido,
  Los párpados bañó á todos arreo.
El mas hambriento se quedó dormido:
  Dos cosas repugnantes, hambre y sueño,
  Privilegio á poetas concedido.
Yo quedé en fin dormido como un leño,
  Llena la fantasia de mil cosas,
  Que de contallas mi palabra empeño,
  Por mas que sean en si dificultosas.

For only smiles, and jests, and laughter rare
    Did such emprises kindle in their soul,
    And so Apollo stooped to grant their prayer;
For Daphne's gallant is unique and sole
    In all the points of courtesy refined,
    And reigns supreme therein from pole to pole.
Forth from the murky cave of horrors blind
    Came languid Morpheus, sprinkler in his hand,
    Wherewith he drugs the senses of mankind;
And with the liquor of Lethean land,
    Which from the fountain of Oblivion flows,
    He bathed the eyelids of the wearied band.
The very hungriest sank to sound repose:
    Hunger and sleep, two things repugnant quite,
    A privilege the poet only knows.
At length I slept, and like a log, that night,
    And of a thousand curious things did dream,
    Which here I pledge mine honour to recite,
However strange or difficult they seem.

CAPITULO VI.

De una de tres causas los ensueños
   Se causan, ó los sueños, que este nombre
   Les dan los que del bien hablar son dueños.
Primera, de las cosas de que el hombre
   Trata mas de ordinario: la segunda
   Quiere la medicina que se nombre
Del humor que en nosotros mas abunda:
   Toca en revelaciones la tercera,
   Que en nuestro bien mas que las dos redunda.
Dormí, y soñé, y el sueño la tercera
   Causa le dió principio suficiente
   A mezclar el ahito y la dentera.
Sueña el enfermo, á quien la fiebre ardiente
   Abrasa las entrañas, que en la boca
   Tiene de las que ha visto alguna fuente.
Y el labio al fugitivo cristal toca,
   Y el dormido consuelo imaginado
   Crece el deseo, y no la sed apoca.

CHAPTER VI.

From one of causes three do night-mares spring,
  Dreams, I should say, for such a name withal
  To ears polite may have a finer ring.
The first concerneth matters that recal
  Our daily life, our customary vein ;
  The second physic wills that we should call
After the fullest humour we contain ;
  The third with revelations hath to do,
  Which touch our welfare more than t'other twain.
I slept and dreamed ; and from the third cause grew
  My dreaming, which had ground enough, I trow,
  In indigestion and tooth-rasping too.
The sick man dreameth, he whose fevered brow
  Withers with fire, that near his mouth there flows
  Some bubbling stream he knows and covets now ;
And while to sip its fleeting stream he goes,
  His restless dreamy strivings are in vain,
  His thirst he slakes not, and his longing grows.

Pelea el valentisimo soldado
   Dormido, casi al modo que despierto
   Se mostró en el combate fiero armado.
Acude el tierno amante á su concierto,
   Y en la imaginacion dormido llega
   Sin padecer borrasca á dulce puerto.
El corazon el avariento entrega
   En la mitad del sueño á su tesoro,
   Que el alma en todo tiempo no le niega.
Yo, que siempre guardé el comun decóro
   En las cosas dormidas y despiertas,
   Pues no soy troglodita ni soy moro;
De par en par del alma abri las puertas,
   Y deje entrar al sueño por los ojos
   Con premisas de gloria y gusto ciertas.
Gocé durmiendo cuatro mil despojos,
   Que los conté sin que faltase alguno,
   De gustos que acudieron a manojos.
El tiempo, la ocasion, el oportuno
   Lugar correspondian al efeto,
   Juntos y por sí solo cada uno.
Dos horas dormi, y mas á lo discreto,
   Sin que imaginaciones ni pavores
   El celebro tuviesen inquïeto.
La suelta fantasia entre mil flores
   Me puso de un pradillo, que exhalaba
   De Pancaya y Sabea los olores.

The slumbering soldier fights his fights again,
  And in his dreaming, as in waking, freaks,
  He wields his trenchant blade, with might and
The tender lover gains what he bespeaks, [main;
  For as he sleeps he nears the wished-for goal,
  And without shipwreck makes the port he seeks;
The dreaming miser, in his restless roll,
  Wraps up his breast within his golden store,
  Where for all time he hath consigned his soul.
I, who am ever decent at the core,
  Alike in dreaming as in waking states,
  Since I am neither Troglodyte nor Moor,
Did of my soul throw open wide the gates,
  And through the eye-lids slumber entered in,
  With glorious promise, spite of all the fates.
Asleep, four thousand triumphs did I win,
  Which I could tell, without in any case
  Missing one single joy that lurked therein;
Time, opportunity, and fitting place,
  Each by itself and all of them in one,
  Produced effects of corresponding grace.
Two hours I slept, more soberly did none,
  No elfish vapours, nor fantastic powers
  Did through my quiet brain unbridled run;
My loosened Fancy strayed mid thousand flowers,
  Which decked a meadow fragrant with the scent
  Of far Panchaian or Sabaean bowers;

El agradable sitio se llevaba
　Tras sí la vista, que durmiendo, viva,
　Mucho mas que despierta se mostraba.
Palpable vi, mas no sé si lo escriba,
　Que á las cosas que tienen de imposibles
　Siempre mi pluma se ha mostrado esquiva.
Las que tienen vislumbre de posibles,
　De dulces, de süaves y de ciertas
　Explican mis borrones apacibles.
Nunca á disparidad abre las puertas
　Mi corto ingenio, y hállalas contino
　De par en par la consonancia abiertas.
¿Cómo puede agradar un desatino
　Si no es que de propósito se hace,
　Mostrándole el donaire su camino?
Que entónces la mentira satisface
　Cuando verdad parece, y está escrita
　Con gracia que al discreto y simple aplace.
Digo, volviendo al cuento, que infinita
　Gente vi discurrir por aquel llano,
　Con algazara placentera y grita:
Con hábito decente y cortesano
　Algunos, á quien dió la hipocresía
　Vestido pobre, pero limpio y sano.
Otros de la color que tiene el dia
　Cuando la luz primera se aparece
　Entre las trenzas de la aurora fria.

My straining vision roamed with great content
   Athwart that beauteous spot, for dreaming sight
   Hath, more than waking, range and wide extent.
What I distinctly saw I fear to write,
   For things impossible to mortal ken
   My prudish quill hath scruples to indite;
What hath a gleam of possible to men,
   The sweet, the smooth, the certain and the sound,
   These are fit topics for my blundering pen.
My narrow wit hath ne'er its gates unbound
   To things incongruous, but welcomes these
   Which keep within the range of reason's bound.
How can Extravaganza hope to please,
   Unless it hath some aim and purpose meet,
   Where humour leads the way and sprightly ease?
For Fiction then is conned with zest complete
   When likest truth, and writ with fitting grace
   To charm at once the simple and discreet!
Returning to my tale: A countless race
   I saw go up and down that meadow green,
   With jocund clamour and with lightsome pace;
Some clad in homely dress, of modish mien,
   To which hypocrisy lent cunning show
   Of poverty, but neat withal and clean;
Others in colours which the day doth know,
   When on the fresh Aurora's locks of gold
   The earliest streak of light begins to glow.

La variada primavera ofrece
   De sus varias colores la abundancia,
   Con que á la vista el gusto alegre crece.
La prodigalidad, la exorbitancia
   Campean juntas por el verde prado
   Con galas que descubren su ignorancia.
En un trono del suelo levantado
   (Do el arte á la materia se adelanta,
   Puesto que de oro y de marfil labrado)
Una doncella vi, desde la planta
   Del pié hasta la cabeza así adornada,
   Que el verla admira, y el oirla encanta.
Estaba en él con majestad sentada,
   Giganta al parecer en la estatura,
   Pero aunque grande, bien proporcionada.
Parecia mayor su hermosura
   Mirada desde léjos, y no tanto
   Si de cerca se ve su compustura:
Lleno de admiracion, colmo de espanto,
   Puse en ella los ojos, y vi en ella
   Lo que en mis versos desmayados canto.
Yo no sabré afirmar si era doncella,
   Aunque he dicho que sí, que en estos casos
   La vista mas aguda se atropella.
Son por la mayor parte siempre escasos
   De razon los juicios maliciosos
   En juzgar rotos los enteros vasos.

The teeming Spring presents a wealth untold
  Of varied hues, and with such beauty graced
  The mind is charmed with what the eyes behold;
There prodigality and wanton waste,
  Holding athwart the plain high revelry,
  Make up in splendour what they lack in taste.
Upon a throne exalted very high,
  (Where Art ruled matter with a power confest,
  Wrought though it was in gold and ivory,)
A maid I saw, in such adornments dressed,
  And eke in every part so wondrous bright,
  The eye was ravished and the ear was blest.
She sat thereon with majesty bedight,
  In stature, as it seemed, a giantess,
  Of fine proportions though of towering height;
With greater lustre shone her loveliness
  When seen from far, for as we nearer draw
  Its power to fascinate grows strangely less.
Entranced with wonder, and o'erwhelmed with awe,
  I fixed my gaze on her, and straight away
  What now my trembling tongue would sing I saw:
If maid or no, I am not free to say,
  Though I've affirmed it, for in such like case
  The keenest sight may haply go astray;
For almost ever those of spiteful race,
  Who brand the vessels cracked that are entire,
  Are scant of reason and devoid of grace.

Altaneros sus ojos y amorosos
　Se mostraban con cierta mansedumbre,
　Que los hacia en todo extremo hermosos.
Ora fuese artificio, ora costumbre,
　Los rayos de su luz tal vez crecian,
　Y tal vez daban encogida lumbre.
Dos ninfas á sus lados asistian,
　De tan gentil donaire y apariencia,
　Que miradas, las almas suspendian.
De la del alto trono en la presencia
　Desplegaban sus labios en razones,
　Ricas en suavidad, pobres en ciencia.
Levantaban al cielo sus blasones,
　Que estaban por ser pocos ó ningunos,
　Escritos del olvido en los borrones.
Al dulce murmurar, al oportuno
　Razonar de las dos, la del asiento,
　Que en belleza jamas le igualó alguno,
Luego se puso en pié, y en un momento
　Me pareció que dió con la cabeza
　Mas allá de las nubes, y no miento:
Y no perdió por esto su belleza,
　Antes miéntras mas grande, se mostraba
　Igual su perfeccion á su grandeza:
Los brazos de tal modo dilataba,
　Que de do nace adonde muere el dia
　Los opuestos extremos alcanzaba.

Bright as a hawk's, and full of amorous fire,
  Her eyes had yet such winning softness too,
  As made them beautiful beyond desire;
Whether to artifice or habit due,
  Their radiant flash at times would grow intense,
  Then change to lustre of a mellower hue.
Beside her stood two nymphs of eminence,
  Of such a lively air and sprightly mien,
  As bound all hearts in wonder and suspense;
To her who on the lofty throne was seen
  They oped their lips, and forth their words did press
  Rich in their sweetness, yet in wisdom mean;
Her titles grand they laboured to express,
  That stood for little or for naught, I trow,
  In the blurred annals of forgetfulness;
And as the twain did whisper soft and low
  Their honied words, she, of the throne on high,
  In beauty unsurpassed before or now,
Rose to her feet; in twinkling of an eye.
  It seemed as if her head would soar upright
  To pierce the clouds; in faith I do not lie;
Yet not one tittle of her charms so bright
  She lost thereby, for, without stint or stay,
  She rose in beauty as she rose in height.
Her arms were lengthened out in such a way,
  As if they would embrace all things that lie
  Betwixt the springing and the dying day;

La enfermedad llamada hidropesía
  Así le hincha el vientre, que parece
  Que todo el mar caber en él podia.
Al modo destas partes así crece
  Toda su compostura; y no por esto,
  Cual dije, su hermosura desfallece.
Yo atónito esperaba ver el resto
  De tan grande prodigio, y diera un dedo
  Por saber la verdad segura, y presto.
Uno, y no sabré quién, bien claro y quedo
  Al oído me habló, y me dijo:—Espera,
  Que yo decirte lo que quieres puedo.
Esta que ves, que crece de manera,
  Que apénas tiene ya lugar do quepa,
  Y aspira en la grandeza á ser primera;
Esta que por las nubes sube y trepa
  Hasta llegar al cerco de la luna
  (Puesto que el modo de subir no sepa),
Es la que confiada en su fortuna
  Piensa tener de la inconstante rueda
  El eje quedo y sin mudanza alguna.
Esta que no halla mal que le suceda,
  Ni le teme atrevida y arrogante,
  Pródiga siempre, venturosa y leda,
Es la que con disinio extravagante
  Dió en crecer poco á poco hasta ponerse,
  Cual ves, en estatura de gigante.

The so-called dropsy, that grave malady,
  So bulged her stomach out, that all the sea
  Might flow therein; so did it strike mine eye.
Each part of all her frame in like degree
  Seemed to increase in bulk, though verily
  Her beauty, as I've said, ne'er ceased to be.
To wait the upshot of such prodigy
  I stood enwrapt, and would have given my thumb
  To know the certain truth, and speedily:
One, whom I know not, to my side did come
  And said in clear and quiet whisper: "Stay,
  Of all that thou would'st know this is the sum!
She, whom thou seest increase in such a way,
  That scarcely hath she further scope to grow,
  And fain the highest part of all would play;
She, who doth scale the clouds and upward go
  The very circle of the moon to gain—
  Although her mode of flight we do not know—
Is one who, of her better fortune vain, [fast
  Would seek to check the inconstant wheel, and
  Its axle fix, thus ever to remain.
She, who hath never felt misfortune's blast,
  Nor fears it now, so daring proud is she,
  Prodigal ever, lustful to the last,
Is one who, with ambition past degree,
  Hath set herself to grow and ever grow,
  Until she is the giantess we see;

No deja de crecer por no atreverse
　　A emprender las hazañas mas notables,
　　Adonde puedan sus extremos verse.
¿No has oido decir los memorables
　　Arcos, anfiteatros, templos, baños,
　　Termas, pórticos, muros admirables,
Que á pesar y despecho de los años,
　　Aun duran sus reliquias y entereza,
　　Haciendo al tiempo y á la muerte engaños?
Yo respondí:—Por mí ninguna pieza
　　Desas que has dicho, dejo de tenella
　　Clavada y remachada en la cabeza.
Tengo el sepulcro de la viuda bella,
　　Y el coloso de Ródas allí junto,
　　Y la lanterna que sirvió de estrella.
Pero vengamos de quién es al punto
　　Esta, que lo deseo.—Haráse luego,—
　　Me respondió la voz en bajo punto.
Y prosiguió, diciendo:—A no estar ciego
　　Hubieras visto ya quién es la dama;
　　Pero en fin, tienes el ingenio lego.
Esta que hasta los cielos se encarama,
　　Preñada, sin saber cómo, del viento,
　　Es hija del Deseo y de la Fama.
Esta fué la ocasion y el instrumento
　　En todo y parte de que el mundo viese
　　No siete maravillas, sino ciento.

And, to increase her growth she is not slow
 To bring her great achievements to the light,
 Whence her extreme of daring men may know !
Hast never heard of those famed works of might,
 The arches, amphitheatres, and fanes,
 Baths, porticoes, and walls of towering height,
Which stand entire, or show their vast remains,
 In spite of gathering years, and seem to hold
 Those fell destroyers, Time and Death, in chains?"
" No scrap," quoth I, "of what thou now hast told,
 But I do hold it in my memory right,
 Well nailed and rivetted from days of old !
I have the lovely widow's tomb in sight,
 With Rhodes' Colossus in the self-same row,
 And eke its lanthorn with the starry light !
But come we to the point I long to know :
 Who may she be?" "Be of an easy mind ! "
 Responded he with acrid voice and low,
" I'll tell thee presently ; but, wert not blind,
 Thou wouldst ere now have recognized the dame,
 But, sooth, thy layman's wit doth lag behind !
She, who to heaven soareth like a flame,
 Pregnant, she knows not how, yet by the wind,
 Is the true daughter of Desire and Fame ;
To her, in whole or part, must be assigned
 The cause why in this world we can, and may,
 Not seven wonders but a hundred find.

Corto número es ciento : aunque dijese
 Cien mil y mas millones, no imagines
 Que en la cuenta del número excediese.
Esta condujo á memorables fines
 Edificios que asientan en la tierra,
 Y tocan de las nubes los confines.
Esta tal vez ha levantado guerra,
 Donde la paz süave reposaba,
 Que en limites estrechos no se encierra.
Cuando Mucio en las llamas abrasaba
 El atrevido fuerte brazo y fiero,
 Esta el incendio horrible resfriaba.
Esta arrojó al romano caballero
 En el abismo de la ardiente cueva,
 De limpio armado, y de luciente acero.
Esta tal vez con maravilla nueva
 (De su ambiciosa condicion llevada)
 Mil imposibles atrevida prueba.
Desde la ardiente Libia hasta la helada
 Citia lleva la fama su memoria,
 En grandiosas obras dilatada.
En fin, ella es la altiva Vanagloria,
 Que en aquellas hazañas se entremete,
 Que llevan de los siglos la vitoria.
Ella misma á sí misma se promete
 Triunfos y gustos, sin tener asida
 A la calva Ocasion por el copete.

Short number is a hundred ; should I say
  A hundred thousand millions, do not fear
  That in the reckoning I go far astray.
She planned and finished, while the world did cheer,
  Structures that sit enthronèd on the ground,
  And to the clouds their soaring summits rear ;
Full often hath she levied war around,
  Where gentle peace lay couched with soft desire,
  Because her limits had too small a bound ;
When 'mid the flames, and ready to expire,
  Bold Mucius let consume his arm of might,
  'Twas she that tempered down the dreadful fire ;
She gave the impulse to the Roman knight
  To leap into the yawning gulf of flame,
  Beclad with flashing steel and armour bright !
Full often, borne away by lust of fame,
  To tempt the impossible she daring goes,
  And on some novel wonder stamps her name ;
From burning Lybia to the Scythian snows,
  Her course is tracked by works immense and hoary,
  Which Fame hath decked with titles grandiose ;
In fine, she is the arrogant Vainglory,
  Who by her grand achievements stuns mankind,
  And binds the ages to rehearse her story !
Herself unto herself gives promise kind
  Of triumphs and of joys ; and in her stress
  She leaves bald Opportunity behind.

Su natural sustento, su bebida,
  Es aire, y así crece en un instante
  Tanto, que no hay medida á su medida.
Aquellas dos del plácido semblante
  Que tiene á sus dos lados, son aquellas
  Que sirven á la máquina de Atlante.
Su delicada voz, sus luces bellas,
  Su humildad aparente, y las lozanas
  Razones, que el amor se cifra en ellas,
Las hacen mas divinas que no humanas,
  Y son (con paz escucha y con paciencia)
  La Adulacion y la Mentira hermanas.
Estas están contino en su presencia,
  Palabras ministrándole al oído,
  Que tienen de prudentes aparencia.
Y ella cual ciega del mejor sentido,
  No ve que entre las flores de aquel gusto,
  El áspid ponzoñoso está escondido.
Y así arrojada con deseo injusto,
  En cristalino vaso prueba y bebe
  El veneno mortal, sin ningun susto.
Quien mas presume de advertido, pruebe
  A dejarse adular, verá cuán presto
  Pasa su gloria como el viento leve.—
Esto escuché, y en escuchando aquesto,
  Dió un estampido tal la Gloria vana,
  Que dió á mi sueño fin dulce y molesto.

Her natural food is air, her drink no less;
    So in a moment to such height she grows
    That in her measure she is measureless!
These at her side, with semblance of repose,
    Are the attendants twain she most doth prize,
    Who bear her Atlas-like where'er she goes;
The thrilling voice, the brilliant beauteous eyes,
    The seeming humbleness, the dulcet play
    Of wanton words where passion hidden lies,
A god-like more than human source betray;
    In sooth they are—with peace and patience hear—
    Falsehood and Flattery, twin sisters they.
They haunt her presence, and are ever near
    With sweetly murmured words of high pretence,
    That have a ring of wisdom to the ear;
And she, quite blind as to the finer sense,
    Sees not the venomous asp that lurking lies
    Beneath the seeming flowers of innocence;
Stung with unhallowed craving, forth she hies
    To taste the deadly poison in its glass
    Of crystal pure, while flash her eager eyes;
Yet, sooth to say, the wariest of his class,
    Who drinks in flattery, finds, before he knows,
    His glories vanish as the light winds pass!"
As rapt I listened, lo! Vainglory rose,
    And burst with an explosion wondrous loud,
    That brought my sweet dream to a bitter close.

Y en esto descubrióse la mañana,
   Vertiendo perlas y esparciendo flores,
   Lozana en vista, y en virtud lozana.
Los dulces pequeñuelos ruiseñores
   Con cantos no aprendidos le decian,
   Enamorados della, mil amores.
Los silgueros el canto repetian,
   Y las diestras calandrias entonaban
   La música que todos componian.
Unos del escuadron priesa se daban,
   Porque no los hallase el dios del dia
   En los forzosos actos en que estaban.
Y luego se asomó su señoria,
   Con una cara de tudesco roja,
   Por los balcones de la aurora fria.
En parte gorda, en parte flaca y floja,
   Como quien teme el esperado trance,
   Donde verse vencido se le antoja.
En propio toledano y buen romance
   Les dió los buenos dias cortesmente,
   Y luego se aprestó al forzoso lance.
Y encima de un peñasco puesto enfrente
   Del escuadron, con voz sonora y grave
   Esta oracion les hizo repente :
—¡ Oh espíritus felices, donde cabe
   La gala del decir, la sutileza
   De la ciencia mas docta que se sabe ;

On this the morning rose without a cloud,
   Arrayed with liquid pearls and scattering flowers,
   Proud in her looks and of her virtue proud;
The tiny nightingales within their bowers,
   With self-taught song, to echo forth her praise,
   Trilled forth their amorous notes in silvery showers;
Caught up the sound the linnets on their sprays,
   The lightsome larks responded from the air,
   And all in concert sung their morning lays!
Some of the squadron started from their lair,
   That the bright god of day they might not meet
   In the constrainèd plight in which they were.
Now at the casements of Aurora sweet,
   With face of Teuton ruddiness, I ween,
   His lordship shewed himself in garb complete;
On one side stout, on t'other limp and lean,
   As one who waits the contest with dismay,
   Wherein as vanquished he may soon be seen.
With courteous air he wished them all, good-day!
   In proper Spanish, and Toledan true,
   And quick prepared him for the coming fray;
Then from a hillock, with his host in view,
   And with a voice that rang from side to side,
   He made them this oration impromptû:
" O spirits fortunate, wherein reside
   The gift of splendid speech, the subtle flow
   Of untold wisdom gathered far and wide,

Donde en su propia natural belleza
  Asiste la hermosa poësía
  Entera de los piés á la cabeza!
No consintais por vida vuestra y mia
  (Mirad con qué llaneza Apolo os habla),
  Que triunfe esta canalla que porfía.
Esta canalla, digo, que se endiabla,
  Que por darles calor su muchedumbre,
  Ya su ruina, ó ya la nuestra entabla.
Vosotros de mis ojos gloria y lumbre,
  Faroles do mi luz de asiento mora,
  Ya por naturaleza, ó por costumbre,
¿Habeis de consentir que esta embaidora,
  Hipócrita gentella se me atreva,
  De tantas necedades inventora?
Haced famosa y memorable prueba
  De vuestro gran valor en este hecho,
  Que á su castigo y vuestra gloria os lleva.
De justa indignacion armad el pecho,
  Acometed intrépidos la turba,
  Ociosa, vagamunda y sin provecho.
No se os dé nada, no se os dé una burba
  (Moneda berberisca, vil y baja)
  De aquesta gente, que la paz nos turba.
El son de mas de una templada caja,
  Y el del pífaro triste y la trompeta,
  Que la cólera sube, y flema abaja,

To which fair poesy, with kindly glow,
  Doth lend her native loveliness divine,
  Perfect in all her parts from top to toe!
Do not permit, upon your life and mine—
  (Mark how Apollo's speech is void of flowers)—
  That that vile crew should sully this fair shrine;
That crew, I say, which girds its fiendish powers,
  And with its countless hordes, inflamed with lies,
  Prepares its ruin, or it may be ours!
Ye, the fond pride and lustre of mine eyes,
  The lanthorns where my light is wont to glow,
  Whether by nature, or through exercise!
Can ye consent that this brute herd and low,
  This knavish, stupid, stuff-inventing race,
  Should beard me here, and in my presence crow?
Give to your powerful arms such ample space,
  That after ages may proclaim aloud
  Your gathered glory, and their fell disgrace;
With righteous wrath your stalwart breasts enshroud,
  And charge with fury, that will never cease,
  That lazy, vagabond, and useless crowd!
Not worth a rush, not worth a *burba* piece,—
  Of Berber coins the very dross and scum—
  Should ye esteem these folk who spoil our peace!
The sound of more than one bemuffled drum,
  The fife's shrill shrieking, and the trumpet's blare,
  That rouse up choler, and make terror dumb,

Así os incite con vertud secreta,
  Que despierte los ánimos dormidos
  En la facion que tanto nos aprieta.
Ya retumba, ya llega á mis oídos
  Del escuadron contrario el rumor grande,
  Formado de confusos alaridos.
Ya es menester, sin que os lo ruegue ó mande,
  Que cada cual como guerrero experto,
  Sin que por su capricho se desmande,
La órden guarde y militar concierto,
  Y acuda á su deber como valiente
  Hasta quedar, ó vencedor, ó muerto.
En esto por la parte de poniente
  Pareció el escuadron casi infinito
  De la bárbara, ciega y pobre gente.
Alzan los nuestros al momento un grito
  Alegre, y no medroso; y gritan arma:
  Arma resuena todo aquel distrito;
  Y aunque mueran, correr quieren al arma.

Let these stir up your secret virtues rare,
    As they arouse the courage, drown the fears
    Of that vexatious swarm who wait us there!
I hear the sound, it strikes upon mine ears,
    The mighty clamour of the marching foe,
    The hubbub wild of martial shouts and cheers!
'Tis needful now, and that full well ye know,
    That each one, with a seasoned warrior's eye,
    Without allowing vain caprice to show,
Should order keep, and stand his comrades by,
    And like a valiant man his duty do,
    Resolved to conquer or at worst to die!"
Then by the western side there rose to view
    A marching squadron great as could be found,
    Of barbarous rabble, blind and ragged too;
Now from our host there rose a mighty sound,
    A joyful, fearless shout: To arms! they cry,
    To arms! re-echoes all the country round,
To arms! To arms! to do or else to die!

CAPITULO VII.

Tú, belígera musa, tú que tienes
  La voz de bronce y de metal la lengua,
  Cuando á cantar del fiero Marte vienes:
Tú, por quien se aniquila siempre y mengua
  El gran género humano: tú, que puedes
  Sacar mi pluma de ignorancia y mengua:
Tú, mano rota, y larga de mercedes,
  Digo en hacellas; una aquí te pido,
  Que no hará que ménos rica quedes.
La soberbia y maldad, el atrevido
  Intento de una gente mal mirada
  Ya se descubre con mortal ruido.
Dame una voz al caso acomodada,
  Una sotil y bien cortada pluma,
  No de aficion ni de pasion llevada,
Para que pueda referir en suma
  Con purísimo y nuevo sentimiento,
  Con verdad clara y entereza suma,

CHAPTER VII.

Thou, martial Muse, who hast, attuned to wars,
  The voice of sounding brass and clarion tongue,
  What time thou sing'st the feats of savage Mars!
Thou, at whose call a countless human throng [bless
  Consumes its strength away! Thou, who canst
  My foolish pen and make it wise and strong!
Thou open hand, with favours and largesse
  So fully fraught, O grant me one, I pray,
  It will not make thy wealthy store the less!
The perverse spirit, insolent display,
  And bold designs of an ill-favoured race,
  With din infernal seek the light of day!
Give me a voice in keeping with the case,
  A well-cut pen with facile point and fleet,
  Exempt from prejudice or passion base,
That in one focus I may cause to meet
  With chastest sentiment of novel kind,
  With perfect frankness and with grasp complete,

El contrapuesto y desigual intento
  De uno y otro escuadron, que ardiendo en ira,
  Sus banderas descoge al vago viento.
El del bando católico, que mira
  Al falso y grande al pié del monte puesto,
  Que de subir al alta cumbre aspira;
Con paso largo y ademan compuesto,
  Todo el monte coronan, y se ponen
  A la furia, que en loca ha echado el resto.
Las ventajas tantean, y disponen
  Los ánimos valientes al asalto,
  En quien su gloria y su venganza ponen.
De rabia lleno y de paciencia falto
  Apolo, su bellísimo estandarte
  Mandó al momento levantar en alto.
Arbolóle un marques, que el propio Marte
  Su briosa presencia representa
  Naturalmente, sin industria y arte.
Poeta celebérrimo y de cuenta,
  Por quien y en quien Apolo soberano
  Su gloria y gusto, y su valor aumenta.
Era la insinia un cisne hermoso y cano,
  Tan al vivo pintado, que dijeras,
  La voz despide alegre al aire vano;
Siguen al estandarte sus banderas
  De gallardos alféreces llevadas,
  Honrosas por no estar todas enteras;

The opposing projects, and conflicting mind
  Of these two squadrons who, with furious cry,
  Display their banners to the fitful wind.
The catholic band regards with steady eye
  The spurious host that lines the mountain's base,
  With foul intent to scale its summit high;
In compact order, and with rapid pace,
  They crown the hill, and to the rage insane
  Of these insensates show determined face;
They seize each coign of vantage, and maintain
  Cool courage for the onset arrogant,
  Where glory and revenge they hope to gain.
With rage o'erflowing, and of patience scant,
  Apollo bids them, with a speedy hand,
  His finest standard on the summit plânt;
Unfurled it is, and by a Marquis grand,
  Whose lordly bearing Mars himself might own,
  Nature's own gift that art can ne'er command;
A poet he of mark, to fame well known,
  In whom Apollo sees, with vigour rare,
  Increase the strength and lustre of his throne;
Thereon was limned a swan, so white and fair,
  So painted to the life, that one might say
  Its joyous cries woke up the listless air.
Behind the standard came a grand array
  Of flags, by gallant ensigns borne on high,
  For all the rents they show, more glorious they!

Las cajas á lo bélico templadas
 Al mílite mas tardo vuelven presto,
 De voces de metal acompañadas.
JERÓNIMO DE MORA llegó en esto,
 Pintor excelentísimo y poeta,
 Apéles y Virgilio en un supuesto.
Y con la autoridad de una jineta
 (Que de ser capitan le daba nombre)
 Al caso acude y á la turba aprieta.
Y porq e mas se turbe y mas se asombre
 El enemigo desigual y fiero,
 Llegó el gran BIEDMA de inmortal renombre.
Y con él GASPAR DE AVILA, primero
 Secuaz de Apolo, á cuyo verso y pluma
 Iciar puede envidiar, temer Sincero.
Llegó JUAN DE MEZTANZA, cifra y suma
 De tanta erudicion, donaire y gala,
 Que no hay muerte ni edad que la consuma.
Apolo le arrancó de Guatimala,
 Y le trujo en su ayuda para ofensa
 De la canalla en todo extremo mala.
Hacer milagros en el trance piensa
 CEPEDA, y acompáñale MEJÍA,
 Poetas dinos de alabanza inmensa.
Clarísimo esplendor de Andalucía,
 Y de la Mancha el sin igual GALINDO
 Llegó con majestad y bizarría.

The tambours, mingling with the battle cry,
  Give speed and vigour to each lagging son,
  While the shrill bugles' pealings rend the sky.
Up doth JERÓNIMO DE MORA run,
  A painter exquisite, and poet sweet,
  A Virgil and Apelles, rolled in one ;
He comes with his *jineta* armed complete,—
  Distinction that bespeaks the captain's name—
  To give his aid and force the foe's retreat.
Still more to awe, and put to very shame
  The pride of that fierce crowd, there hither sped
  The grand BIEDMA of undying fame,
With GASPAR DE AVILA, a chief and head
  Of Phœbus' body-guard, whose winged plume
  Iciar might envy, and Sincerus dread.
JUAN DE MEZTANZA came, the very bloom
  And sum of so much learning, wit, and grace,
  That Death can touch it not, nor Time consume;
Apollo gave him a distinguished place,
  And had him brought from Guatimala's land,
  To do despite to that detested race.
CEPEDA thinks to make a wondrous stand
  In this encounter, and MEJIA too,
  True poets both, who boundless praise command.
Now came GALINDO, peerless to the view,
  La Mancha's star, and Andalusia's light,
  Whose manly stride bespeaks his valour true.

De la alta cumbre del famoso Pindo
   Bajaron tres bizarros lusitanos,
   A quien mis alabanzas todas rindo.
Con prestos piés y con valientes manos
   Con FERNANDO CORREA DE LA CERDA,
   Pisó RODRIGUEZ LOBO monte y llanos.
Y porque Febo su razon no pierda,
   El grande DON ANTONIO DE ATAIDE
   Llegó con furia alborotada y cuerda.
Las fuerzas del contrario ajusta y mide
   Con las suyas Apolo, y determina
   Dar la batalla, y la batalla pide.
El ronco son de mas de una bocina,
   Instrumento de caza y de la guerra,
   De Febo á los oídos se avecina.
Tiembla debajo de los piés la tierra
   De infinitos poetas oprimida,
   Que dan asalto á la sagrada sierra.
El fiero general de la atrevida
   Gente que trae un cuervo en su estandarte,
   Es ARBOLÁNCHES, muso por la vida.
Puestos estaban en la baja parte,
   Y en la cima del monte frente á frente
   Los campos de quien tiembla el mismo Marte:
Cuando una, al parecer discreta gente,
   Del católico bando el enemigo
   Se pasó, como en número de veinte.

Came down from far-famed Pindus' lofty height
  Three Lusitanians of consummate skill,
  Who well may claim my highest praise by right;
With ready feet, and with determined will,
  CORREA DE LACERDA lighted there,
  And with RODRIGUEZ LOBO trod the hill;
And that Apollo might have force to spare,
  ANTONIO DE ATAIDE joined the band,
  Inflamed with ardour, wise as it was rare.
When Phœbus had the opposing forces scanned,
  And weighed them with his own, he in his scorn
  Resolves to fight, and battle doth demand;
The hoarse rough sound of more than one shrill horn,
  An instrument of chase and war, I trow,
  On to Apollo's deafened ears is borne;
The frightened earth begins to tremble now,
  As countless poets tramp along the plain,
  And rush to scale the sacred Mountain's brow.
The fierce commander of that daring train,
  Whose standard bears the semblance of a Crow,
  Is ARBOLÁNCHES, very rogue in grain.
So did these armies twain, one down below,
  One at the mountain-top, stand face to face,
  While Mars grew faint to see the fearsome show;
When lo! a troop, that seemed not void of grace,
  In number twenty, left the Catholic band,
  To swell the numbers of the spurious race.

Yo con los ojos su carrera sigo,
   Y viendo el paradero de su intento,
   Con voz turbada al sacro Apolo digo:
¿Qué prodigio es aqueste? ¿Qué portento?
   O por mejor decir, ¿que mal agüero,
   Que asi me corta el brio y el aliento?
Aquel transfuga que partió primero,
   No solo por poeta le tenia,
   Pero tambien por bravo churrullero.
Aquel lijero que tras él corria,
   En mil corrillos en Madrid le he visto
   Tiernamente habla en la poesia.
Aquel tercero que partió tan listo,
   Por satírico necio y por pesado
   Sé que de todos fué siempre malquisto.
No puedo imaginar cómo ha llevado
   Mercurio estos poetas en su lista.
   —Yo fuí, respondió Apolo, el engañado;
Que de su ingenio la primera vista
   Indicios descubrió que serían buenos
   Para facilitar esta conquista.
—Señor, repliqué yo, creí que ajenos
   Eran de las deidades los engaños,
   Digo, engañarse en poco mas ni ménos.—
La prudencia que nace de los años,
   Y tiene por maestra la experiencia,
   Es la deidad que advierte destos daños.

With straining eyes I marked them on their course,
 And when I saw the end of their intent,
 I to Apollo cried with accents hoarse:
"What prodigy is this, what strange event?
 Or better said, what omen big with bale,
 That takes my breath away, and leaves me spent?
That base deserter there, who first turned tail,
 I reckoned him a bard, nor that alone,
 But a brave twaddler on the largest scale!
That light-toed one, who at his heels hath flown,
 I've heard, in thousand circles of Madrid,
 Trill out his verses with the tenderest tone!
The third, who left with such uncommon speed,
 Hath by the wise been ever ill-received,
 Satiric fool, unbearable indeed!
It is a thing not easily conceived
 Why Mercury inscribed them on his roll!"
"I" quoth Apollo, "was the one deceived;
At the first blush they gave such proofs of soul,
 That worthy adjutants they seemed to me
 To bring this emprise to the wished-for goal!"
"My lord, I thought that deities were free
 And safe from such deceptions," I replied,
 "I mean deceptions in the least degree!
The prudence, born of years and knowledge wide,
 Is the divinity, within our ken,
 That wards off such misjudgments from our side!"

Apolo respondió:—Por mi conciencia,
    Que no te entiendo,—algo turbado y triste
    Por ver de aquellos veinte la insolencia.
Tú, sardo militar, LOFRASO, fuiste
    Uno de aquellos bárbaros corrientes,
    Que del contrario el número creciste.
Mas no por esta mengua los valientes
    Del escuadron católico temieron,
    Poetas madrigados y excelentes.
Antes tanto coraje concibieron
    Contra los fugitivos corredores,
    Que riza en ellos y matanza hicieron.
¡Oh falsos y malditos trovadores,
    Que pasais plaza de poetas sabios,
    Siendo la hez de los que son peores!
Entre la lengua, paladar y labios
    Anda contino vuestra poesía,
    Haciendo á la virtud cien mil agravios.
Poetas de atrevida hipocresía,
    Esperad, que de vuestro acabamiento
    Ya se ha llegado el temeroso dia.
De las confusas voces el concento
    Confuso por el aire resonaba
    De espesas nubes condensando el viento.
Por la falda del monte gateaba
    Una tropa poética, aspirando
    A la cumbre, que bien guardada estaba.

Apollo answered: "On my conscience then,
  I understand thee not!" and knit his brow,
  To see the daring of these twenty men.
LOFRASO, soldier of Sardinia, thou
  Wert one of those barbarian runaways,
  That swelled the numbers of the foe, I trow!
But such desertion had no power to raise
  One spark of terror in the catholic band,
  Well-seasoned poets, worthy of all praise;
Nay, such resentment did they show off-hand
  Against these light-heeled gentry, void of grace,
  That hip and thigh they smote them from the land.
O false, accursèd, troubadouring race,
  That fain would pass for poets wise and strong,
  Being the very scum of all that's base!
Between the palate, tongue, and lips, your song
  Comes surging forth in never-ending blast,
  Affronting Virtue with unmeasured wrong!
Ye poets, in deception unsurpassed,
  Beware, for now the awful threatened day
  That seals your final doom hath come at last!
The sounds confused, that wildering winged their way
  Aloft to heaven, condensed in middle air,
  And formed of murky clouds a thick array.
The steep hill-side a troop of rhymesters rare
  Climbed up like cats, and cleared the broken ground,
  To gain the summit, though well-guarded there;

P

Hacian hincapié de cuando en cuando,
    Y con hondas de estallo y con ballestas
    Iban libros enteros disparando.
No del plomo encendido las funestas
    Balas pudieran ser dañosas tanto,
    Ni al disparar pudiera ser mas prestas.
Un libro mucho mas duro que un canto
    A JUSEPE DE VARGAS dió en las sienes,
    Causándole terror, grima y espanto.
Gritó, y dijo á un soneto :—Tú, que vienes
    De satírica pluma disparado,
    ¿Por qué el infame curso no detienes?
Y cual perro con piedras irritado,
    Que deja al que las tira, y va tras ellas,
    Cual si fueran la causa del pecado,
Entre los dedos de sus manos bellas
    Hizo pedazos al soneto altivo,
    Que amenazaba al sol y á las estrellas.
Y díjole Cilenio :—O rayo vivo
    Donde la justa indignacion se muestra
    En un grado y valor superlativo,
La espada toma en la temida diestra,
    Y arrójate valiente y temerario
    Por esta parte, que el peligro adiestra.
En esto del tamaño de un breviario
    Volando un libro por el aire vino,
    De prosa y verso que arrojó el contrario.

From time to time they took a leap and bound,[might,
   And from their slings and cross-bows, plied with
Whole books came flying with a whizzing sound;
Not balls of gleaming lead, that fearful sight,
   Have on their way such dire confusion sown,
Nor reached their destined goal with speedier flight.
A book, much harder than the hardest stone,
   Struck JUSEPE DE VARGAS on the brow,
And caused him terror grim, and many a groan;
He howled, and to a Sonnet cried : " O thou,
   Who hither com'st shot from satiric quill,
Why dost not stay thy foul careering now ! "
Like pelted dog, that vents its fierce ill-will
   Upon the stones, not him who threw the same,
As if they were the authors of the ill,
With fingers fine he seized it as it came,
   And into pieces tore that sonnet great,
That menaced sun, and moon, and starry frame.
Mercurius cried : " O living bolt of fate,
   Whose righteous indignation moves aright,
In lofty sweep, and with tremendous weight !
Grasp now the falchion in thy dreaded right,
   And launch thee, with impetuous bravery,
Where peril looms in thickest of the fight !"
On this came whizzing, like a bird on high,
   A Book in prose and verse, shot by our foes,
In bulk and height a very Breviary ;

De verso y prosa el puro desatino
   Nos dió á entender que de ARBOLÁNCHES eran
   Las Avidas pesadas de contino.
Unas rimas llegaron, que pudieran
   Desbaratar el escuadron cristiano,
   Si acaso vez segunda se imprimieran.
Dióle á Mercurio en la derecha mano
   Una sátira antigua licenciosa,
   De estilo agudo, pero no muy sano.
De una intricada y mal compuesta presa,
   De un asunto sin jugo y sin donaire,
   Cuatro novelas disparó PEDROSA.
Silbando recio, y desgarrando el aire,
   Otro libro llegó de rimas solas
   Hechas al parecer como al desgaire;
Viólas Apolo, y dijo, cuando viólas:
   —Dios perdone á su autor, y á mí me guarde
   De algunas rimas sueltas españolas.—
Llegó el PASTOR DE IBERIA, aunque algo tarde,
   Y derribó catorce de los nuestros,
   Haciendo de su ingenio y fuerza alarde.
Pero dos valerosos, dos maestros,
   Dos lumbreras de Apolo, dos soldados,
   Unicos en hablar, y en obrar diestros;
Del monte puestos en opuestos lados
   Tanto apretaron á la turba multa,
   Que volvieron atras los encumbrados.

From its extravagance in verse and prose,
  'Twas ARBOLANCHES' work, we well could guess,
  His dull " Avidas," heavy to the close.
Some Rhymes were hurled, that boded much distress
  And great disaster to the Christian band,
  Had they but gone a second time to press;
Mercurius got a blow on his right hand
  From an old Satire, rotten at the core,
  Piquant in style, but of unsavoury brand.
Of tangled prose, and ill-digested lore,
  With subject quite devoid of sense or grace,
  PEDROSA launched at us his ' Novels four ! '
With a sharp hiss, and cleaving empty space,
  Another book, with nought but rhymes, was sped,
  With modesty self-conscious on its face ;
Apollo looked at them, and looking said :
  " God shrive their author, and preserve my pate
  From certain Spanish verses, blank as lead !"
The SHEPHERD OF IBERIA came, though late,
  Attacked fourteen of ours and beat them too,
  A striking proof of wit and valour great.
But now two men of heart, great masters two,
  Two of Apollo's luminaries bright,
  Two soldiers quick to speak and prompt to do,
From sides opposing of the mountain's height,
  Pressed back the surging mass, which grew so weak
  That all the foremost turned and took to flight ;

Es Gregorio de Angulo el que sepulta
   La canalla, y con él Pedro de Soto,
   De prodigioso ingenio y vena culta.
Doctor aquel, estotro único y doto
   Licienciado, de Apolo ambos secuaces,
   Con raras obras y ánimo devoto.
Las dos contrarias indignadas haces
   Ya miden las espadas, ya se cierran
   Duras en su teson y pertinaces.
Con los dientes se muerden, y se aferran
   Con las garras, las fieras imitando;
   Que toda piedad de sí destierran.
Haldeando venia y trasudando
   El autor de *La Picara Justina*,
   Capellan lego del contrario bando.
Y cual si fuera de una culebrina
   Disparó de sus manos su librazo,
   Que fué de nuestro campo la ruina.
Al buen Tomas Gracian mancó de un brazo,
   A Medinilla derribó una muela,
   Y le llevó de un muslo un gran pedazo.
Una despierta nuestra centinela
   Gritó:—Todos abajen la cabeza,
   Que dispara el contrario otra novela.—
Dos pelearon una larga pieza,
   Y el uno al otro con instancia loca
   De un envion, con arte y con destreza,

GREGORIO DE ANGULO, and eke
  PEDRO DE SOTO did that deed of fate,
  Men of high culture and of wit unique;
That one a Doctor, this Licentiate
  Of high degree, both in Apollo's guard,
  Great in their works, and in devotion great.
The ranks opposing, fierce in their regard,
  Now measure swords, and now keep closer file,
  In action stolid and in purpose hard;
They use their teeth to bite, and in fierce style
  They rive with pointed nails like beasts of prey,
  As void of pity as they're full of guile.
At tip-top speed, and sweating by the way,
  LA PICARA JUSTINA'S author came,[13]
  The laic chaplain of the rude array;
As if despatched from mortar's mouth of flame,
  He launched his big and monstrous tome on high,
  And as it fell our camp a wreck became:
Good TOMAS GRACIAN lost an arm thereby,
  Poor MEDINILLA mourned a molar dear,
  And eke a goodly portion of one thigh.
A wakeful sentinel of ours gave cheer,
  And cried: "Heads down, my comrades all,
  The foe hath launched another Novel here!"
Two wrestled with each other for a fall,
  When lo! the one, in his insensate rage,
  And with a dexterous art that was not small,

Seis seguidillas le encajó en la boca,
   Con que le hizo vomitar el alma,
   Que salió libre de su estrecha roca.
De la furia el ardor, del sol la calma
   Tenia en duda de una y otra parte
   La vencedora y pretendida palma.
Del cuervo en esto el lóbrego estandarte
   Cede al del cisne, porque vino al suelo
   Pasado el corazon de parte á parte.
Su alférez, que era un andaluz mozuelo,
   Trovador repentista, que subia
   Con la soberbia mas allá del cielo,
Helósele la sangre que tenia,
   Murióse cuando vió que muerto estaba,
   La turba, pertinaz en su porfia.
Puesto que ausente el gran LUPERCIO estaba
   Con un solo soneto suyo hizo
   Lo que de su grandeza se esperaba.
Descuadernó, desencajó, deshizo
   De opuesto escuadron catorce hileras,
   Dos criollos mató, hirió un mestizo.
De sus sabrosas burlas y sus véras
   El magno cordobes un cartapacio
   Disparó, y aterró cuatro banderas.
Daba ya indicios de cansado y lacio
   El brio de la bárbara canalla,
   Peleando mas flojo y mas despacio.

Forced down the other's throat, at the last stage,
   Six *Seguidillas*; on the which his soul
   Leapt lightly out, and left its narrow cage.
There fury raged, here reigned a calm control,
   And still through all the ranks the question ran,
   Which side will gain the palm, the victor's goal!
When lo! the Crow, that decked the banner wan,
   With stricken heart and piercèd thro' and through,
   Fell to the ground and yielded to the Swan!
Its ensign was an Andalusian true,
   A stripling poet, improvising wight,
   Whose pride soared to the sky, and topped it too;
His blood congealed as he beheld the sight,
   And when he died, that pertinacious race
   Saw ruin face them on the field of fight.
Though empty was the grand LUPERCIO'S place,
   One of his Sonnets did for him a deed,
   In keeping quite with its astounding grace;
It broke, it shattered, caused to fly with speed
   Fourteen good files of the opposing band,
   Slew two Creoles, and wounded one half-breed!
The great Cordovan, note-book in his hand,
   Full of his sappy jests and serious wit,
   Discharged it, and there fell four banners grand!
Now tired and worn, there oozed out bit by bit
   The courage of that barbarous canaille,
   More and more pithless grew each aimless hit;

Mas renovóse la fatal batalla
  Mezclándose los unos con los otros,
  Ni vale arnes, ni presta dura malla.
Cinco melifluos sobre cinco potros
  Llegaron, y embistieron por un lado,
  Y lleváronse cinco de nosotros.
Cada cual como moro ataviado,
  Con mas letras y cifras que una carta
  De príncipe enemigo y recatado,
De romances moriscos una sarta,
  Cual si fuera de balas enramadas,
  Llega con furia y con malicia harta.
Y á no estar dos escuadras avisadas
  De las nuestras del recio tiro y presto,
  Era fuerza quedar desbaratadas.
Quiso Apolo indignado echar el resto
  De su poder y de su fuerza sola,
  Y dar al enemigo fin molesto.
Y una sacra cancion, donde acrisola
  Su ingenio, gala, estilo y bizarría
  BARTOLOMÉ LEONARDO DE ARGENSOLA,
Cual si fuera un petrarte Apolo envía
  Adonde está el teson mas apretado,
  Mas dura y mas furiosa la porfía.
Cuando me paro á contemplar mi estado,
  Comienza la cancion, que Apolo pone
  En el lugar mas noble y levantado.

But once again rose up the battle's wail,
  In confused melée all together strive,
  No armour saves, nor hardest coat of mail.
Astride five colts, five honied bards arrive,
  And making quite a sudden charge in flank,
  They of our men bear off in triumph five ;
In robes Moresque they show full many a prank,
  With more of mystic scroll than missive sent
  By some old wily foe of princely rank.
On this a shower of Moorish ballads rent
  The air, like missiles formed of chained shot,
  That rained in fury and with vile intent ;
Had not two bands of ours due notice got
  Of that most sudden and most bitter fire,
  Ruin and speedy death had been their lot.
Now in Apollo's breast raged fierce desire
  To show the full resources of his might,
  And crush his enemies with righteous ire ;
An ode divine, where shone the genius bright,
  The strength and grandeur of that poet true,
  BARTOLOMÉ DE ARGENSOLA hight,
Apollo launched ; and like a bomb it flew,
  And ploughed the ranks with most unerring shot,
  Where fought most fiercely that malignant crew ;
" *When I sit down to muse upon my lot,*"
  Begins the Song which, by Apollo's grace,
  Received the crown of honour on the spot.

Todo lo mira, todo lo dispone
  Con ojos de Argos, manda, quita y veda,
  Y del contrario á todo ardid se opone.
Tan mezclados están, que no hay quien pueda
  Discernir cuál es malo, ó cuál es bueno,
  Cuál es GARCILASISTA Ó TIMONEDA.
Pero un mancebo de ignorancia ajeno,
  Grande escudriñador de toda historia,
  Rayo en la pluma y en la voz un trueno,
Llegó tan rica el alma de memoria,
  De sana voluntad y entendimiento,
  Que fué de Febo y de las musas gloria.
Con este aceleróse el vencimiento,
  Porque supo decir: Este merece
  Gloria, pero aquel no, sino tormento.
Y como ya con distincion parece
  El justo y el injusto combatiente,
  El gusto al paso de la pena crece.
Tú, PEDRO MANTUANO el excelente,
  Fuiste quien distinguió de la confusa
  Máquina el que es cobarde del valiente.
JULIAN DE ALMENDARIZ no rehusa,
  Puesto que llegó tarde, en dar socorro
  Al rubio Delio con su ilustre musa.
Por las rucias que peino, que me corro
  De ver que las comedias endiabladas,
  Por divinas se pongan en el corro

The god with Argus' eyes surveys the chase,
   He bids, forbids, disposes all anew,
   And to the foeman shows his sternest face.
So mingled are they, none have knowledge true
   To tell the good from bad, or to make known
   Who GARCILASO, TIMONEDA who;
Till came a youth, to ignorance unknown,
   A mighty sifter of historic lore,
   Flash in his pen, and thunder in his tone;
Whose memory teemeth with such wealthy store
   That Phœbus and the Muses all revere
   His sound firm judgment, healthy to the core;
Thanks to his aid, the victory comes near,
   For he could say, what none could better know:
   " This merits praise, that punishment severe!"
And as the difference begins to show
   Betwixt the boastful champions and the brave,
   The pleasure grows with each descending blow;
O PEDRO MANTUANO, wise and grave,
   'Twas thou who, out of these conflicting views,
   Didst separate the true man from the knave!
DE ALMENDARIZ could not well refuse,
   Though late he came, to give his succour free
   To ruddy Phœbus with his far-famed Muse.
By the red hairs I comb, I blush to see
   How the bedevilled Comedies do raise
   Their heads aloft and claim divine to be;

Y á pesar de las limpias y atildadas
   Del cómico mejor de nuestra Hesperia,
   Quieren ser conocidas y pagadas.
Mas no ganaron mucho en esta feria,
   Porque es discreto el vulgo de la corte,
   Aunque le toca la comun miseria.
De llano no le déis, dadle de corte,
   Estancias Polifemas, al poeta
   Que no os tuviere por su guia y norte.
Inimitables sois, y á la discreta
   Gala que descubris en lo escondido,
   Toda elegancia puede estar sujeta.
Con estas municiones el partido
   Nuestro se mejoró de tal manera,
   Que el contrario se tuvo por vencido.
Cayó su presuncion soberbia y fiera,
   Derrúmbanse del monte abajo cuantos
   Presumieron subir por la ladera.
La voz prolija de sus roncos cantos
   El mal suceso con rigor la vuelve
   En interrotos y funestos llantos.
Tal hubo, que cayendo se resuelve
   De asirse de una zarza, ó cabrahigo,
   Y en llanto, á lo de Ovidio, se disuelve.
Cuatro se arracimaron á un quejigo
   Como enjambre de abejas desmandada,
   Y le estimaron por el lauro amigo.

And, spite of all the pure and high-toned plays
  Of our Hesperia's highest comic son,
  Aspire to solid gain as well as praise;
But much in such a mart will not be won,
  Our honest town's folk are too shrewd by far,
  Although the common stress they cannot shun!
Ye Polyphemian stanzas, leave your scar,
  And with the sharp edge, on the poet's face
  Who will not take you as his guiding star!
Your matchless splendour, fraught with hidden grace,
  Proclaim you as the standard at all cost,
  To which all other elegance gives place!
Thus reinforced, our strong embattled host
  Grew stronger still, with such o'erwhelming might,
  That our dashed foes gave up their cause as lost.
Their proud presumption was in woeful plight,
  For headlong down the precipice were thrown
  As many as presumed to scale the height;
Their rude hoarse chaunting, with its dreary drone,
  Was changed by the disaster of that day
  To dismal sobbing, and convulsive moan.
One, as he fell, contrived his fall to stay,
  And, as to some wild fig or thorn he clung,
  He melted in Ovidian tears away;
Four, like a swarm of bees, suspended hung
  From a gnarled oak, beneath whose friendly shade
  They thought themselves the laurel leaves among;

Otra cuadrilla vírgen, por la espada,
   Y adúltera de lengua, dió la cura
   A sus piés de su vida almidonada.
BARTOLOMÉ llamado DE SEGURA
   El toque casi fué del vencimiento:
   Tal es su ingenio, y tal es su cordura.
Resonó en esto por el vago viento
   La voz de la vitoria repetida
   Del número escogido en claro acento.
La miserable, la fatal caida
   De las musas del limpio tagarete
   Fué largos siglos con dolor plañida.
A la parte del llanto (¡ay me!) se mete
   Zapardiel, famoso por su pesca,
   Sin que un pequeño instante se quïete.
La voz de la vitoria se refresca,
   Vitoria suena aquí, y allí vitoria,
   Adquirida por nuestra soldadesca,
   Que canta alegre la alcanzada gloria.

Another company, with virgin blade
  And harlot tongue, betook themselves to flight,
  To save their lives they called their feet to aid.
BARTOLOMÉ, he DE SEGURA hight,
  Struck the last note of victory complete,
  His wit and wisdom had such wondrous might.
The listening hills unto the skies repeat
  The voice of triumph, as it rang elate
  From thousand lips in accents clear and sweet;
The final fall, the miserable fate,
  Of these the Muses of the savoury drain,
  Was wailed for many an age with dolour great.
There stands (alack!) among this weeping train
  Zapardiel, renowned for fishery,
  Who not one instant can her tears restrain!
The day is ours; and "Victory" is the cry,
  From mouth to mouth the stirring accents run,
  The Victory of our gallant soldiery,
  Who chaunt with joy the glory they have won!

CAPITULO VIII.

Al caer de la máquina excesiva
  Del escuadron poético arrogante
  Que en su no vista muchedumbre estriba:
Un poeta, mancebo y estudiante,
  Dijo:—Caí, paciencia; que algun dia
  Será la nuestra, mi valor mediante.
De nuevo afilaré la espada mia,
  Digo mi pluma, y cortaré de suerte
  Que dé nueva excelencia á la porfía.
Que ofrece la comedia, si se advierte,
  Largo campo al ingenio, donde pueda
  Librar su nombre del olvido y muerte.
Fué desto ejemplo JUAN DE TIMONEDA,
  Que con solo imprimir, se hizo eterno,
  Las comedias del gran LOPE DE RUEDA.
Cinco vuelcos daré en el propio infierno
  Por hacer recitar una que tengo
  Nombrada: *El gran Bastardo de Salerno.*

CHAPTER VIII.

When fell the vast and overgrown machine
  Of that poetic insolent array,
  Whose like for numbers never yet was seen,
A poet, fresh from school, was heard to say:
  "Have patience, comrades, trust my valour fine,
  The time will come when we shall have our day!
Anew I'll sharpen up this blade of mine,
  My pen, I mean, and slash to such degree
  Will make our cause with novel lustre shine;
For Comedy doth offer, one can see,
  Large scope for genius, such as may suffice
  To keep its name from death and darkness free;
'Twas thus that TIMONEDA won the prize,
  Who put to press, to his undying fame,
  Great LOPE DE RUEDA'S Comedies;
Five skips I'd give, and in the nether flame,
  To get recited one that I have here,
  "*Salerno's mighty Bastard*" is its name;

Guarda, Apolo, que baja guarde rengo
   El golpe de la mano mas gallarda
   Que ha visto el tiempo en su discurso luengo.—
En esto el claro son de una bastarda,
   Alas pone en los piés de la vencida
   Gente del mundo perezosa y tarda.
Con la esperanza del vencer perdida,
   No hay quien no atienda con lijero paso,
   Si no á la honra, á conservar la vida.
Desde las altas cumbres de Parnaso
   De un salto uno se puso en Guadarrama,
   Nuevo, no visto y verdadero caso.
Y al mismo paso la parlera fama
   Cundió del vencimiento la alta nueva,
   Desde el claro Caïstro hasta Jarama.
Lloró la gran vitoria el turbio Esgueva,
   Pisuerga la rió, rióla Tajo,
   Que en vez de arena granos de oro lleva.
Del cansancio, del polvo y del trabajo
   Las rubicundas hebras de Timbreo,
   Del color se pararon de oro bajo.
Pero viendo cumplido su deseo,
   Al son de la guitarra mercuriesca
   Hizo de la gallarda un gran paseo.
Y de Castalia en la corriente fresca
   El rostro se lavó, y quedó luciente
   Como de acero la segur turquesca.

Phœbus beware, from me thou hast to fear
   A sharp back-stroke, the finest and the first
   That Time hath seen in all his long career!"
On this a bomb with mighty clatter burst,
   Which urged the flight of that defeated race,
   In all the world the laziest and the worst.
No hope had they to wipe out their disgrace,
   They fled the spot with swift and smoking feet,
   And life, not honour, held the foremost place.
A certain one, from high Parnassus' seat,
   Reached Guadarrama with one leap in air,
   A new, unheard of, ay, and genuine feat.
With equal speed did babbling rumour bear
   The news of triumph to the listening land,
   From clear Caïstro to Jarama fair;
Dark Esgueva mourned the victory grand,
   Pisuerga smiled, old Tagus laughing rolled
   Down to the sea his grains of golden sand.
With weariness, and dust, and toil untold,
   Apollo's locks, that erst were ruby bright,
   Were dashed with colour of the dullest gold;
But well content that all had ended right,
   While gay Mercurius thrummed the light guitar,
   He danced a galliard with supreme delight;
And in Castalia's stream, the coolest far,
   He laved his face, which shone as brightly now
   As polished steel of Turkish scimitar;

Pulióse luego, y adornó su frente
  De majestad mezclada con dulzura,
  Indicios claros del placer que siente.
Las reinas de la humana hermosura
  Salieron de do estaban retiradas
  Miéntras duraba la contienda dura:
Del árbol siempre verde coronadas,
  Y en medio la divina Poesía,
  Todas de nuevas galas adornadas.
Melpómene, Tersícore, y Talía,
  Polimnia, Urania, Erato, Euterpe y Clio,
  Y Caliope, hermosa en demasía,
Muestran ufanas su destreza y brio,
  Tejiendo una entricada y nueva danza
  Al dulce son de un instrumento mio.
Mio, no dije bien, mentí á la usanza
  De aquel que dice propios los ajenos
  Versos, que son mas dinos de alabanza.
Los anchos prados, y los campos llenos
  Están de las escuadras vencedoras
  (Que siempre van á mas, y nunca á ménos):
Esperando de ver de sus mejoras
  El colmo con los premios merecidos
  Por el sudor y aprieto de seis horas.
Piensan ser los llamados escogidos,
  Todos á premios de grandeza aspiran,
  Tiénense en mas del lo que son tenidos:

He rubbed him deftly down, and decked his brow
   With blended majesty and sweetest grace,
   Clear tokens of the joy he felt, I trow.
The Queens of human beauty left the place,
   Where they in sure and safe retreat had been,
   While raged the battle and the furious chase ;
With wreaths plucked from the tree, the evergreen,
   They stood encircling god-like Poesy,
   All dressed in newest robes of brightest sheen ;
Thalia, Terpsichoré, Melpomene,
   Erato, Urania, Polyhymnia fine,
   Euterpe, Clio, and Calliope ;
Proud of their lithesome step, the tuneful Nine
   Tripped lightly through a new and mazy dance,
   To the sweet sound of instrument of mine,
Mine, did I say, I do but lie perchance,
   Like him who calls another's rhymes his own,
   If they be fit his honour to advance !
The meadows and the plain immense are strown
   With the battalions of the conquering powers,
   That swell and ever swell to force unknown ;
All eager to receive the welcome showers
   Of crowning honours, due to toil unbated,
   Through all the sweat and anguish of six hours ;
The "called" as "chosen" fain would be instated,
   All look for highest places on the roll,
   And rate themselves far higher than they're rated ;

Ni á calidades ni riquezas miran,
　　A su ingenio se atiene cada uno,
　　Y si hay cuatro que acierten, mil deliran.
Mas Febo, que no quiere que ninguno
　　Quede quejoso dél, mandó á la Aurora
　　Que vaya y coja *in tempore oportuno*
De las faldas floríferas de Flora
　　Cuatro tabaques de purpúreas rosas,
　　Y seis de perlas de las que ella llora.
Y de las nueve por extremo hermosas
　　Las coronas pidió, y al darlas ellas
　　En nada se mostraron perezosas.
Tres, á mi parecer, de las mas bellas
　　A Parténope sé que se enviaron,
　　Y fué Mercurio el que partió con ellas.
Tres sugetos las otras coronaron,
　　Allí en el mesmo monte peregrinos,
　　Con que su patria y nombre eternizaron.
Tres cupieron á España, y tres divinos
　　Poetas se adornaron la cabeza,
　　De tanta gloria justamente dinos.
La envidia monstruo de naturaleza
　　Maldita y carcomida, ardiendo en saña
　　A murmurar del sacro don empieza.
Dijo:—¿Será posible que en España
　　Haya nueve poetas laureados?
　　Alta es de Apolo, pero simple hazaña.—

Not rank, nor riches, but the wealth of soul
  Is all their claim, they make no other, none :
  For four that hit, a thousand miss the goal.
But Phœbus, who would fain all quarrel shun,
  Gave mandate, and forthwith Aurora hies
    To gather, at a season opportune,
From wealth of flowers on Flora's lap that lies,
  Four baskets-full of roses purpurine,
  And six of pearls dropped from her tearful eyes.
He begged the crowns, the fairest ever seen,
  The tuneful Nine upon their temples wear,
  Who gave them up with sweet and cheerful mien;
Three, to my mind, the fairest of the fair,
  To Naples went, I'm certain of the same ;
  For Mercury himself conveyed them there ;
Three other poets gained three crowns of fame,
  Who then were pilgrims at the sacred shrine,
  With deathless honour to their land and name ;
Three came to Spain ; and lo ! three bards divine
  Entwined them round their brows ; and verily
  Upon their heads with fitting grace they shine !
But now did Envy, Nature's prodigy,
  Cursèd, corroding, stung with rage insane,
  Against the sacred gift raise murmuring cry:
" And is it possible," she said, " that Spain
  Should have and boast nine poets laureate ?
  Great is Apollo, but his judgment's vain !"

Los demas de la turba, defraudados
   Del esperado premio, repetian
   Los himnos de la envidia mal cantados.
Todos por laureados se tenian
   En su imaginacion, ántes del trance,
   Y al cielo quejas de su agravio envían.
Pero ciertos poetas de romance
   Del generoso premio hacer esperan,
   A despecho de Febo presto alcance.
Otros, aunque latinos, desesperan
   De tocar del laurel solo una hoja,
   Aunque del caso en la demanda mueran.
Véngase ménos el que mas se enoja,
   Y alguno se tocó sienes y frente,
   Que de estar coronado se le antoja.
Pero todo deseo impertinente
   Apolo repartió, premiando á cuantos
   Poetas tuvo el escuadron valiente.
De rosas, de jazmines y amarantos
   Flora le presentó cinco cestones,
   Y la Aurora de perlas otros tantos.
Estos fuéron, letor dulce, los dones
   Que Delio repartió con larga mano
   Entre los poetísimos varones.
Quedando alegre cada cual y ufano
   Con un puño de perlas y una rosa,
   Estimando este premio sobrehumano;

The remnant of the crowd, with looks irate,
    Defrauded of their long expected prize,
    Took up the jarring strain of envious hate ;
Before the fight began, their dazzled eyes
    Beheld them hailed as laureates of song,
    And now to heaven their shouts for "justice" rise.
But certain poets of the vulgar tongue
    Hope still, and soon, to wrest that honour rare,
    In spite of Phœbus and his tuneful throng ;
Others, though worthy latinists, despair
    To pluck one leaflet from the laurel down,
    Though till their dying day they urge their prayer.
Those least avenge themselves who most do frown ;
    And one was seen to press his throbbing brow,
    As if he fancied he might touch the crown.
This most unseemly strife Apollo now
    Cooled down at once, and gave rewards galore
    To every poet in the band, I vow ;
Flora brought out five baskets from her store,
    Of Jasmines, Amarynths, and Roses fair,
    Aurora of her pearls as many more.
These were, sweet reader mine, the guerdons rare
    Which Phœbus scattered with a lavish hand
    Amongst the most poetic poets there ;
They were, in sooth, a proud and happy band ;
    A string of pearls, and eke a single rose,
    Were in their eyes a gift divinely grand.

Y porque fuese mas maravillosa
   La fiesta y regocijo, que se hacia
   Por la vitoria insigne y prodigiosa,
La buena, la importante Poesía
   Mandó traer la bestia, cuya pata
   Abrió la fuente de Castalia fria.
Cubierta de finisima escarlata,
   Un lacayo la trujo en un instante,
   Tascando un freno de bruñida plata.
Envidiarle pudiera Rocinante
   Al gran Pegaso de presencia brava,
   Y aun Brilladoro el del señor de Anglante.
Con no sé cuántas alas adornaba
   Manos y piés, indicio manifiesto
   Que en lijereza al viento aventajaba.
Y por mostrar cuán ágil y cuán presto
   Era, se alzó del suelo cuatro picas,
   Con un denuedo y ademan compuesto.
Tú, que me escuchas, si el oído aplicas
   Al dulce cuento deste gran Viaje,
   Cosas nuevas oirás de gusto ricas.
Era del bel troton todo el herraje
   De durísima plata diamantina,
   Que no recibe del pisar ultraje.
De la color que llaman columbina,
   De raso en una funda trae la cola,
   Que suelta, con el suelo se avecina.

And that the joyous festival might close
 With one more great and yet more marvellous thing,
 In honour of that triumph grandiose,
Sweet Poesy, the radiant, bade them bring   [light,
 The wondrous brute whose hoof-prints brought to
 And made to gush Castalia's limpid spring ;
A lackey brought him in an instant quite,
 With finest scarlet covered o'er and o'er,
 Champing his silver bit of gleaming white ;
Sooth, Rozinante might have envied sore
 The mighty Pegasus his matchless breed,
 And eke my lord D'Anglante's Brilliadore.
I do not know how many wings indeed
 Bedecked his feet, proof positive and sound,
 That he could top the very wind in speed ;
To show how quick and agile was his bound,
 He sprang four pike-lengths from the earth upright,
 With towering vigour and a calm profound.
Thou, who art listening, if thou heed aright
 The sweet recital of this Journey grand,
 Shalt hear new things of exquisite delight.
This trotter's trappings, every plate and band,
 Were sparkling silver, hard as could be found,
 And fit the utmost tear and wear to stand ;
His tail in sling of satin fine was bound,
 Of colour that is known as columbine,
 But let it loose 'twould sweep the very ground ;

Del color del carmin ó de amapola
  Eran sus clines, y su cola gruesa,
  Ellas solas al mundo, y ella sola.
Tal vez anda despacio, y tal apriesa,
  Vuela tal vez, y tal hace corvetas,
  Tal quiere relinchar, y luego cesa.
¡Nueva felicidad de los poetas!
  Unos sus excrementos recogian
  En dos de cuero grandes barjuletas.
Pregunté para qué lo tal hacian,
  Respondióme Cilenio á lo bellaco,
  Con no sé qué vislumbres de ironía:
—Esto que se recoge, es el tabaco,
  Que á los vaguidos sirve de cabeza
  De algun poeta de celebro flaco.
Urania de tal modo lo adereza,
  Que puesto á las narices del doliente,
  Cobra salud, y vuelve á su entereza.—
Un poco entónces arrugué la frente,
  Ascos haciendo del remedio extraño,
  Tan de los ordinarios diferente.
—Recibes, dijo Apolo, amigo engaño
  (Leyóme el pensamiento). Este remedio
  De los vaguidos cura y sana el daño.
No come este rocin lo que en asedio
  Duro y penoso comen los soldados,
  Que están entre la muerte y hambre en medio

With hair of poppy-red or dark carmine
  Was decked his mane, and eke his massy tail,
  In all the world was nothing half so fine.
At times he moveth swift, then slow as snail,
  Sometimes he curvets, sometimes cleaves the air,
  At times he neighs, and then is still and stale.
New poet's luxury! Enjoyment rare!
  For some, in two big bags of leather dry,
  Collect his droppings with the utmost care!
"What are they doing?" I enquired, "and why?"
  Mercurius answered me right brusque enough,
  And yet with humorous gleamings in his eye:
" That which they gather is Tobacco snuff,
  Which for a poet with a weakly brain,
  To cure its giddiness, is rare good stuff!
Urania makes it, in such happy vein,
  That when the sufferer's nostrils sniff the scent,
  He gains his health and is himself again!"
I knit my brows, and with a shrug gave vent
  To my disgust at such peculiar cure,
  From those in common use so different.
"Thou art in error, friend, this stuff, be sure,"
  Apollo said, to whom my thoughts lay bare,
  "Cures all head-swimmings, and makes health
This charger is not fed on such coarse fare [secure!
  As soldiers at some direful siege do eat,
  When death or hunger they are doomed to bear;

Son deste tal los piensos regalados,
    Ambar y almizcle entre algodones puesto,
    Y bebe del rocío de los prados.
Tal vez le damos de almidon un cesto,
    Tal de algarrobas con que el vientre llena,
    Y no se estriñe, ni se va por esto.
—Sea, le respondí, muy norabuena,
    Tieso estoy de celebro por ahora,
    Vaguido alguno no me causa pena.—
La nuestra en esto universal señora,
    Digo la Poesía verdadera,
    Que con Timbreo y con las musas mora,
En vestido subcinto, á la lijera
    El monte discurrió y abrazó á todos,
    Hermosa sobre modo, y placentera.
—¡Oh sangre vencedora de los godos!
    Dijo : de aquí adelante ser tratada
    Con mas süaves y discretos modos
Espero ser, y siempre respetada
    Del ignorante vulgo, que no alcanza,
    Que puesto que soy pobre, soy honrada.
Las riquezas os dejo en esperanza,
    Pero no en posesion, premio seguro
    Que al reino aspira de la inmensa holganza.
Por la belleza deste monte os juro,
    Que quisiera al mas mínimo entregalle
    Un privilegio de cien mil de juro.

His rations are of daintiness complete,
  Amber and musk enwrapped in cotton wool,
  His drink the dew-drops of the meadow sweet;
At times of starch he hath a basket full,
  Or else of carobs, which his hunger stay,
  And do not puff him up, but keep him cool!"
I answered sharp: "Let that be as it may,
  My brain till now is good and sound withal,
  Head-swimmings cause me not the least dismay!"
On this our Sovereign lady, whom we call
  True Poesy, the bosom friend by right
  Of great Apollo and the Muses all,
With kilted garments, and with speed of light,
  Coursed o'er the mountain, and in merry vein
  Embraced each one, and said with great delight:
"O conquering blood, of purest Gothic strain,
  Now do I hope, and better than before,
  A wise and generous treatment to obtain,
And be respected ever more and more
  By the dull crowd, who cannot understand
  That though I'm poor I'm honest to the core!
I leave you wealth in hope, and not in hand;
  A guerdon rich, full of the highest cheer
  That all the realm of Fancy can command!
Now do I swear, and by this mountain dear,
  That were it mine, I'd give the meanest e'en
  An income of a hundred thousand clear;

R

Mas no produce minas este valle,
 Aguas sí, salutíferas y buenas,
 Y monas que de cisnes tienen talle.
Volved á ver, ó amigos, las arenas
 Del aurifero Tajo en paz segura,
 Y en dulces horas de pesar ajenas.
Que esta inaudita hazaña os asegura
 Eterno nombre en tanto que dé Febo
 Al mundo aliento, y luz serena y pura.—
¡Oh maravilla nueva, oh caso nuevo,
 Digno de admiracion que cause espanto,
 Cuya extrañeza me admiró de nuevo!
Morfeo, el dios del sueño, por encanto
 Allí se apareció, cuya corona
 Era de ramos de beleño santo.
Flojísimo de brio y de persona,
 De la pereza torpe acompañado,
 Que no le deja á vísperas ni á nona.
Traia al Silencio á su derecho lado,
 El Descuido al siniestro, y el vestido
 Era de blanda lana fabricado.
De las aguas que llaman del olvido,
 Traia un gran caldero, y de un hisopo
 Venía como aposta prevenido.
Asia á los poetas por el hopo,
 Y aunque el caso los rostros les volvia
 En color encendida de piropo,

But in our vales no mines are to be seen,
  We've only waters limpid, good, and sane,
  And apes that take the form of swans, I ween!
Return, O friends, to see the sands again
  Of golden Tagus, and may peace secure
  Be yours, and happy hours that know no pain;
For now to you these matchless feats assure
  Eternal fame, while Phœbus holds his reign,
  To flood the world with light serene and pure!"
O marvel new! O novelty most plain!
  Worthy of wonder dashed with horror too,
  Whose strangeness makes me marvel yet again!
Morpheus, the god of slumber, came to view
  As if by magic; on his head was worn
  A wreath of henbane leaves, of saintly hue;
He had a long-drawn stride, a look forlorn,
  And in his wake came Sloth, that sluggish eft,
  Who leaves him not at even-song or morn;
At his right side stood Silence, at his left
  Was Negligence; his loosely flowing dress
  Was woven of softest wool, both woof and weft.
Full of the waters of Forgetfulness
  He bore a cauldron, and from bed to bed
  He came with sprinkler wherewithal to bless;
Right by the scruff he seized each poet's head,
  And, though their faces changed into the hue
  Of pyrop stone, a bright and fiery red,

El nos bañaba con el agua fria,
　Causándonos un sueño de tal suerte,
　Que dormimos un dia y otro dia.
Tal es la fuerza del licor, tan fuerte
　Es de las aguas la virtud, que pueden
　Competir con los fueros de la muerte.
Hace el ingenio alguna vez que queden
　Las verdades sin crédito ninguno,
　Por ver que á toda contingencia exceden.
Al despertar del sueño así importuno,
　Ni vi monte, ni monta, dios, ni diosa,
　Ni de tanto poeta vide alguno.
Por cierto extraña y nunca vista cosa;
　Despabilé la vista, y parecióme
　Verme en medio de una ciudad famosa.
Admiracion y grima el caso dióme;
　Torné á mirar, porque el temor ó engaño
　No de mi buen discurso el paso tome.
Y díjeme á mi mismo: No me engaño:
　Esta ciudad es Nápoles la ilustre,
　Que yo pisé sus ruas mas de un año:
De Italia gloria, y aun del mundo lustre,
　Pues de cuantas ciudades él encierra
　Ninguna puede haber que asi le ilustre.
Apacible en la paz, dura en la guerra,
　Madre de la abundancia y la nobleza,
　De elíseos campos y agradable sierra.

With water cool he laved us, and there grew
   Over each sense a drowsiness so long
   We slept that day and eke another too.
Such is its strength, such virtues strange belong
   To that rare liquor, that in very deed
   The rights of death itself are not more strong !
Full many things there be that far exceed
   The common faith, which genius stamps as true :
   The vulgar pass them by, and do not heed !
Waking from that sound sleep there met my view
   No hill nor hillock, god nor goddess round,
   Nor any poet of the countless crew.
Strange matter truly, passing every bound !
   I rubbed mine eyes, and seemed transported thence
   Into the centre of some town renowned ;
With some disgust, with wonder most intense,
   I turned to look, lest some deluding fear
   Had gained the vantage o'er my better sense :
And inly said : " There's no deception here,
   'Tis Naples' self, that city of great fame,
   Whose streets I paced for better than a year.
Italia's pride, that sets the world aflame,
   For of all famous cities near and far
   Not one possesses such a glorious name !
Soft in the time of peace, and strong in war,
   Mother of all abundance and noblesse,
   Elysian fields, and sweetest hills that are !

Si vaguidos no tengo de cabeza,
   Paréceme que está mudada en parte,
   De sitio, aunque en aumento de belleza.
¿Qué teatro es aquel, donde reparte
   Con él cuanto contiene de hermosura,
   La gala, la grandeza, industria y arte?
Sin duda el sueño en mis párpebras dura,
   Porque este es edificio imaginado,
   Que excede á toda humana compostura.
Llegóse en esto á mí disimulado
   Un mi amigo, llamado Promontorio,
   Mancebo en dias, pero gran soldado.
Creció la admiracion viendo notorio
   Y palpable que en Nápoles estaba,
   Espanto á los pasados accesorio.
Mi amigo tiernamente me abrazaba,
   Y con tenerme entre sus brazos, dijo,
   Que del estar yo allí mucho dudaba,
Llamóme padre, y yo lláméle hijo,
   Quedó con esto la verdad en punto,
   Que aquí puede llamarse punto fijo.
Díjome Promontorio:—Yo barrunto,
   Padre, que algun gran caso á vuestras canas
   Las trae tan léjos ya semidifunto.
—En mis horas tan frescas y tempranas
   Esta tierra habité, hijo, le dije,
   Con fuerzas mas briosas y lozanas.

If giddy thoughts do not my brain distress,
  It seems that she hath changed her site in part,
  But to the increase of her loveliness.
What theatre is this, within whose heart
  Such wondrous stores of beauty seem to rest,
  Such splendour, grandeur, industry and art?
Doubtless my eyelids still with sleep are pressed,
  For such a structure only Fancy rears,
  Not human science even at its best!
On this up-gliding at my side appears
  A friend of mine, one PROMONTORIO hight,
  A right good soldier, though a youth in years;
My wonder grew, and to its greatest height,
  To see him verily in Naples here—
  To the past marvels fit companion quite.
My friend embraced me with a hug full dear,
  And, holding me, to question he begun
  Whether 'twas I myself he held so near;
He called me "father," and I called him "son,"
  And so the truth was placed in sudden light,
  Or sunny light, to use a homely pun;
Said PROMONTORIO: "Tell me if I'm right
  That some misfortune, father, brings thee here,
  With hairs so grey, and in this half-dead plight?"
"My son," I said, "I trod this country dear
  In happier hours, and in a merrier vein,
  While yet my powers were fresh, my vision clear;

Pero la voluntad que á todos rige,
   Digo, el querer del cielo, me ha traido
   A parte que me alegra mas que aflige.—
Dijera mas, sino que un gran ruido
   De pifanos, clarines y tambores
   Me azoró el alma, y alegró el oído;
Volvi la vista al son, vi los mayores
   Aparatos de fiesta que vió Roma
   En sus felices tiempos y mejores.
Dijo mi amigo:—Aquel que ves que asoma
   Por aquella montaña contrahecha,
   Cuyo brio al de Marte oprime y doma,
Es un alto sugeto, que deshecha
   Tiene á la envidia en rabia, porque pisa
   De la virtud la senda mas derecha.
De gravedad y condicion tan lisa,
   Que suspende y alegra á un mismo instante,
   Y con su aviso al mismo aviso avisa.
Mas quiero, ántes que pases adelante
   En ver lo que veras, si estás atento,
   Darte del caso relacion bastante.
Será DON JUAN DE TASIS de mi cuento
   Principio, porque sea memorable,
   Y lleguen mis palabras á mi intento.
Este varon, en liberal notable,
   Que una mediana villa le hace conde,
   Siendo rey en sus obras admirable:

But that same will, that doth all wills constrain,
　I mean the will of heaven, hath held me bound
　To seek it now with greater joy than pain ;"
More had I said, when lo ! a mighty sound
　The fifes and horns and kettledrums did raise,
　My ear to gladden and my soul confound !
I turned me, and I saw more grand displays
　Of festive jubilee than Rome could show
　E'en in her grandest and her happiest days !
Quoth he, my friend : " He whom thou seest go
　With ardour to ascend that tortuous hill,
　Whose vigour gives to Mars himself a blow,
A soaring spirit is, who treads with skill
　The clear straight path that leads to Virtue's goal,
　And sends through Envy's heart a furious thrill ;
Of grave demeanour, yet of sweetest soul,
　He fills each heart with wonder and delight,
　And by his wit doth wisdom's self control !
But ere thou passest on to see the sight
　That now awaits thee, if thou so incline,
　On this great show I fain would shed some light:
I give DON JUAN DE TASIS foremost line
　In this my tale, that it may better ring,
　And that my words may square with my design.
This gentleman, of gifts a living spring,
　Whom VILLAMEDIANA made a Count,
　Although already by his works a King ;

Este, que sus haberes nunca esconde,
    Pues siempre los reparte, ó los derrama,
    Ya sepa adónde, ó ya no sepa adónde:
Este, á quien tiene tan en fil la fama,
    Puesta la alteza de su nombre claro,
    Que liberal y pródigo se llama,
Quiso pródigo aqui, y allí no avaro,
    Primer mantenedor ser de un torneo,
    Que á fiestas sobrehumanas le comparo.
Responden sus grandezas al deseo
    Que tiene de mostrarse alegre, viendo
    De España y Francia el regio himeneo.
Y este que escuchas, duro, alegre estruendo,
    Es señal que el torneo se comienza,
    Que admira por lo rico y estupendo.
Arquímedes el grande se avergüenza
    De ver que este teatro milagroso
    Su ingenio apoque, y á sus trazas venza.
Digo pues, que el mancebo generoso,
    Que allí desciende de encarnado y plata,
    Sobre todo mortal curso brioso,
Es el CONDE DE LEMOS, que dilata
    Su fama con sus obras por el mundo,
    Y que lleguen al cielo en tierra trata:
Y aunque sale el primero, es el segundo
    Mantenedor, y en buena cortesia
    Esta ventaja califico y fundo.

He who, of goods and wealth a very fount,
  Likes not to hoard, but scatters them with glee,
  Hither or thither, 'tis of no account;
He, to whom Fame hath given, in such degree,
  To his clear name a loftiness serene,
  That he is styled the prodigal and free,
Hath so decreed, for honour ever keen,
  To be the first defender in the plain
  Of a grand Tourney—grandest ever seen!
His lofty greatness makes the passage plain
  To his desire, with joy to celebrate
  The regal nuptials that bind France and Spain.
The sound thou hearest is the sign we wait,
  That the grand Tourney will commence amain,
  That well may stun thee with its pomp and state;
Great Archimedes' self would writhe in pain
  To see how this miraculous display
  Beggars his plans, makes his inventions vain.
Observe the youth, the generous and the gay,
  Who lighteth down, in vigour reaching high
  Above the rest, in crimson bright array;
The COUNT DE LEMOS he, whose deeds do fly
  On wings of fame through all the world we see,
  Making fleet commerce 'twixt the earth and sky;
Though first he comes, the second champion he,
  Which place he takes, if I do err not far,
  To suit the just demands of courtesy.

El DUQUE DE NOCERA, luz y guia
   Del arte militar, es el tercero
   Mantenedor deste festivo dia.
El cuarto, que pudiera ser primero,
   Es DE SANTELMO el fuerte CASTELLANO,
   Que al mesmo Marte en el valor prefiero.
El quinto es otro Enéas el troyano,
   ARROCIOLO, que gana en ser valiente
   Al qué fué verdadero, por la mano.—
El gran concurso y número de gente
   Estorbó que adelante prosiguiese
   La comenzada relacion prudente.
Por esto la pedí que me pusiese
   Adonde sin ningun impedimento
   El gran progreso de las fiestas viese.
Porque luego me vino al pensamiento
   De ponerlas en verso numeroso,
   Favorecido del febeo aliento.
Hizolo así, y yo vi lo que no oso
   Pensar, que no decir, que aquí se acorta
   La lengua y el ingenio mas curioso.
Que se pase en silencio es lo que importa
   Y que la admiracion supla esta falta,
   El mesmo grandïoso caso exhorta.
Puesto que despues supe que con alta
   Magnífica elegancia milagrosa,
   Donde ni sobra punto ni le falta,

El DUQUE DE NOCERA, guiding star
  In military art, holds the third place
  As champion in this glorious festive war;
The fourth, who might be first in point of grace,
  Is Fort St. Elmo's mighty Castellan,
  Who Mars himself might vanquish in the race;
The fifth is ARROCIOLO, valiant man
  Who equals great Æneas, him of Troy,
  And e'en o'ertops him by a goodly span!"
The mighty numbers, which did there deploy,
  Brought to a speedy end his tale of grace,
  Whose grave recital filled my heart with joy.
On this I begged him he would find a place,
  Where undisturbed, as on some vantage tower,
  I might survey the wondrous festive race;
For it had struck me, in a happy hour,
  That I might put it into sounding verse,
  If Phœbus would but kindly give me power.
This did he; and I saw what to rehearse
  I do not dare, for thought and language fail,
  And keenest wit must suffer a reverse;
'Tis needful then that Silence tell the tale,
  For, sooth, it was a magnifique affair,
  And Fancy can supply each rich detail.
Since then I've heard that, with a curious care,
  With elegance supreme and grandiose,
  That heightened nothing and left nothing bare,

El curioso Don Juan de Oquina en prosa
 La puso, y dió á la estampa para gloria
 De nuestra edad, por esto venturosa.
Ni en fabulosa ó verdadera historia
 Se halla que otras fiestas hayan sido,
 Ni pueden ser mas dignas de memoria.
Desde allí, y no sé cómo, fuí traido
 Adonde ví al gran Duque de Pastrana
 Mil parabienes dar de bien venido;
Y que la fama en la verdad ufana
 Contaba que agradó con su presencia,
 Y con su cortesía sobrehumana:
Que fué nuevo Alejandro en la excelencia
 Del dar, que satisfizo á todo cuanto
 Puede mostrar real magnificencia;
Colmo de admiracion, lleno de espanto,
 Entré en Madrid en traje de romero,
 Que es granjería el parecer ser santo.
Y desde léjos me quitó el sombrero
 El famoso Acevedo, y dijo:—*A Dio,
Voi siate il ben venuto, cavaliero;
So parlar zenoese, e tusco anch'io.*—
 Y respondi:—*La vostra signoria
Sia la ben trovata, padron mio.*—
Topé á Luis Velez, lustre y alegria,
 Y discrecion del trato cortesano,
 Y abracéle en la calle á mediodía.

DON JUAN DE OQUINA told it all in prose,
  And gave it to the press to grace our age,
  In this most lucky we may well suppose;
For, not in story fabulous nor sage,
  Hath such like festival been ever found,
  None worthier of a place in History's page.
From this I reached, I know not how, the ground
  Where I could see received, with welcome grand,
  El DUQUE DE PASTRANA the renowned;
Fame, winged with truth, did publish o'er the land
  How much he charmed with wondrous courtesy,
  And stately bearing fitted to command;
How, like a second Alexander, he
  With regal hand, where meanness left no taint,
  Did carry splendour to the last degree.
O'erwhelmed with awe, and eke with wonder faint,
  I reached Madrid in pilgrim's dress severe,
  For much it profiteth to seem a saint;
There doffed his hat to me, as he came near,
  The famous ACEVEDO and did cry:
  "A Dio, you are the well-come, Cavalier,
I speak ze Zenoese, the Tuscan I!"
  "Padron, you are the well-found!" I did say;
  And as I turned I met, and eye to eye,
With LUIS VELEZ, model fine and gay
  Of courtly polished wit, and kissed his face
  In open street, and in the blaze of day;

El pecho, el alma, el corazon, la mano
　Di á PEDRO DE MORALES, y un abrazo,
　Y alegre recebí á JUSTINIANO.
Al volver de una esquina sentí un brazo
　Que el cuello me ceñia, miré cúyo,
　Y mas que gusto me causó embarazo,
Por ser uno de aquellos (no rehuyo
　Decirlo) que al contrario se pasaron,
　Llevados del cobarde intento suyo.
Otros dos al del Layo se llegaron,
　Y con la risa falsa del conejo,
　Y con muchas zalemas me hablaron.
Yo socarron, yo poeton ya viejo
　Volvíles á lo tierno las saludes,
　Sin mostrar mal talante ó sobrecejo.
No dudes, ó letor caro, no dudes,
　Sino que suele el disimulo á veces
　Servir de aumento á las demas virtudes.
Dínoslo tú, David, que aunque pareces
　Loco en poder de Aquís, de tu cordura
　Fingiendo el loco, la grandeza ofreces.
Dejélos esperando coyuntura
　Y ocasion mas secreta para dalles
　Vejámen de su miedo, ó su locura.
Si encontraba poetas por las calles,
　Me ponia á pensar, si eran de aquellos
　Huidos, y pasaba sin hablalles.

My heart and hand I gave, and warm embrace
  To PEDRO DE MORALES, and with right
  JUSTINIANO claimed like friendly place.
At turning of a street there grasped me tight
  Around my neck an arm—I wondered whose;
  And, more to my confusion than delight,
(To speak right out I cannot well refuse,)
  He was a renegado of the band,
  Who did the coward's work in coward's shoes.
Two others of these LAICS came to hand,
  And with a grinning, hypocritic smile,
  And much salaaming, spoke me fair and bland.
I, an old poet, with sardonic wile
  Returned their bows, with courtesy in chief,
  Nor showed my pique, nor raised my brows the while.
Let it not, tender reader, give thee grief,
  Dissimulation hath at times its place
  To set the other virtues in relief;
O David, tell us, was not this thy case,
  When thou, in power of Achish, play'dst the fool,
  And feigned folly showed thy wisdom's grace?
I left them, biding fitting time and cool
  To brand their folly and their cowardice,
  And fill their cup of chastisement right full;
If in the high street poets met mine eyes,
  I stopped to think if they were runaways,
  And without speech I passed them in a trice;

S

Poníanseme yertos los cabellos
   De temor no encontrase algun poeta,
   De tantos que no pude conocellos,
Que con puñal buïdo, ó con secreta
   Almarada me hiciese un agujero
   Que fuese ál corazon por via reta,
Aunque no es este el premio que yo espero
   De la fama, que á tantos he adquirido
   Con alma grata y corazon sincero.
Un cierto mancebito cuellierguido,
   En profesion poeta, y en el traje
   A mil leguas por godo conocido,
Lleno de presuncion y de coraje
   Me dijo:—Bien sé yo, señor Cervántes,
   Que puedo ser poeta, aunque soy paje.
Cargastes de poetas ignorantes,
   Y dejástesme á mí, que ver deseo
   Del Parnaso las fuentes elegantes.
Que caducais sin duda alguna creo:
   Creo, no digo bien: mejor diria
   Que toco esta verdad, y que la veo.—
Otro, que al parecer, de argentería,
   De nácar, de cristal, de perlas y oro
   Sus infinitos versos componia,
Me dijo bravo, cual corrido toro:
   —No sé yo para qué nadie me puso
   En lista con tan bárbaro decoro.

My hair stood up on end, in homely phrase,
　Lest I should meet some poet by the way
　Of those I did not know, or did not praise ;
Who, with a poignard, or with secret play
　Of some sharp dirk, might stab me from behind,
　And take my life without a moment's stay.
Such meed of fame, sooth, fear I not to find,
　Who have received so many in my day,
　With guileless soul and with a grateful mind.
A certain stiff-necked stripling stopped the way,
　A bard to trade, with dress that's all the rage,
　And stamps him Goth a thousand leagues away ;
Who said with all the pertness of his age :
　" Hark'ee, Señor Cervantes, well I know
　I can a poet be, though I'm a page ;
With loads of witless poets didst thou go,
　And left me out, who fain would see, I vow,
　The dainty springs that in Parnassus flow !
I do believe thou art a dotard, thou ;
　Believe ! I said not well, I'd better say,
　I've hit the very mark, and see it now ! "
Another there, whose verses made display
　Of silver, mother-o'-pearl, and crystal too,
　Of pearls and gold, in wildering array,
Like baited bull, came fiercely to my view ;
　" With gauds like these, can any tell me why
　They gave me not a place among the crew ?"

—Así el discreto Apolo lo dispuso,
  A los dos respondí, y en este hecho
  De ignorancia ó malicia no me acuso.—
Fuíme con esto, y lleno de despecho
  Busqué mi antigua y lóbrega posada,
  Y arrojéme molido sobre el lecho;
  Que cansa cuando es larga una jornada.

FIN.

So cried he ; and to both I gave reply :
 "It was the wise Apollo's wish," I said,
 "No malice, nay, nor ignorance had I!"
On this, with smothered ire, I turned and fled,
 And to my old and sombre home retired,
 And flung me worn and shattered on my bed ;
For when a journey's long one feels so tired.

FINIS.

APPENDIX
TO THE
"PARNASSUS."

ADJUNTA AL PARNASO.

Algunos dias estuve reparándome de tan largo viaje, al cabo de los cuales salí á ver y á ser visto, y á recebir parabienes de mis amigos, y malas vistas de mis enemigos; que puesto que pienso que no tengo ninguno, todavía no me aseguro de la comun suerte.

Sucedió pues que saliendo una mañana del monasterio de Atocha, se llegó á mí un mancebo al parecer de veinte y cuatro años poco mas ó ménos, todo limpio, todo aseado y todo crujiendo gorgoranes, pero con un cuello tan grande y tan almidonado, que creí que para llevarle fueran menester los hombros de un Atlante. Hijos deste cuello eran dos puños chatos, que comenzando de las muñecas, subian y trepaban por las canillas del brazo arriba, que parecia que iban á dar asalto á las barbas. No he visto yo hiedra tan codiciosa de subir desde el pié de la muralla donde se arrima, hasta las almenas, como el ahinco que llevaban estos puños á ir á darse de

APPENDIX TO THE "PARNASSUS."

CERTAIN days did I remain recruiting myself after so long a journey, at the end of which I sallied forth to see and to be seen, to receive good greetings from my friends and evil glances from my enemies; for though I have none that I know of, I do not hold me exempt from the common lot.

And so it happened that, going forth one morning from the monastery of Atocha, I was accosted by a youth of some four-and-twenty summers, a few more or less; cleanly withal, and arrayed to the full in garments of rustling silk, but with a ruff so large, and so bestarched, that the shoulders of an Atlas seemed needful to bear it. To match this ruff were two flat cuffs, which, beginning with the wrists, went creeping up the brachial bones, as if eager to assail the whiskers. Never have I seen Ivy more ambitious of climbing up its supporting wall to the topmost battlements, than were these cuffs in their eager

puñadas con los codos. Finalmente, la exorbitancia del cuello y puños era tal, que en el cuello se escondia y sepultaba el rostro, y en los puños los brazos.

Digo pues que el tal mancebo se llegó á mí, y con voz grave y reposada me dijo: ¿Es por ventura vuestra merced el señor Miguel de Cervántes Saavedra, el que há pocos dias que vino del Parnaso?

A esta pregunta creo sin duda que perdí la color del rostro, porque en un instante imaginé y dije entre mí: ¿Si es este alguno de los poetas que puse, ó dejé de poner en mi *Viaje*, y viene ahora á darme el pago que él se imagina se me debe?

Pero sacando fuerzas de flaqueza, le respondí: "Yo, señor, soy el mesmo que vuestra merced dice: ¿qué es lo que se me manda?"

El luego en oyendo esto, abrió los brazos, y me los echó al cuello, y sin duda me besara en la frente, si la grandeza del cuello no lo impidiera, y díjome: "Vuestra merced, señor Cervántes, me tenga por su servidor y por su amigo, porque há muchos dias que le soy muy aficionado, así por sus obras como por la fama de su apacible condicion."

Oyendo lo cual respiré, y los espíritus que andaban alborotados, se sosegaron; y abrazándole yo tambien con recato de no ajarle el cuello, le dije:

Appendix to the Parnassus. 267

desire to come to fisticuffs with the elbows. In short, the enormity of the ruff and cuffs was such, that the face lay hid and buried in the ruff, and the arms in the cuffs.

As I was saying, this same youth accosted me, and said with grave and quiet voice: "Is your worship, perchance, the Señor Miguel de Cervantes who arrived from Parnassus a few days ago?"

At this inquiry I verily believe that my face lost colour, for in a twinkling I found me saying to myself: "May this be one of the poets whom I put, or refrained from putting, into my *Journey*, and who comes now to pay me off as he fancies I deserve?"

But gathering strength from weakness, I replied: "I, Señor, am the same of whom your worship speaks; what would you with me?"

On hearing this, he straightway opened his arms and threw them round my neck, and would doubtless have kissed my brow, had not the bigness of his ruff hindered, and said to me: "Let your worship, Señor Cervantes, esteem me as your servant and friend; seeing I have been these many days your admirer, both for your works' sake, and the well-known kindliness of your disposition."

On hearing this, I breathed again, and my disturbed spirits revived; and embracing him, with due respect

"Yo no conozco á vuestra merced si no es para sirvirle; pero por las muestras bien se me trasluce que vuestra merced es muy discreto y muy principal: calidades que obligan á tener en veneracion á la persona que las tiene."

Con estas pasamos otras corteses razones, y anduvieron por alto los ofrecimientos, y de lance en lance, me dijo: "Vuestra merced sabrá, señor Cervántes, que yo por la gracia de Apolo soy poeta, ó á lo ménos deseo serlo, y mi nombre es Pancracio de Roncesvalles."

MIGUEL. "Nunca tal creyera, si vuestra merced no me lo hubiera dicho por su mesma boca."

PANCRACIO. "¿Pues por qué no lo creyera vuestra merced?"

MIGUEL. "Porque los poetas por maravilla andan tan atildados como vuestra merced, y es la causa, que como son de ingenio tan altaneros y remontados, ántes atienden á las cosas del espíritu, que á las del cuerpo."

"Yo, señor," dijo él, "soy mozo, soy rico y soy enamorado: partes que deshacen en mí la flojedad que infunde la poesía. Por la mocedad tengo brio; con la riqueza, con que mostrarle; y con el amor, con que no parecer descuidado."

"Las tres partes del camino," le dije yo, "se tiene vuestra merced andadas para llegar á ser buen poeta."

to the integrity of his ruff, I said to him: "I do not know your worship, save as your humble servant; but from visible proofs I am assured that you are very discreet, and distinguished: qualities which constrain me to respect the person who possesses them."

On this we exchanged other courteous phrases, and went to extremes in compliments, until, from one thing to another, he said: " Your worship, Señor Cervantes, should know that I, by Apollo's grace, am a poet, or at least desire to be one, and my name is Pancracio de Roncesvalles."

MIGUEL. "I should never have believed it, had you not told it me with your own mouth."

PANCRACIO. "Why, then, should you not have believed it?"

MIGUEL. "Because seldom or never do poets go so finely arrayed as you do; and the reason is, that, as their genius is ever soaring aloft, they pay more heed to the things of the spirit, than to those of the body."

"I, Señor," quoth he, "am young, rich, and in love, qualities which undo in me the negligence which poetry engenders. My youth gives me vigour, my wealth the means of displaying it, and my love saves me from all appearance of untidiness."

"Your worship," I replied, " has already gone three parts of the way towards being a good poet."

PANCRACIO. "¿Cuáles son?"

MIGUEL. "La de la riqueza y la del amor. Porque los partos de los ingenios de la persona rica y enamorada son asombrós de la avaricia, y estímulos de la liberalidad, y en el poeta pobre la mitad de sus divinos partos y pensamientos se los llevan los cuidados de buscar el ordinario sustento. Pero dígame vuestra merced, por su vida: ¿de qué suerte de menestra poética gasta ó gusta mas?"

PANCRACIO, "No entiendo eso de menestra poética."

MIGUEL. "Quiero decir, que á qué género de poesía es vuestra merced mas inclinado, al lírico, al heróico, ó al cómico."

PANCRACIO. "A todos estilos me amaño; pero en el que mas me ocupo es en el cómico."

MIGUEL. "Desa manera habrá vuestra merced compuesto algunas comedias."

PANCRACIO. "Muchas, pero solo una se ha representado."

MIGUEL. "¿Pareció bien?"

PANCRACIO. "Al vulgo no."

MIGUEL. "¿Y á los discretos?"

PANCRACIO. "Tampoco."

MIGUEL. "¿La causa?"

PANCRACIO. "La causa fué, que la achacaron que era larga en los razonamientos, no

PANCRACIO. "What may these be?"

MIGUEL. "Those of riches and love; for the fruits of the rich, enamoured one's genius avarice stunts not, but liberality quickens; while the half of the poor poet's divine fruits and fancies miscarry by reason of his anxious care to win his daily bread. But tell me, for dear life, what kind of poetic pottage do you relish most?"

PANCRACIO. "I understand not what you mean by poetic pottage."

MIGUEL. "I would say, what kind of poetry do you most affect, the lyric, the heroic, or the comic?"

PANCRACIO. "I am apt at all styles, but that which engages me most is the comic."

MIGUEL. "Your worship, then, will have written some comedies?"

PANCRACIO. "Many, but only one of them has been put upon the stage."

MIGUEL. "Was it well received?"

PANCRACIO. "By the vulgar, no."

MIGUEL. "And by the enlightened?"

PANCRACIO. "As little."

MIGUEL. "And the reason?"

PANCRACIO. "The reason was, that they blamed it for being long-winded in its speeches, not too chaste in its verses, and altogether void of invention."

muy pura en los versos, y desmayada en la invencion."

"Tachas son estas," respondí yo, "que pudieran hacer parecer malas las del mesmo Plauto."

"Y mas," dijo él, "que no pudieron juzgalla, porque no la dejaron acabar segun la gritaron. Con todo esto, la echó el autor para otro dia; pero porfiar que porfiar: cinco personas vinieron apénas."

"Créame vuestra merced," dije yo, "que las comedias tienen dias, como algunas mujeres hermosas; y que esto de acertarlas bien, va tanto en la ventura, como en el ingenio: comedia he visto yo apedreada en Madrid, que la han laureado en Toledo: y no por esta primer desgracia deje vuestra merced de proseguir en componerlas; que podrá ser que cuando ménos lo piense, acierte con alguna que le dé crédito y dineros."

"De los dineros no hago caso," respondió él; "mas preciaria la fama, que cuanto hay; porque es cosa de grandísimo gusto, y de no ménos importancia ver salir mucha gente de la comedia, todos contentos, y estar el poeta que la compuso á la puerta del teatro, recibiendo parabienes de todos."

"Sus descuentos tienen esas alegrías," le dije yo, "que tal vez suele ser la comedia tan pésima, que no hay quien alce los ojos á mirar al poeta, ni aun él para cuatro calles del coliseo, ni aun los alzan los

Appendix to the Parnassus.

"Blemishes these," I replied, "that would have damned the comedies of Plautus himself!"

"And all the more," he rejoined, "that they left themselves no means of judging it, for they hooted it off the stage before it was half-finished. The manager reserved it for another day: but worse and worse, for scarcely five persons came."

"Believe me," I said to him, "that comedies have their times as beautiful women have; and chance, as well as wit, plays a part in hitting these precisely. I have seen a comedy pelted in Madrid, which was crowned in Toledo. Let not your worship, then, be discouraged by the first failure, but proceed to compose others; for when you least dream of it you may succeed with one which will bring you in both credit and coin."

"Of the coin I make no account," he replied, "but fame I would prize, be it much or little. For it is a thing of exquisite delight, and no less importance, to see crowds of people issuing from the comedy, all in fine humour, and the poet who wrote it standing at the door of the theatre, receiving congratulations from all around."

"Such pleasures have their drawbacks," I said to him, "for sometimes the comedy may be so wretchedly bad, that no one will care to cast eyes on the poet, as he rushes headlong five streets'

que la recitaron, avergonzados y corridos de haberse engañado y escogídola por buena."

"Y vuestra merced, señor Cervántes," dijo él, "¿ha sido aficionado á la carátula? ¿ha compuesto alguna comedia?"

"Sí," dije yo: "muchas; y á no ser mias, me parecieran dignas de alabanza, como lo fuéron: *Los Tratos de Argel, La Numancia, La gran Turquesca, La Batalla Naval, La Jerusalen, La Amaranta ó La del Mayo, el Bosque amoroso, La Unica y la Bizarra Arsinda,* y otras muchas de que no me acuerdo; mas la que yo mas estimo, y de la que mas me precio, fué y es, de una llamada *La Confusa,* la cual, con paz sea dicho de cuantas comedias de capa y espada hasta hoy se han representado, bien puede tener lugar señalado por buena entre las mejores."

PANCRACIO. "¿Y agora tiene vuestra merced algunas?"

MIGUEL. "Seis tengo con otros seis entremeses."

PANCRACIO. "¿Pues por qué no se representan?"

MIGUEL. "Porque ni los autores me buscan, ni yo les voy á buscar á ellos."

PANCRACIO. "No deben de saber que vuestra merced las tiene."

MIGUEL. "Sí saben, pero como tienen sus poetas

Appendix to the Parnassus. 275

length from the building; not even the players thereof, who stand blushing and mortified at their deception in having accepted the play as good!"

"Has your worship, Señor Cervantes," said he, "affected the playwright's art? Have you composed any comedy?"

"Yes," said I, "many; and, had they not been mine, I should have held them worthy of praise, as indeed they were: *The Manners of Algiers*, *Numancia*, *The grand Sultana*, *The Naval Combat*, *Jerusalem*, *Amaranta or the May-flower*, *The Amorous Grove*, *The rare and matchless Arsinda*, and many others that have slipped from my memory. But that which I most esteem, and still pride myself upon, was, and is one styled *The Confused Lady*, which, with peace be it spoken, may rank as good among the best of the comedies of the 'Cloak and Sword,' which have hitherto been represented."

PANCRACIO. "Has your worship at present any on hand?"

MIGUEL. "I have six, and as many more interludes."

PANCRACIO. "Why, then, are they not being acted?"

MIGUEL. "Because neither do the managers come to seek me, nor do I go to seek them."

paniaguados, y les va bien con ellos, no buscan pan de trastrigo; pero yo pienso darlas á la estampa, para que se vea de espacio lo que pasa apriesa, y se disimula, ó no se entiende cuando las representan; y las comedias tienen sus sazones y tiempos, como los cantares."

Aquí llegábamos con nuestra plática, cuando Pancracio puso la mano en el seno, y sacó dél una carta con su cubierta, y besándola, me la puso en la mano: leí el sobrescrito, y vi que decia desta manera:

" A Miguel de Cervántes Saavedra, en la calle de las Huertas, frontero de las casas donde solia vivir el príncipe de Marruecos, en Madrid." Al porte: medio real, digo diez y siete maravedís.

Escandalizóme el porte, y de la declaracion del medio real, digo diez y siete. Y volviéndosela le dije:

" Estando yo en Valladolid llevaron una carta á mi casa para mí, con un real de porte: recebióla y pagó el porte una sobrina mia, que nunca ella le pagara; pero dióme por disculpa, que muchas veces me habia oido decir que en tres cosas era bien gastado el dinero: en dar limosna, en pagar al buen médico, y en el porte de las cartas, ora sean de amigos, ó de enemigos, que las de los amigos avisan, y de las de los enemigos se puede tomar algun indicio de sus pensamientos. Diéronmela,

Appendix to the Parnassus. 277

PANCRACIO. "Haply they know not that you have them?"

MIGUEL. "Yes, they know it; but as they have their own household poets, who bring grist to the mill, they do not seek finer cern than the finest. I have thoughts, however, of giving them to the press, that people may see at their leisure what passes hurriedly, inaccurately, and often unintelligibly when acted on the stage. And comedies have their times and seasons as popular songs have."

We had reached this point of our dialogue, when Pancracio thrust his hand into his bosom, and drew therefrom a letter with its envelope, and kissing it, he placed it in my hands. I read the superscription and found it to run thus:

"To Miguel de Cervantes Saavedra, in Orchard Street, fronting the house where the Prince of Morocco used to live, in Madrid." For postage: half a real, I mean, seventeen maravedis.

I boggled at the postage, and its imposition of "half a real, I mean, seventeen maravedis." So, returning the letter to him, I said:

"While I was living in Valladolid a letter was brought to my house for me, with a real for postage. A niece of mine received it and paid the postage, which she never ought to have paid. But she tendered as excuse, that she had often heard me say

y venía en ella un soneto malo, desmayado, sin garbo ni agudeza alguna, diciendo mal del *Don Quijote;* y de lo que me pesó fué del real, y propuse desde entónces de no tomar carta con porte: así que, si vuestra merced le quiere llevar desta, bien se la puede volver, que yo sé que no me puede importar tanto como el medio real que se me pide."

Rióse muy de gana el señor Roncesvalles, y díjome: "Aunque soy poeta, no soy tan mísero que me aficionen diez y siete maravedís. Advierta vuestra merced, señor Cervántes, que esta carta por lo ménos es del mesmo Apolo: él la escribió no há viente dias en el Parnaso, y me la dió para que á vuestra merced la diese: vuestra merced la lea, que yo sé que le ha de dar gusto."

"Haré lo que vuestra merced me manda," respondí yo; "pero quiero que ántes de leerla, vuestra merced me le haga de decirme, cómo, cuándo, y á qué fué al Parnaso."

Y él respondió: "Cómo fuí, fué por mar, y en una fragata que yo y otros diez poetas fletamos en Barcelona; cuándo fuí, fué seis dias despues de la batalla que se dió entre los buenos y los malos poetas; á qué fuí, fué á hallarme en ella, por obligarme á ello la profesion mia."

"A buen seguro," dije yo, "que fuéron vuestras mercedes bien recebidos del señor Apolo."

that money was well spent in doing three things: in giving alms, in feeing a good doctor, and in paying the postage of letters, whether from friends or enemies; for those of friends give goodly counsel, while those of enemies may afford some clue to their designs. I opened the missive, and there dropped from it a bad, pithless, graceless, pointless Sonnet in dispraise of the 'Don Quixote.' But what weighed most on my soul was the matter of the real, and I resolved that after this I would take in no letter bearing postage. So if your worship means to exact it, you may take the letter back, for I have strong suspicion that to me it is not worth the half real you ask for it!"

Whereupon Señor Roncesvalles laughed heartily, and said to me: "Albeit I am a poet, I am not so badly off as to higgle about seventeen maravedis. Your worship, Señor Cervantes, must understand that this letter is from no less a personage than Apollo himself. He wrote it in Parnassus not twenty days ago, and gave it me to give to you. Read it, for well I know it will give you pleasure."

"I will do," said I, "what your worship requests, but, before reading it, would you inform me how, when, and wherefore you went to Parnassus?"

To which he replied: "*How* I went, was by Sea, and in a frigate chartered by me, and ten other poets, in Barcelona; *when* I went, was six days after the

PANCRACIO. "Sí fuimos, aunque le hallamos muy occupado á él, y á las señoras Piérides, arando y sembrando de sal todo aquel término del campo donde se dió la batalla. Preguntéle para qué se hacia aquello, y respondióme, que así como de los dientes de la serpiente de Cadmo habian nacido hombres armados, y de cada cabeza cortada de la hidra que mató Hércules habian renacido otras siete, y de las gotas de la sangre de la cabeza de Medusa se habia llenado de serpientes toda la Libia; de la mesma manera de la sangre podrida de los malos poetas que en aquel sitio habian sido muertos, comenzaban á nacer del tamaño de ratones otros poetillas rateros, que llevaban camino de henchir toda la tierra de aquella mala simiente, y que por esto se araba aquel lugar, y se sembraba de sal, como si fuera casa de traidores."

En oyendo esto, abrí luego la carta, y vi que decia:

Appendix to the Parnassus.

battle waged between the good and bad poets; *wherefore* I went, was to fulfil the obligation imposed on me by my profession."

"Then of a surety," said I, "your worship was well received by my lord Apollo?"

"We were indeed: though we found his lordship, and the ladies Pierides, very much busied in ploughing and sowing with salt that portion of the field where the battle took place. I asked him why he was doing this, and he answered, that just as from the teeth of the dragon of Cadmus there sprung up armed men, and from each severed head of the Hydra slain by Hercules seven others were produced, and from the blood-clots of Medusa's head the whole of Lybia became peopled with serpents; so in like manner from the putrid blood of the bad poets, done to death on that field, a whole crop of little poets, small as mice, began already to peer forth, so that the whole country-side was threatened with the plague of that evil seed. For this reason, he said, he was ploughing up the spot, and sowing it with salt, as if it were a house of traitors!"

On hearing this I forthwith opened the letter, and found its contents to be these:

APOLO DELFICO

Á MIGUEL DE CERVANTES SAAVEDRA.

SALUD.

El señor Pancracio de Roncesvalles, llevador desta, dirá á vuestra merced, señor Miguel de Cervántes, en qué me halló ocupado el dia que llegó á verme con sus amigos. Y yo digo, que estoy muy quejosa de la descortesía que conmigo se usó en partirse vuestra merced deste monte sin despedirse de mí, ni de mis hijas, sabiendo cuánto le soy aficionado, y las Musas por el consiguiente; pero si se me da por disculpa que le llevó el deseo de ver á su Mecénas el gran conde de Lemos, en las fiestas famosas de Nápoles, yo la acepto, y le perdono.

Despues que vuestra merced partió deste lugar, me han sucedido muchas desgracias, y me he visto en grandes aprietos, especialmente por consumir y acabar los poetas que iban naciendo de la sangre e los malos que aquí murieron, aunque ya, gracias al cielo y á mi industria, este daño está remediado.

APOLLO DELPHICUS

TO MIGUEL DE CERVANTES SAAVEDRA.

HEALTH.

Señor Pancracio de Roncesvalles, the bearer of this, will tell your worship, Señor Miguel de Cervantes, how he found me employed on that day when he came with his friends to visit me. Let me say, that I am greatly vexed by the discourtesy with which you treated me, when you left this mount without taking leave of me and my daughters; knowing how much I, and the Muses of course, are attached to you. But if you tender as excuse, that you were borne away by the desire of visiting your Maecenas, the great Count de Lemos, during the famous feasts of Naples, I accept it and pardon you.

Since your worship left this place many unpleasant things have befallen me, and I have found me in great straits, especially in putting a final end to the poets, who kept sprouting up from the blood of the bad ones who died here; though, thanks to Heaven and mine own good husbandry, that damage has been remedied.

No sé si del ruido de la batalla, ó del vapor que arrojó de sí la tierra, empapada en la sangre de los contrarios, me han dado unos vaguidos de cabeza, que verdaderamente me tienen como tonto, y no acierto á escribir cosa que sea de gusto ni de provecho: asi, si vuestra merced viere por allá que algunos poetas, aunque sean de los mas famosos, escriben y componen impertinencias y cosas de poco fruto, no los culpe, ni los tenga en ménos, sino que disimule con ellos: que pues yo, que soy el padre y el inventor de la poesía, deliro y parezco mentecato, no es mucho que lo parezcan ellos.

Envio á vuestra merced unos privilegios, ordenanzas y advertimientos, tocantes á los poetas: vuestra merced los haga guardar y cumplir al pié de la letra, que para todo ello doy á vuestra merced mi poder cumplido cuanto de derecho se requiere.

Entre los poetas que aquí vinieron con el señor Pancracio de Roncesvalles, se quejaron algunos de que no iban en la lista de los que Mercurio llevó á España, y que así vuestra merced no los habia puesto en su *Viaje*. Yo les dije, que la culpa era mia, y no de vuestra merced; pero que el remedio deste daño estaba en que procurasen ellos ser famosos por sus obras, que ellas por sí mismas les darian fama y claro renombre, sin andar mendigando ajenas alabanzas.

Appendix to the Parnassus. 285

Whether caused by the din of battle or the steaming vapours from the earth soaked with the blood of the slain, I know not, but I feel certain swimmings of the head, which hold me as one distraught, unable to write anything either for pleasure or profit. So, if you should find over there that certain poets (be they even of the most famous) are writing or composing needless things to little purpose, do not blame them or esteem them less, but bear with them; for if I, who am the father and inventor of poesy, seem to be lightheaded, it is no wonder that they also should seem so.

I send your worship certain privileges, decrees, and warnings, appertaining to the poets. Be pleased to see that they observe and fulfil them to the letter; and for this purpose I invest you with plenary powers to take all lawful measures.

Of the poets who came hither with Señor Pancracio de Roncesvalles, certain complained that they were not found in the list of those which Mercury carried to Spain, and were therefore not inserted by you in your *Journey*. I told them that the fault was mine and not yours; but that the remedy for this wrong lay in their seeking to become famous through their works; that these of themselves would give them fame and clear renown, without gadding about to beg praise from others.

De mano en mano, si se ofreciere ocasion de mensajero, iré enviando mas privilegios, y avisando de lo que en este monte pasare. Vuestra merced haga lo mesmo, avisándome de su salud y de la de todos los amigos.

Al famoso Vicente Espinel dará vuestra merced mis encomiendas, como á uno de los mas antiguos y verdaderos amigos que yo tengo.

Si D. Francisco de Quevedo no hubiere partido para venir á Sicilia, donde le esperan, tóquele vuestra merced la mano, y dígale que no deje de llegar á verme, pues estarémos tan cerca ; que cuando aquí vino, por la súbita partida no tuve lugar de hablarle.

Si vuestra merced encontrare por allá algun tránsfuga de los veinte que se pasaron al bando contrario, no les diga nada, ni los aflija, que harta mala ventura tienen, pues son como demonios, que se llevan la pena y la confusion con ellos mesmos do quiera que vayan.

Vuestra merced tenga cuenta con su salud, y mire por sí, y guárdese de mí, especialmente en los caniculares, que aunque le soy amigo, en tales dias no va en mi mano, ni miro en obligaciones, ni en amistades.

Al señor Pancracio de Roncesvalles téngale vuestra merced por amigo, y comuníquelo: y pues es rico, no se le dé nada que sea mal poeta. Y con esto nuestro Señor guarde á vuestra merced como puede y yo deseo.

If I should find a handy messenger, I shall go on sending you, from time to time, more privileges, and apprise you of all that takes place on this hill. Let your worship do the same, giving me tidings of your health, and that of all my friends.

Give my warmest regards to the famous Vicente Espinel, as to one of the oldest and staunchest friends I have.

If D. Francisco de Quevedo hath not left for Sicily, where they await him, seize him by the hand, and tell him he must not fail to visit me in a neighbourly way; for his late sudden departure gave me no time to talk with him.

If your worship should meet with any deserters of the twenty who went over to the enemy, say nothing to them, nor vex them, for hard enough is their fate, seeing they are like unto demons, who bear pain and punishment in their bosoms, wherever they go.

Let your worship take heed to your health, and look to yourself, and beware of me, especially during the dog-days; for though I be your friend, on such days I am not master of myself, and regard neither duties nor friendships.

Hold Señor Pancracio de Roncesvalles as your friend, and confide in him; and, since he is rich, let it not concern him that he is a poor poet. And so may our Lord guard your worship as he can, and as I desire.

Del Parnaso á 22 de julio, el dia que me calzo las espuelas para subirme sobre la Canícula, 1614.

Servidor de vuestra merced,

APOLO LUCIDO.

En acabando la carta, vi que en un papel aparte venía escrito:

PRIVILEGIOS, ORDENANZAS Y ADVERTENCIAS, QUE APOLO ENVÍA Á LOS POETAS ESPAÑOLES.

Es el primero, que algunos poetas sean conocidos tanto por el desaliño de sus personas, como por la fama de sus versos.

Item, que si algun poeta dijere que es pobre, sea luego creido por su simple palabra, sin otro juramento ó averiguacion alguna.

Ordénase, que todo poeta sea de blanda y de suave condicion, y que no mire en puntos, aunque los traiga sueltos en sus medias.

Item, que si algun poeta llegare á casa de algun su amigo ó conocido, y estuviere comiendo y le convidare, que aunque él jure que ya ha comido, no se le crea en ninguna manera, sino que le hagan

From Parnassus, this 22nd of July, the day when I buckled on my spurs to mount the Dog-star, 1614.

Your worship's obedient Servant,
APOLLO LUCIDUS.

On finishing the letter I found, on a separate sheet, writing to this effect:

PRIVILEGES, DECREES, AND WARNINGS, WHICH APOLLO SENDS TO THE SPANISH POETS.

The first is, that any poets may be known, as well by the untidiness of their persons, as by the fame of their verses.

Item, that if any poet should affirm that he is poor, he shall forthwith be believed on his simple word, without other oath or affidavit whatsoever.

It is decreed, that every poet be of a mild and genial disposition, and stand not on points, albeit he may go with holes in his stockings.

Item, that if any poet should arrive at the house of a friend or acquaintance, and find him at dinner and be invited to eat, though he should swear that he has already dined, he shall in no wise be believed,

comer por fuerza, que en tal caso no se le hará muy grande.

Item, que el mas pobre poeta del mundo, como no sea de los Adanes y Matusalenes, pueda decir que es enamorado, aunque no lo esté, y poner el nombre á su dama como mas le viniere á cuento, ora llamándola Amarili, ora Anarda, ora Clori, ora Fílis, ora Fílida, ó ya Juana Tellez, ó como mas gustare, sin que desto se le pueda pedir ni pida razon alguna.

Item, se ordena que todo poeta, de cualquier calidad y condicion que sea, sea tenido y le tengan por hijodalgo, en razon del generoso ejercicio en que se ocupa, como son tenidos por cristianos viejos los niños que llaman de la piedra.

Item, se advierte que ningun poeta sea osado de escribir versos en alabanzas de príncipes y señores, por ser mi intencion y advertida voluntad, que la lisonja ni la adulucion no atraviesen los umbrales de mi casa.

Item, que todo poeta cómico, que felizmente hubiere sacado á luz tres comedias, pueda entrar sin pagar en los teatros, si ya no fuere la limosna de la segunda puerta, y aun esta sí pudiese ser, la excuse.

Item, se advierte que si algun poeta quisiere dar á la estampa algun libro que él hubiere compuesto, no se dé á entender que por dirigirle á algun monarca, el tal libro ha de ser estimado, porque si él no es

but be made to sit down by force, for in such case no great amount will be needed.

Item, that the poorest poet in the world, provided he be not one of the Adams or Methusalems, may declare himself enamoured, though he be not so, and may give such name to his mistress as shall best suit his fancy, calling her Amaryllis, or Anarda, or Chloris, or Phyllis, or Filida, or even Joan Tellez, at his own pleasure, without reason given or required.

Item, it is decreed, that every poet, of whatsoever quality or condition, may be and should be esteemed an "Hidalgo," by virtue of the gentle profession he follows; just as children,—so-called of the gutter,—are held to be sound old Christians.

Item, warning is given, that no poet shall dare to write verses in praise of princes and lords, since it is my declared will and intention that neither wiles nor flattery shall pass the threshold of my house.

Item, that every comic poet, who has brought out three successful comedies, shall have the entry of the theatres without payment, unless it be the pittance for the poor at the second door, and even this, if need be, shall be excused him.

Item, warning is given, that if any poet shall go to press with any work he may have composed, he is in no wise to presume that, by dedicating it to some monarch, said book must needs be applauded, for,

bueno, no le adobará la dirección, aunque sea hecha al prior de Guadalupe.

Itcm, se advierte que todo poeta no se desprecie de decir que lo es; que si fuere bueno, será digno de alabanza; y si malo, no faltará quien lo alabe; que cuando nace la escoba, etc.

Item, que todo buen poeta pueda disponer de mí y de lo que hay en el cielo á su beneplácito: conviene á saber, que los rayos de mi cabellera los pueda trasladar y aplicar á los cabellos de su dama, y hacer dos soles sus ojos, que conmigo serán tres, y así andará el mundo mas alumbrado; y de las estrellas, signos y planetas puede servirse de modo, que cuando ménos lo piense, la tenga hecha una esfera celeste.

Item, que todo poeta á quien sus versos le hubieren dado á entender que lo es, se estime y tenga en mucho, ateniéndose á aquel refran: Ruin sea el que por ruin se tiene.

Item, se ordena que ningun poeta grave haga corrillo en lugares públicos, recitando sus versos; que los que son buenos, en las aulas de Aténas se habian de recitar, que no en las plazas.

Item, se da aviso particular que si alguna madre tuviere hijos pequeñuelos, traviesos y llorones, los pueda amenazar y espantar con el coco, diciéndoles: Guardáos, niños, que viene el poeta fulana, que os

if it be not good, no dedication will better it, even though it be addressed to the Prior of Guadalupe.

Item, warning is given, that no poet shall disdain to avow his title ; for, if he be a good poet, he is worthy of praise, and, if a bad one, he will not lack admirers ; for " with the thistle grows the ass," &c.

Item, that every good poet may dispose of me, and of all that is in heaven, at his own pleasure. He may, forsooth, take the beams of my locks, and transfer them to the tresses of his mistress ; he may make two suns of her eyes, which, with me, will make three, and so shall the world be flooded with light. In like manner may he avail himself of the stars, signs, and planets, and fashion thereof, ere he dream of it, a whole celestial globe.

Item, that every poet, whose verses give him reason to think himself such, may hold himself in high respect, remembering the old adage : " Low is he who holds himself in low esteem."

Item, it is decreed, that no grave poet shall form a circle in public places, reciting therein his verses ; for those which are good should be declaimed in the halls of Athens, and not in the city squares.

Item, be it known in particular, that if any mother have small, fidgetty, squalling children, she may frighten them with the bogie in these terms : " Take heed, boys, for Mr. poet So-and-so is coming

echará con sus malos versos en la sima de Cabra, ó en el pozo Airon.

Item, que los dias de ayuno no se entienda que los ha quebrantado el poeta que aquella mañana se ha comido las uñas al hacer de sus versos.

Item, se ordena que todo poeta que diere en ser espadachin, valenton y arrojado, por aquella parte de la valentía se le desagüe y vaya la fama que podia alcanzar por sus buenos versos.

Item, se advierte que no ha de ser tenido por ladron el poeta que hurtare algun verso ajeno, y le encajare entre los suyos, como no sea todo el concepto y toda la copla entera, que en tal caso tan ladron es como Caco.

Item, que todo buen poeta, aunque no haya compuesto poema heróico, ni sacado al teatro del mundo obras grandes, con cualesquiera, aunque sean pocas, pueda alcanzar renombre de divino, como le alcanzaron Garcilaso de la Vega, Francisco de Figueroa, el Capitan Francisco de Aldana y Hernando de Herrera.

Item, se da aviso que si algun poeta fuere favorecido de algun príncipe, ni le visite á menudo, ni le pida nada, sino déjese llevar de la corriente de su ventura; que el que tiene providencia de sustentar las sabandijas de la tierra y los gusarapos del agua, la tendrá de alimentar á un poeta, por sabandija que sea.

to drop you, with his bad verses, into Cabra's cavern, or Airon's well!"

Item, that on a Fast-day it shall not be presumed that a poet hath broken it, because that morning he may have chewed his nails in making his verses.

Item, it is decreed, that every poet, who sets himself up as a swashbuckler, bully, and dare-devil, shall, for that display of valour, be clean emptied of the fame he may have gained by his good verses.

Item, be it known to all, that no poet is to be held as a purloiner, who shall take the verse of some one else and insert it amongst his own; provided it be not the whole idea or the entire stanza, in which case he must be branded as a very Cacus.

Item, that every good poet, though he may not have composed a heroic poem or given great works to the world's stage, may with any works, however small, achieve the distinction of "divine;" in like manner as it was gained by Garcilaso de la Vega, Francisco de Figueroa, Captain Francisco de Aldana, and Hernando de Herrera.

Item, warning is given, that if any poet be favoured of any prince, he is not to weary him with visits, nor dun him for anything, but let himself be borne on the current of his luck; for he who caters for the worms of the earth and the small fry of the sea, will be mindful of a poet, worm though he be.

En suma, estos fuéron los privilegios, advertencias y ordenanzas que Apolo me envió, y el señor Pancracio de Roncesvalles me trujo, con quien quedé en mucha amistad, y los dos quedamos de concierto de despachar un propio con la respuesta al señor Apolo, con las nuevas desta corte. Daráse noticia del dia, para que todos sus aficionados le escriban.

FIN DE LA ADJUNTA.

Such, in brief, were the privileges, warnings, and decrees which Apollo sent me by the hand of Señor Pancracio de Roncesvalles. He and I are now firm friends ; and are minded to dispatch a familiar to my lord Apollo, bearing our answer, with the news of the town. Due notice will be given of the day, so that all his devoted friends may write to him.

END OF THE APPENDIX.

LETTER OF CERVANTES TO MATEO VAZQUEZ.

WRITTEN DURING THE SECOND YEAR OF HIS CAPTIVITY IN ALGIERS.

1575-80.

Twas in the fight when that famed bolt of war,
The Austrian Eagle's son that scorned to yield,
Plucked from the Asian King, of luckless star,
Bright leaves of laurel on the billowy field—
'Twas then that envious fate, with cruel stroke,
Struck down CERVANTES and bemaimed his hand;
When lo! his genius in its strength awoke,
And changed dull lead to purest diamond,
Chaunting such sweet, refined, sonorous verse,
As after ages will for aye rehearse;
For men will tell how one hand, maimed in strife,
Could give its master an immortal life!

       LOPE DE VEGA,
        Laurel de Apolo.
        1630.

PREFATORY NOTE.

This remarkable letter of Cervantes, addressed to Mateo Vazquez de Leca Colona, Secretary of State to Philip II., after the downfall of Antonio Perez, is now for the first time presented to English readers in its entirety, with a transcript of the antique text, and a literal version in the metre of the original. It was discovered at Madrid in the beginning of April, 1863, among the archives of the Count of Altamira, by the distinguished academician, D. Tomás Muñoz y Romero, through an official of the household, D. Luis Buitrago y Peribañez. It was found amongst a bundle of papers, labelled "Divers Matters of Curiosity," which also contained an autograph MS. of Lope de Vega's Comedy, *Los Benavides*. Such wide-spread interest did the discovery of this letter excite, that it was submitted for critical inspection to Señor Hartzenbusch, Director of the Royal Library of Madrid, who, convinced of its authenticity, published it for the first time in the ninth number of the "Boletin Bibliografico Español" for 1863. He afterwards appended it to the fourth volume of his charming bijou edition of the "Don Quixote," (Argamasilla, 4 vols., 1863); and it was finally inserted in Rivadeneyra's magnificent edition of the collected works of Cervantes (Madrid, 12 vols., 1863-4), as a genuine relic of the " prince of Spanish wits." The letter consists of eighty tercets and a quatrain. The last sixty-seven lines, containing the impassioned appeal to Philip II., are to be found almost verbatim in the first Act of Cervantes' Comedy, *El Trato de Argel*.

Although addressed to Philip's Secretary of State, it does not seem to have been laid before the King himself, and instead of being consigned to the archives of Simancas, it found its way into those of the house of Altamira, with which noble family Mateo Vazquez was connected by marriage. When the library of the family was dispersed a few years ago, a vast number of Vazquez's State papers and correspondence were ruthlessly disposed of for the price of waste paper (nine reals the *arroba!*). A portion of these was eventually purchased by the British Museum, but the famous letter is, unfortunately, not among the number. It is at present, we believe, in the possession of the Duke of Baena.

Prefatory Note.

Such is a short account of the history of this interesting epistle, which forms a worthy pendant to the "Viaje del Parnaso," both from a literary and biographical point of view. It is the first noted poem of Cervantes, of any great length, that has come down to us. Though he himself tells us,

> From earliest years I loved with passion rare
> The winsome art of Poesy the gay,

yet none of his youthful compositions have survived, save a few mediocre sonnets and redondillas contributed, when he was twenty-two years of age, to the curious work of his Master in Arts, Juan Lopez de Hoyos, on the "Death and Obsequies of Queen Isabella of Valois." He also gives us in the "Viaje" a mysterious intimation of the composition of a pastoral poem in the heyday of his youth:

> To rival Phyllis my Phylena gay
> Hath carolled through the woods, whose leafy land
> Gave forth the sound of many a merry lay.

But poor Phylena seems to have lost herself in the woods, for she has never been seen nor heard of since. During his lengthened stay in Italy as a soldier, he was a passionate student of the masters of Italian poetry, notably of Ariosto, but his own poetic genius lay unproductive. Algiers, strange to say, was the cradle of his muse as it was the mould of his character. Even amid the terrible sufferings of their slavery, the Spanish captives were in the habit, when occasion offered, of giving dramatic representations, wherein they recited their national romances, and danced their national dances, to keep alive the flame of their patriotism. Cervantes was the life and soul of this movement. In his Comedy, *Los Baños de Argel*, he gives a mirthful account of the acting of one of Lope de Rueda's quaint colloquies in the country dialect, under like circumstances. Of the "numberless romances" which he tells us he composed in his lifetime, most, doubtless, were written to amuse and stir up his despairing fellow-sufferers. And perhaps too that simple little drama called *The Comedy of the Sovereign Virgin of Guadalupe, and her miracles*, which is now generally attributed to Cervantes, was written by him for the prison-theatre of Algiers. But his poetical epistle is the finest product of his captive pen. It is full of pathos, a very cry "from out the depths." Never were the melody and power of the *terza rima* used by Cervantes with more skill or to nobler purpose.

The insinuating, yet delicate and ingenuous flattery with which he seeks to gain the ear of the royal favourite; the matchless vigour of expression with which he goes on to recount the horrors and triumphs of Lepanto, the capture of the galley *Sol*, and the intolerable barbarities endured by himself and fellow-captives; to crown all, the clear ringing tone, like a trumpet-call, with which he summons King Philip to come to the rescue of 20,000 Spanish Christians, and attach Algiers to the Spanish crown; all these combined give a thrilling interest to this unique letter.

The appeal was fruitless, but the honour of the effort remains with Cervantes. Mateo Vazquez might bury the letter in his portfolio, and belie the encomiums of his former admirer, but Cervantes' noble description of the "Perfect Statesman" is still worthy of perusal for itself alone. Philip, too, might remain deaf to the appeal, and waste his strength in petty wars, and his substance in raising up that monument of ostentation the Escurial; but there were some even of his contemporaries bold enough to say, that had the one-handed captive been duly seconded, Christendom might have been avenged, and Spain enriched with a new province. For Cervantes was not a man of mere words. He had the courage to dare great things as well as the spirit to plan them. In after life he was accustomed to speak with special pride of the part he played, and the wounds he received in the great combat of Lepanto; but his countrymen may be prouder still of the bearing he showed during the five years of his sore captivity. The indomitable daring of the man, the steadfast purity of his life, the self-sacrificing generosity he lavished on his comrades, and withal, the inborn gaiety that enabled him to bear all and dare all with a gallant heart; these combined acted like a magic spell over friends and oppressors, and clearly marked him out as one born to be a leader of men.

But neither in the State nor in literature was such a leadership ever vouchsafed him during his lifetime. And as he himself naïvely tells us, the sole outcome of those five years of cruel suffering, and fruitless daring was, that he was thereby enabled during his whole career to reduce to perfect practice the hardest of all lessons, viz.: to bear poverty and neglect with patience. He might also have added that the manly independence of thought and action, which pervaded his writings as it did his life, was due in no small measure to the stern schooling of his slavery in Algiers.

This idea is gracefully wrought out in one of the laudatory sonnets prefixed to Cervantes' *Galatea*, published in 1584, four years after his return from captivity. The writer was a friend and fellow-townsman of his own, author of the *Pastor de Filida*, which received honourable mention in the celebrated scrutiny of Don Quixote's library. Although a "laudatory sonnet," it has a greater ring of truth-

Prefatory Note.

fulness and sincerity than belonged to most of the
tribe. It is thus entitled :

LUIS GALVEZ DE MONTALVO

TO CERVANTES.

What time the Moormen held thy body chained,
   And pressed thy captive neck beneath their feet,
   Whereas thy soul, with rigour more complete
Bound fast to Faith, a higher freedom gained,
All heaven rejoiced ; but this our land remained
   Without thee widowed, and the royal seat
   Bewailed the absence of our Muses sweet,
While in its halls a cheerless silence reigned ;
But now thou bringest to our country dear
   An unchained body, and a healthy mind,
Freed from the trammels of a savage host,
Heaven draws the veil that hid thy merit clear ;
   The land receives thee with a welcome kind,
And Spain regains the Muses she had lost.

                                   J. Y. G.

DE MIGUEL DE CERUANTE, CAPTIUO:
Á M. VAZQUEZ, MI SR.

Si el baxo son de la çampoña mia,
   Señor, a vro. oydo no hay llegado
   En tiempo que sonar mejor deuia,
No ha sido por la falta de cuydado,
   Sino por sobra del que me ha traydo
   Por estraños caminos desuiado.
Tambien por no adquirirme de attreuido
   El nombre odioso, la cansada mano
   A encubierto las faltas del sentido.
Mas ya que el valor vio sobre humano
   De quien tiene noticia todo el suelo,
   La graciosa altivez, el trato llano
Anichilan el miedo y el recelo,
   Que ha tenido hasta aquí mi humilde pluma,
   De no quereros descubrir su buelo.
De vra. alta bondad y virtud summa
   Diré lo ménos, que lo más, no siento
   Quien de cerrarlo en verso se presuma.

FROM MIGUEL DE CERVANTES, CAPTIVE :
TO MY LORD, M. VAZQUEZ.

If the low piping of my homely reed
    Hath failed, Señor, to strike upon your ear,
    What time its notes were sweeter far indeed,
It was not that my wish was dull and sere,
    But that the stress of cares hath urged my flight
    Through strange and devious paths this many a year;
And haply too, lest I should merit quite
    The intruder's hateful name, my faltering hand
    Declined to cypher what I fain would write.
But now that I, with all the wondering land,
    Your more than human merit recognize,
    That gracious dignity, these manners bland
Bid me throw off the tremor and disguise,
    Which suffered not my pen, in other time,
    To wing its humble flight before your eyes.
Your sovereign goodness, and your virtue prime
    I can but glance at, for 'twere vain, I know,
    To seek to fetter them in bonds of rhyme.

Aquel que os mira en el subido assiento
 Do el humano fauor puede encumbrarse
 Y que no cessa el fauorable viento,
Y él se vé entre las ondas anegarse
 Del mar de la priuança, do procura
 O por *fas* ó por *nefas* leuantarse,
¿ Quién dubda que no dize : " La ventura
 Ha dado en leuantar este mancebo
 Hasta ponerle en la mas alta altura ?
Ayer le vimos inexperto y nueuo
 En las cosas que agora mide y trata
 Tan bien, que tengo embidia y las apprueuo."
Desta manera se congoxa y mata
 El embidioso, que la gloria agena
 Le destruye, marchita y desbarata.
Pero aquel que con mente mas serena
 Contempla vro. trato y vida honrrosa,
 Y el alma dentro de virtudes llena,
No la inconstante rueda presurosa
 De la falsa fortuna, suerte, o hado,
 Signo, ventura, estrella, ni otra cosa,
Dize q. es causa que en el buen estado
 Que agora posseeis os aya puesto
 Con esperança de mas alto grado,
Mas solo el modo del viuir honesto,
 La virtud escogida que se muestra
 En vras. obras y apazible gesto.

The man who sees you as you upward go
  To climb the highest summit man can gain,
  Where the propitious breezes ever blow,
And sees himself gulphed in the surging main
  Of courtly favour, whence to rise at last,
  Per fas aut nefas, he doth strive in vain,--
Sooth, such an one will say: "'Tis Fortune's cast
  That gave this modest youth the means to raise
  Himself to such high honour unsurpassed;
But yesterday so new to courtly ways,
  And now he treats of high affairs right well;
  I envy him, though I be forced to praise!"
Thus doth the envious man to bursting swell
  With jealous thoughts, and cheapens with dispraise
  Another's glories which his own excel;
But he who with a calmer mind surveys
  The tenour of your life, the soul within,
  With honour fraught that stoops to nothing base,
Will frankly own: Not any fickle spin
  Of Fortune's wheel, not hazard, luck, nor fate,
  Nor sign, nor happy star, nor aught akin,
Hath placed you firmly in the good estate
  You have attained and occupy to-day,
  With goodly hope of station still more great;
But 'twas your honest life, straightforward way,
  That virtue rare, which, in your every deed
  And gentle bearing, seeks the light of day:

Esta dize, Señor, que os da su diestra
   Y os tiene assido con sus fuertes laços
   Y a mas y a mas subir siempre os adiestra.
! O sanctos, o, agradables dulces braços
   De la sancta virtud, alma y diuina,
   Y sancto quien recibe sus abraços !
Quien con tal guia como vos camina,
   ¿ De qué se admira el ciego vulgo baxo
   Si a la silla mas alta se auezina ?
Y puesto que no ay cosa sin trabajo,
   Quien va sin la virtud va por rodeo,
   Que el que la lleua va por el attajo.
Si no me eñgana la experiençia, creo
   Que se vee mucha gente fatigada
   De vn solo pensamiento y un desseo.
Pretenden mas de dos llaue dorada,
   Muchos un mesmo cargo, y quien aspira
   Á la fideladad de vna embaxada.
Cada qual por si mesmo al blanco tira
   Do assestan otros mil, y solo es vno
   Cuya saeta dio do fue la mira.
Y este quiça q. a nadie fué importuno
   Ni a la soberbia puerta del priuado
   Se hallo, despues de visperas, ayuno,
Ni dió ni tuuo a quien pedir prestado,
   Solo con la virtud se entretenia,
   Y en Dios y en ella estaua confiado.

This, would he say, gives all the strength you need,
　Surrounds you with restraints both good and wise,
　And by the hand to higher things doth lead.
Blessed are the arms, and passing sweet the ties
　Of holy virtue, heavenly and refined,
　And blessed is he who on her bosom lies!
Why stands amazed the common herd and blind,
　That one who walks, like you, with such a guide,
　Should near the throne his fitting office find?
Though toil and moil all good success decide,
　Who journeys without virtue goes astray,
　He goes direct who travels by her side.
If my experience err not, in our day
　Full many with but one desire we see,
　In whose pursuit they wear their lives away.
Some two or three aim at the golden key,
　At like posts others, while one gives his soul
　To gain some confidential embassy.
Each for himself, a unit in the whole,
　Covets what thousands wish, though one alone
　Can hit the mark, or reach the wished-for goal;
And he, it may be, ne'er used whining tone,
　Nor lingered at some favourite's portal cold,
　His fast unbroken till the day be gone;
He haply never gave nor borrowed gold,
　Nor from the line of honour true did glide,
　Of God and virtue keeping steadfast hold.

Vos sois, Sr. por quien dezir podria
    (Y lo digo y dire sin estar mudo)
    Que sola la virtud fue vra. guia,
Y que ella sola fue bastante, y pudo
    Leuantaros al bien do estais agora,
    Priuado humilde, de ambicion desnudo.
¡ Dichosa y felizíssima la hora
    Donde tuuo el real conoscimiento
    Notiçia del valor que anida y mora
En vro. reposado entendimiento,
    Cuya fidelidad, cuyo secreto
    Es de vras. virtudes el cimiento!
Por la senda y camino mas perfecto
    Van vros. piés, que es la que el medio tiene,
    Y la que alaba el seso mas discreto.
Quien por ella camina, vemos viene
    Á aquel dulce suaue paradero
    Que la felizidad en si contiene.
Yo que el camino mas baxo y grosero
    He caminado en fria noche escura,
    He dado en manos del atolladero;
Y en la esquiua prision, amarga y dura,
    Adonde agora quedo, estoy llorando
    Mi corta infelizissima ventura,
Con quexas tierra y cielo importunando,
    Con sospiros al ayre escuresciendo,
    Con lágrimas el mar accrescentando.

Letter of Cervantes. 315

Of you, Señor, it may be published wide,
  (And I'll repeat it now nor silent be,)
  That virtue solely was your constant guide ;
And this sufficed to compass the degree
  Of goodly honour where this day you rest,
  A modest favourite, from ambition free !
Thrice happy was the lucky hour and blest,
  Which carried tidings to the royal ear
  Of that high merit, which doth build its nest
Within your intellect profound and clear ;
  Whose strict fidelity, reserve complete,
  Bind all your talents in one rounded sphere !
From day to day you tread, with steady feet,
  That perfect way, which keeps the happy mean,
  Held most in honour by the most discreet ;
Who travels on this way at last is seen
  To reach that sweet and pleasant resting-place,
  Within whose portals reigns a joy serene !
I, who have trod the vulgar road and base,
  Beneath a bitter night, where star was not,
  Have stumbled in the mire, in woeful case ;
And in this gloomy prison, dismal spot,
  Where now I find me, nought remains to me
  But to bemoan my most unhappy lot.
I weary heaven and earth with many a plea,
  The air is darkened with my bitter breath,
  And with my tears I help to swell the sea.

Vida es esta, Sr. do estoy muriendo,
　　Entre bárbara gente descreida
　　La mal lograda juuentud perdiendo.
No fué la causa aquí de mi venida
　　Andar vagando por el mundo a caso
　　Con la verguença y la razon perdida.
Diez años ha que tiendo y mudo el passo
　　En seruiçio del gran Philippo nro.,
　　Y con descanso, y cansado y laso;
Y en el dichoso dia que siniestro
　　Tanto fué el hado á la enemiga armada,
　　Quanto á la nra. fauorable y diestro,
De temor y de esfuerço acompañada,
　　Presente estuuo mi persona al hecho,
　　Mas de sperança que de hierro armada.
Vi el formado esquadron roto y deshecho,
　　Y de barbara gente y de christiana
　　Roxo en mil partes de Neptuno el lecho,
La muerte ayrada con su furia insana
　　Aquí y allí con priessa discurriendo,
　　Mostrandose á quien tarda á quien temprana,
El son confuso, el espantable estruendo,
　　Los gestos de los tristes miserables
　　Que entre el fuego y el agua iuan muriendo,
Los profundos sospiros lamentables,
　　Que los heridos pechos despedian,
　　Maldiciendo sus hados detestables.

This life, Señor, is but a living death,
  Where, 'mid a barbarous misbelieving race,
  My ill-starred youth drags out and withereth.
No random wandering brought me to this place,
  No vagabond desires with me were rife,
  Right reason gone, nor shame upon my face!
These ten years gone I led a soldier's life
  In our great Philip's service; now in state
  Of sweet repose, now worn with toil and strife;
And on that happy day, when dubious Fate
  Looked on the foeman's fleet with baleful eye,
  On ours with smiling glance and fortunate,
Inspired with mingled dread and courage high,
  In thickest of the direful fight I stood,
  My hope still stronger than my panoply.
I marked the shattered host melt like a flood,
  And thousand spots upon old Neptune's breast
  Dyed red with heathen and with Christian blood;
Death, like a fury, running with foul zest
  Hither and thither, sending crowds in ire
  To lingering torture, or to speedy rest;
The cries confused, the horrid din and dire,
  The mortal writhings of the desperate,
  Who breathed their last 'mid water and 'mid fire;
The deep-drawn sighs, the groanings loud and great
  That sped from wounded breasts, in many a throe,
  Cursing their bitter and detested fate.

Eloseles la sangre que tenian
    Quando en el son de la trompeta nra.
    Su daño y nra. gloria conoscian.
Con alta voz de vencedora muestra,
    Rompiendo el aire claro, el son mostraua
    Ser vencedora la christiana diestra.
A esta dulce sazon yo, triste, estaua
    Con la una mano de la espada assida,
    Y sangre de la otra derramaua.
El pecho mio de profunda herida
    Sentia llagado, y la siniestra mano
    Estaua por mill partes ya rompida.
Pero el contento fué tan soberano,
    Q. á mi alma llegó viendo vençido
    El crudo pueblo infiel por el christiano,
Que no echaua de ver si estaua herido,
    Aunque era tan mortal mi sentimiento,
    Que á veces me quitó todo el sentido.
Y en mi propia cabeça el escarmiento
    No me pudo estoruar que el segundo año
    No me pusiesse á discrecion del viento,
Y al bárbaro, medroso, pueblo estraño,
    Vi recogido, triste, amedrentado,
    Y con causa temiendo de su daño.
Y al reino tan antiguo y celebrado,
    Á do la hermosa Dido fué vendida
    Al querer del troyano desterrado,

The blood that still was left them ceased to flow,
  What time our trumpets, pealing far and near,
  Proclaimed our glory and their overthrow;
The sounds triumphant, ringing loud and clear,
  Bore through the smitten air, in jubilant flood,
  The Christians' victory from ear to ear!
At this sweet moment I, unlucky, stood
  With one hand buckled firmly to my blade,
  The other dripping downward streams of blood;
Within my breast a cruel thrust had made
  A deep and gaping wound, and my left hand
  Was bruised and shattered, past all human aid;
Yet such was the delicious joy and grand
  That thrilled my soul, to see the faithless foe
  Crushed by the valour of the Christian band,
I hardly knew if I were hurt or no,
  Although my anguish, cutting and unkind,
  At times with mortal swooning laid me low.
Yet all I suffered could not move my mind,
  Which led me on, within the second year,
  To yield to the discretion of the wind;
And to that people, barbarous and austere,
  A cowering, crouching, timid race I came,
  Who well might dread to find their downfall near.
And in that ancient kingdom, known to fame,
  Where beauteous Dido to the love did yield
  Of Troy's great exile, and was put to shame,

Tambien, vertiendo sangre aun la herida,
   Mayor con otras dos, quise ir y hallarme,
   Por ver ir la morisma de vencida.
Dios sabe si quisiera allí quedarme
   Con los que allí quedaron esforçados,
   Y perderme con ellos o ganarme;
Pero mis cortos implacables hados
   En tan honrrosa empresa no quisieron
   Q. acabase la vida y los cuydados;
Y al fin, por los cabellos me truxeron
   Á ser vencido por la valentia
   De aquellos que despues no la tuuieron.
En la galera *Sol*, que escurescia
   Mi ventura su luz, á pesar mio
   Fue la pérdida de otros y la mia;
Valor mostramos al principio y brio,
   Pero despues, con la experiençia amarga,
   Conoscimos ser todo desuario.
Senti de ageno yugo la gran carga,
   Y en las manos sacrílegas malditas
   Dos años ha que mi dolor se alarga.
Bien se que mis maldades infinitas
   Y la poca attricion que en mi se encierra
   Me tiene entre estos falsos Ismaelitas.
Quando llegué vencido y vi la tierra
   Tan nombrada en el mundo, q. en su seno
   Tantos piratas cubre, acoge, y cierra,

Although my ancient wound was still unhealed,
  With two besides, I joyed upon the spot
  To see the Moormen vanquished on the field.
God knows if I had earnest wish or not
  To share my brave and gallant comrades' fate,
  And live or die with them, whate'er their lot!
But destiny, in her relentless hate,
  Willed not that I, in this renowned affair,
  Should end my being and my sufferings great;
And finally she dragged me by the hair
  To yield me to a power I could not quell,
  Whose after prowess was but scant and spare;
For in the galley *Sol*, whose lustre fell
  By my ill-fortune, I was doomed to see
  My comrades' ruin, and mine own as well.
At first our valour shone in high degree,
  Until by sad experience we awoke
  To see how mad was all our bravery!
These two long years I've borne a foreign yoke,
  And my o'erburdened neck hath felt the gall
  Of an accursèd sacrilegious folk.
My countless sins and my contrition small,
  I know full well, have bound me, scant of grace,
  To grind beneath this Ismaëlitish thrall.
When I arrived in chains, and saw the place,
  So noted in the world, whose teeming breast
  Hath nursed the fierce swarms of a pirate race,

No pude al llanto detener el freno,
  Que á mi despecho, sin saber lo que era,
  Me vi el marchito rostro de agua lleno.
Ofresciése á mis ojos la ribera
  Y el monte donde el grande Cárlos tuuo
  Leuantada en el ayre su vandera,
Y el mar que tanto esfuerço no sostuuo,
  Pues mouido de embidia de su gloria,
  Ayrado entonces mas q. nunca estuuo.
Estas cosas boluiendo en mi memoria,
  Las lágrimas truxeron á los ojos,
  Mouidas de desgraçia tan notoria.
Pero si el alto Cielo en darme enojos
  No esta con mi ventura conjurado,
  Y aqui no lleua muerte mis despojos,
Quando me vea en mas alegre estado,
  Si vra. intercession, Sr. me ayuda
  A verme ante Philippo arrodillado,
Mi lengua balbuziente y quasi muda
  Pienso mouer en la Real presencia,
  De adulacion y de mentir desnuda.
Diciendo: "Alto Sr., cuya potencia
  Sujetas trae mil barbaras Naciones
  Al desabrido yugo de obediencia,
A quien los Negros Indios con sus dones
  Reconoscen honesto vassallage,
  Trayendo el oro acá de sus rincones:

My bitter lamentation found no rest;
    And, ere I knew, the tears coursed at their ease
    Adown my haggard cheeks, and unrepressed.
My straining eyes were fixed upon the seas,
    The strand, and hill whereon our Charles the Great
    Unfurled his royal banner to the breeze;
I saw the main which, chafing 'neath the weight
    Of so much glory, rose in fierce array,
    And foamed with envious, unexampled hate;
And as I mused, and memory cast its ray
    Upon the scene, my tears seemed charged with fire
    And shame, at thought of that disastrous day.
But if high Heaven should not with Fate conspire
    To heap still greater sorrows on my head,
    And Death should not despoil me in his ire;
And should, in happier days, my steps be led
    To royal Philip's throne, and by your aid
    I find me kneeling in that presence dread;
Then do I hope to speak, nor feel afraid,
    Though haply with a stammering, faltering tongue,
    Yet not with lies or flattery arrayed,
And thus entreat: "Most mighty Sire, whose strong
    And powerful arm doth hold in subject sway
    Of nations barbarous a countless throng;
To whom the swarthy Indians homage pay,
    And drag the gold from out its rocky nest,
    Their wealth of tribute at thy feet to lay;

Despierte en tu Real pecho el gran coraje
 La gran soberbia con que una vicoca
 Aspira de contino á hazerte vltraje.
La gente es mucha, mas su fuerça es poca,
 Desnuda, mal armada, que no tiene
 En su defensa fuerte muro o roca.
Cada vno mira si tu armada viene,
 Para dar á sus pies cargo y cura
 De conseruar la vida que sostiene.
Del' amarga prision triste y escura,
 Adonde mueren veinte mill christianos,
 Tienes la llave de su cerradura.
Todos (qual yo) de alla, puestas las manos,
 Las rodillas por tierra, solloçando
 Cercados de tormentos inhumanos,
Valeroso Señor, te están rogando
 Bueluas los ojos de misericordia
 Á los suyos que están siempre llorando.
Y pues te dexa agora la discordia,
 Que hasta aquí te ha opprimido y fatigado,
 Y gozas de pacífica concordia;
Haz, o buen Rey, q. sea por ti acabado
 Lo que con tanta audaçia y valor tanto
 Fue por tu amado padre començado.
Solo en pensar que vas pondrá vn espanto
 En la enemiga gente, que adeuino
 Ya desde aquí su pérdida y quebranto."

Letter of Cervantes. 325

Let the proud daring of that pirate pest,
   Who braves thy potence to this very hour,
   Rouse noble wrath within thy royal breast!
The folk be many, though but scant their power,
   Naked, ill-armed, for them no refuge lies
   Behind the rampart, or the battled tower;
They all across the main, with straining eyes,
   Are watching till thy coming fleet be nigh,
   With ready feet to save the lives they prize.
Thou hast the keys, within thy hand they lie,
   To unlock the prison, dismal and profound,
   Where twenty thousand Christians pine and die.
They all, as I, are groaning on the ground,
   Pressing with hands and knees the cursed place,
   With most inhuman tortures girdled round!
Most potent Sire, they beg thee of thy grace
   To turn, and that right soon, thy pitying eyes
   On theirs, whence tears do run in endless chase.
Since now from out thy land pale Discord flies,
   Which hitherto hath wearied out thy heart,
   And peace unbroken all around thee lies,
Be thine the task, good King, with fitting art
   To end the work, in which with courage high
   Thine honoured father took the foremost part.
The rumours of thy coming, as they fly,
   Will strike the foe with awe, for well they know
   The hour of their perdition draweth nigh!"

¿ Quién dubda q. el Real pecho benino
  No se muestre, escuchando la tristeza
  En que estan estos miseros contino?
Bien paresce q. muestro la flaqza.
  De mi tan torpe ingenio, q. pretende
  Hablar tan baxo ante tan alta Alteza;
Pero el justo desseo la defiende. . . .
  Mas á todo silencio poner quiero
  Que temo q. mi pluma ya os offende,
  Y al trabajo me llaman donde muero.

FIN.

Who doubts that through the royal breast will flow
  Sweet thoughts of pity, while he hears the sigh
  Of these poor wretches buried in their woe?
Although, methinks, I but display my dry
  And sluggish wit, presuming thus to use
  Such lowly words before a prince so high,
My just desire may well my fault excuse!
  Here will I pause, and henceforth silent be,
  Nor with my pen your kindliness abuse,
  For now they call me to the gang, ah me!

FINIS.

NOTES AND ILLUSTRATIVE PIECES.

NOTES AND ILLUSTRATIVE PIECES.

NOTE 1. PAGE 9.

A certain Corporal. Cervantes here makes a punning play on the name of Cesare Caporali, whose poem, *Viaggio di Parnaso*, suggested his own. In English the pun seems rather far-fetched, and perhaps the name itself had better have been introduced. Caporali's poem first appeared in a collection of poems by various authors, thus entitled : *Raccolta di alcune rime piacevoli*, Parma, 1582. A complete annotated edition of his works was published at Perugia, in 1651, under the title of *Rime di Cesare Caporali*. The annotator, Carlo Caporali, quotes the first three lines of Cervantes' poem as highly complimentary to his kinsman, in this curious note: "Il Cervantes, Poeta non oscuro tra Spagnuoli, ne da tal guidicio:

"Un quidam Caporale, Italiano," &c.

NOTE 2. PAGE 9.

Where an old mule he bought him for the tour. As a specimen of Caporali's versification we may as well give his own description of his mule, which varies materially from that of Cervantes :—

> Comprai anco una mula, e accio gli interni
> Pensier communicar potessi seco
> L'accapai da consigli, e da governi ;
> La qual, per quel di ella poi disse meco,
> Scese in Italia gia con Carl' Ottavo,
> Con le bagaglie d'un Trombetta Greco ;
> Havea una sella, e finimento bravo,
> Era di coda lunga, e vista corta,
> Nata di madre Sarda, e padre Schiavo.

Which may be roughly rendered thus :—

> For needful ends I also bought a mule,
> And, that her inmost thoughts might outward leak,
> I hedged her in with sage advice and rule ;
> With Charles the Eighth she came down, so to speak,
> Times gone to Italy, and in the hire'
> And service of a Trumpeter, a Greek.
> She had a saddle, trappings to admire,
> Her tail was long, and eke her vision short,
> Born of Sardinian dam and Sclavic sire.

Note 3. Page 16.

Con ocho mis de queso. *Mis* is a colloquial contraction for *maravedis*. The maravedi as a coin is now obsolete in Spain. It had varying values according to the metal in which it was coined ; the copper maravedi was worth the thirty-fourth part of a real. We may therefore render this line in English : *With eight mites' worth of cheese.*

Note 4. Page 17.

Farewell Madrid. This adieu to Madrid is highly characteristic of Cervantes. With a few humorous and piquant touches he presents a complete picture of the surroundings of the city, its humours, its literary life, the state of its theatres, the politics of the hour, the pinched life of its poets, and of himself in particular—and all in his peculiar light-hearted vein. Gongora, who was also a martyr to the general neglect of literary men, gives us a curious picture of the life of the Court in his celebrated burlesque sonnet on Madrid. As it may be interesting to compare the spirit and temper with which two distinguished contemporaries treat the same theme, we present it to our readers. Gongora fairly bears off the palm for concentrated bitterness :—

MADRID.

A BURLESQUE SONNET.

A bestial life, in witchery enshrined ;
   Harpies that prey on purses, and all grades
   Of wrecked ambitions lurking in the shades,
Might make a grave judge talk, and raise the wind ;
Broad-ways with coaches, lacqueys, pages lined ;
   Thousands of uniforms with virgin blades ;
   Ladies loquacious, legates, broking trades ;
Faces like masks, and rogueries refined ;
Lawyers long-robed, most bare-faced lies that are ;
   Clerics on she mules, mulish tricks and ways ;
   Streets paved with mud, and filth of endless smell ;
Bemaimed and battered heroes of the war ;
   Titles and flatteries and canting phrase :
   This is Madrid, or better said, 'tis Hell !

This version of the Sonnet is given by Mr. Duffield ("Don Quixote : His Critics," &c., p. 93) without the translator's permission.

Note 5. Page 19.

Farewell, St. Philip's broad-way of the town. The battlements of the retaining wall of the Convent of San Felipe (now demolished) formed the promenade of the fashionable idlers and scandal-mongers in the time of Cervantes. It was approached on either side by a spacious flight of steps, hence its name *Las Gradas de San Felipe.* Its common and more appropriate title was *El Mentidero,* Lie-Walk or Scandal-Alley.

Note 6. Page 23.

Like Dante's. This is a slight, and we hope pardonable, addition to the original, under stress of rhyme. It only means, what Cervantes doubtless meant, that Mercury addressed him in the finest *terza rima.* It is also quite in keeping with other humorous phrases in the book; as, for instance, when Apollo at the head of his soldiers is represented as addressing them—*in proper Spanish and good Toledese.*

Note 7. Page 27.

A swarm of verses formed the whole array. Though Cervantes did not borrow from Caporali the conception of his rhythmic ship, inasmuch as that daring voyager took passage both for himself and mule in a prosaic merchant-vessel, from the port of Ostia to Messina and the Gulf of Corinth, yet Caporali has certainly the merit of having first employed the same curious materials, in the construction of the four gates of his allegorical Temple of Poesy, described in the second part of his *Viaggio di Parnaso*.

It would be out of place to attempt any description of the poetic forms and measures here mentioned by Cervantes. The literature of Spain is peculiarly rich in these. Some, like the Sonnet, the *Terza* and *Ottava Rima*, are borrowed from the Italians; others, like the Redondilla, the Letrilla, the Decima, are exclusively Spanish. Lope de Vega, in his *Arte nuevo de hacer Comedias*, has summed up the peculiarities of some of these in their adaptation to the drama :—

> The Decimas are good for plaintive wails,
>   The Sonnet answers well for those who wait;
> Romances are designed for stirring tales,
>   Although in Octaves they have lustre great;
> For matters grave the Tercets fitting prove,
> And Redondillas for the affairs of love.

NOTE 8. PAGE 27.

Glosses . . . to grace Malmaridada's wedding-day. The art of glossing favourite songs and ballads was held in high estimation amongst the Spaniards when the art of producing original ones had died out. Depping likens it to the absurdity of serving up piquant and savoury dishes in watery gravy. It served, however, one very useful purpose, though undesigned. It helped to preserve snatches of old ballads that would otherwise have been lost, and oftentimes these glosses give valuable various readings of those that still exist. Of this truth the Romance of "La bella Malmaridada" is a striking instance. It was so celebrated that it gave motive to innumerable glosses and imitations. Duran affirms, that he has been enabled to reconstruct the true old romance mainly through a gloss, which a certain Quesada made of it, and published in a *Pliego suelto*. It was first printed by Sepulveda in his *Romances, nuevamente sacados de historias antiguas*, Anvers, 1551. We spare our readers any of the glosses, and give instead an attempted version of the original ballad. Its antique simplicity, however, is hardly reproduced:—

LA BELLA MALMARIDADA.

"O lady, fairest I have seen, so fair and yet ill-married,
Thy cheeks are pale with grief, I ween, say, has thy bliss miscarried?

"If thou wouldst burn with other flames, on me bestow compassion,
To flaunt and flirt with other dames, thy husband sets the fashion;

"They kiss and court from night to morn, with slander he doth treat thee,
And he hath sworn and better sworn, when he comes home to beat thee!"

Outspake the lady with delight, and thus addressed her lover:
"O carry me hence, thou good Sir Knight, where none shall us discover!

"Thy home where'er it be is mine, and I will serve thee ever,
I'll make for thee the bed so fine, where we shall sleep together;

"Thy supper I shall well prepare, with hands so neat and dainty,
With chickens good and capons rare, and thousand things in plenty;

"I'll be no more my husband's wife, no more shall stay beside him,
He leads me such a dismal life, I cannot, sooth, abide him!"

They prattled thus in merry mood, and passed the time with glee,
When lo! her husband near them stood, a furious man was he:

" What art thou doing, traitress, say? To-day thou hast to die!"
" For what, my lord, for what, I pray? I merit it, no, not I!

" Myself have never kissed a man, although a man hath kissed me,
I'll bear his punishment as I can; my lord, I prithee list me!

" With horse's bridle thou dost hold, my lord, I prithee stroke me,
And with these cords of silk and gold, my lord, I prithee choke me;

" And to the orange-garden cold, alive, I prithee, hurry me,
Within a sepulchre of gold and ivory there bury me;

" And place this motto on my tomb, that passers-by may read it,
And reading it may know my doom, and knowing it may heed it:

" ' The flower of flowers here doth lie, for very love she died;
Whoever else for love shall die, be buried by her side!' "

NOTE 9. PAGE 27.

Of Sonnets bastard and legitimate. This is hardly a literal rendering of the original, but seems to be the meaning of the passage. Cervantes himself set the fashion of the illegitimate form of Sonnet, in his famous one on the Catafalque of Philip II., which consists of sixteen lines and a half. Quevedo also wrote sonnets of eleven lines. Though Spain has produced no Petrarch, the Sonnet occupies a very important place in its poetry. Garcilaso de la Vega, and the brothers Argensola, are specially distinguished for classical elegance and strict adherence to the Italian method. Lope de Vega, who aspired to the mastery in this, as in all departments of poetry, without conspicuous success, gives the following amusing

SONNET ON THE SONNET.

To write a sonnet doth Juana press me,
   I've never found me in such stress or pain;
   A sonnet numbers fourteen lines, 'tis plain,
And three are gone, ere I can say, God bless me!
I thought that spinning rhymes might sore oppress me,
   Yet here I'm midway in the last quatrain;
   And if the foremost tercet I can gain,
The quatrains need not any more distress me.
To the first tercet I have got at last,
   And travel through it with such right good will,
   That with this line I've finished it, I ween;
I'm in the second now, and see how fast
   The thirteenth line runs tripping from my quill;
   Hurrah, 'tis done! Count if there be fourteen!

NOTE 10. PAGE 33.

Coritos too, and dwellers in Biscay. Coritos was the name given in old times to Montañeses and Biscayans. According to the Academy's dictionary, it is probably derived from the Latin *corium*, equivalent to the Spanish *cuero* or skin—the material used for the protection of their bodies. At present the name is given by way of ridicule to the Asturians.

The Yanguesians, Biscayans, and Coritos, the hardy highlanders of Spain, were more famous as porters and carriers than as poets, and as such Cervantes has immortalized them in the *Don Quixote*. And yet it is curious that in the very heart of the Asturias the people now-a-days use a dialect, known by the name of *Bable*, which represents the very language spoken in Spain during the

Notes and Illustrative Pieces. 339

middle ages ; and many phrases and turns of expression found in the " Poema del Cid " are familiar in the mouths of the Asturian peasantry. It is a very sonorous and smooth-going language, though not particularly rich in expression. It has a small literature of its own, composed chiefly of songs and romances, sung by the people to accompany the very ancient circular dance, peculiar to the natives of those regions, known by the name of *danza prima*. As a specimen of the old Asturian romances we give the following, taken from the collection of Don Pedro José Pidal. (See Duran, *Romancero General*, Tom. 1. Madrid, 1849.)

ROMANCE OF THE SAILOR.

Upon a morning of Saint John,
  A sailor fell into the sea ;
" What wilt thou give me, sailor mine,
  From out the waves to ransom thee?"

" I'll give thee all my sailing ships,
  Laden with gold and silver free ! "
" Not any ships of thine I want,
  Nor silver fine, nor gold from thee !

"One thing I wish, when thou shalt die,
  That thou wilt give thy soul to me !"
His soul, he gave it up to God,
  His body to the salt, salt sea !

NOTE II. PAGE 35.

I scanned the list, and first upon the leet. Leet is an old Scottish legal term, commonly used in Scotland at the present day to denote a list or roll of candidates for election. We hope we may be pardoned for introducing it here, as it is both appropriate and poetical. This is the second list of distinguished living poets which Cervantes framed in his day. Just thirty years before, in 1584, he published in his *Galatea* the "Canto de Caliope," wherein he introduces the names of some eighty poets, whom he covers with indiscriminate praise. This was in the early days of his literary career, before hard experience had damped his enthusiasm. This ungrateful task, as may well be supposed, brought him little comfort of mind, giving satisfaction to few and deadly offence to many. The present list contains only eight or nine out of the vast number then commented on; most of the rest had already gone to the majority. Herrera, Gongora, Lope de Vega, the Argensolas, Articda, &c., are again introduced, but Quevedo is the only commanding genius that appears for the first time. Calderon de la Barca was then but a youth of fourteen, pursuing his studies at Salamanca. Out of the 150 names introduced into the poem our limits will only allow us to touch on the more eminent, especially those who came into immediate contact with Cervantes, either as friends or foes. Those who are interested will find full information concerning the rest, in the catalogue given at the end of the collected edition of Cervantes' works in twelve volumes, published in Madrid, 1863-4; and also at the end of M. Guardia's French translation.

NOTE 12. PAGE 39.

Known wide as Miguel Cid. This Sevilian poet, of whom Guardia declares he could learn nothing, was celebrated for his "devotion to the Mother of God in the mystery of her immaculate conception," and in 1610 published the famous *coplas* beginning

> Todo el mundo en general
> A voces, reina escogida,
> Dice que sois concebida
> Sin pecado original.

He was a very pious man, and, though a simple weaver of rugs, he enjoyed great celebrity amongst his townsmen, who often embraced and applauded him in the public streets. He died in 1617, and the common people were sure he had predicted the day of his death. He was buried in the Cathedral of Seville. The Chapter ordered that a picture of the *Purisima Concepcion* should be placed over his tomb, containing amongst other figures a portrait of the poet, with his famous *coplas* in his hand. This was painted by Francisco Pacheco, and Sr. Asensio assures us that it is still to be seen in the Sacristy of our Lady de la Antigua. His collected poems were published thirty years after his death, by his son, under this title: "Sacred Joustings of the illustrious and memorable poet Miguel Cid, published by his son, inheritor of the same name: dedicated to the most Holy Virgin Mary, our Lady, conceived without spot of original sin.—Printed at Seville, by Simon Fajardo, 1647."

NOTE 13. PAGE 39.

Don Luis de Gongora. It is hard to tell how much of Cervantes' eulogium is sincere praise, and how much fine irony. No doubt there is a mixture of both; for

Gongora, though a sort of demigod, was a very Janus. On one side of him we see the man of clear subtle intellect, yet, withal, curiously sensitive soul, whose satires for vigour and incisive touch were unmatched; whose odes and romances have the true patriotic ring and cadence; and whose *letrillas* and *villancicos*, now playful, now pathetic, like the music of silver bells, give us to know the resources of the Spanish tongue both in its sweetness and strength. Such was Gongora in the vigour of early manhood. On the other side of him we see a man, who in his later years wrapped himself in mystery and posed as a very angel of darkness; who invented a new literary tongue; founded a new school, the pestilent sect of the *Cultos;* and gave forth as his Koran those awfully mysterious poems called the *Polifemo* and the *Soledades*, which it required the labours of three laborious commentators during his lifetime to explain to the uninitiated. To refine the Castilian tongue by Latinizing it; to banish commonplace by the use of metaphorical, uncouth, and mysteriously bombastic phrases; and, in fine, to reach the sublime by a species of mechanical inflation; these were the characteristics of what was called in derision *Culteranismo*. What led Gongora to such a perversion of his consummate talents it would be hard to say. No doubt he was soured by a life of poverty and neglect; but, after all, there was a kind of literary contagion afloat in the atmosphere of Europe during his age; and Gongorism in Spain, Marinism in Italy, Euphuism in England, were but different phases of the same disease. This worship of the unintelligible became the fashion, and one of its first converts was the notorious Count of Villamediana. Of course the wits of the old school (such as Jáuregui, Lope de Vega, and Quevedo) assailed it with their choicest invective and ridicule. Here is one of the current epigrams :—

> Our poet *Soledad*, the able,
> Hath writ a most romantic ditty,
> In dreary length a very city,
> In sheer bewilderment a Babel.

Lope winds up one of his most sarcastic sonnets, full of the most outrageous Gongorism, in this style :—

> "Dost apprehend it? Fabius, be candid."
> "Of course I do!" "O Fabius, thou liest,
> For I who wrote it do not understand it."

And in another place he gives this advice to his comrades :—

> Meanwhile to shelter our *Pegasus*
> From the bad odour of the cultish jargon,
> Come, let us burn pastilles of *Garcilasos*.

Gongora, who was quite a match for Lope in the art of satiric fencing, gave vent to his wrath in this fashion :—

> Dicen que hace Lopico
> Contra mi versos adversos,
> Pero, si yo versifico,
> Con el pico de mis versos
> A' este Lopico lo pico.

Cervantes does not seem to have taken any special part in this war of wits; though the exaggeration of the compliment he here pays him, just in those points where Gongora was weakest, betrays the " pinch or two of salt." His general estimate of Gongora's powers as a poet may be learned from the eulogy he passes on him in the *Canto de Caliope*, when he was twenty-three years of age. It is the goddess herself who addresses the shepherds and shepherdesses:—

> In Don Luis de Gongora I present
>   A quick ripe genius, rare as can be found;
> His works do give me wealth and sweet content,
>   Nor me alone, but the wide world around;
> Give me one favour for the love I've lent,
>   Cause that his soaring knowledge and profound
> Be of your warm applause the constant breath,
> Defying light-winged Time, and ruthless Death.

The only return which Gongora gave (so far as we know) for this handsome compliment was an exceedingly shabby one. It is contained in that famous sonnet of his, which he made on the festivities held at Valladolid in honour of the baptism of Philip IV., christened Felipe Domenico Victor, on which occasion was present Admiral Charles Howard, with 600 English gentlemen, who had come to ratify the preliminaries of peace concluded in London with James I. It runs thus:—

> The queen brought forth. The Lutheran came here,
>   Six hundred heretics and heresies
>   To boot. In fifteen days a million flies
> To give them jewels, wine, and all good cheer.
> We gave a grand parade—a farce, I fear—
>   And certain feasts, which were but flummeries,
>   To please the English legate and his spies,
> Who swore on Calvin peace had brought him here.
> Then we baptized the babe Dominican,
>   Born to become our Dominus in Spain.
>   We gave a masque might for enchantment pass;
> Poor we became, Luther a wealthy man,
>   And all these feats they bade be written plain
>   By one Don Quixote, Sancho, and his ass.

Notes and Illustrative Pieces. 345

Except for this paltry fling at Cervantes, we should never have known that, in the very year when the first part of the *Don Quixote* appeared, Cervantes was appointed *pro tem.* Court Chronicler ; and actually brought out (though anonymously) a book thus entitled : " Narrative of events in the City of Valladolid, from the time of the most auspicious birth of the Prince Don Felipe Domenico Victor, till the conclusion of the joyous festivities in honour thereof. Valladolid, 1605." This is now included in his collected works, though being but a barren record of Court Ceremonial it bears few traces of the hand of the great master. Gongora was born, in 1561, at Cordova, in the Calle de Marcial. The Spaniards often style him the Martial of Spain. His works, however, were published immediately after his death under this strange title : " Works in verse of the Spanish Homer, collected by Juan Lopez de Vicuña, Madrid, 1627."

NOTE 14. PAGE 39.

O soul divine, &c. Of Hernando de Herrera, who, as a poet, achieved the appellation of Divine, Cervantes had a most exalted opinion. Born at Seville in the early part of the sixteenth century, he was a young man when Boscan and Garcilaso de la Vega were in their prime ; and during the active part of his career he was the contemporary of Diego de Mendoza, and of Fray Luis de Leon, who was also a native of Seville. He died in 1597, and with his death ended that series of distinguished poets, who, by the introduction of classical and Italian forms, changed the current of Spanish poetry from its old homely channel, and gave it fresh spirit and a higher life. The purity and fervour of Herrera's style had great attraction for Cervantes in his earlier days, and he thus eulogizes him in the *Canto de Caliope:*—

> It little boots that I should now proclaim
>   The praises of Herrera the Divine;
> If to the fifth sphere I exalt his name,
>   But little fruit will yield this pain of mine.
> But if as friend I'm jealous for his fame,
>   His works will tell this tale in every line:
> In knowledge reigns Hernando monarch sole,
> From Nile to Ganges, and from pole to pole.

Cervantes also must have had a personal knowledge of this learned ecclesiastic during his sojourn in Seville, and most likely made his acquaintance in the studio of Pacheco the painter, where all who were distinguished in poetry, art, or science, held common rendezvous. In a MS. codex of the year 1631, which contains various poems, collected apparently by Francisco Pacheco, there is one by Cervantes on the death of Herrera which has this very interesting note appended to it by himself:—

"*Miguel de Cervantes, author of Don Quixote:*

"This sonnet I made on the death of Hernando de Herrera, and to understand the first quatrain I may mention that he used to celebrate in his verses a lady under the name of LUZ. I think it one of the good ones I have made during my life:—

> "The man who climbed, by paths as yet unknown,
>   The sacred mountain to its topmost height;
>   Who on one *Light* did lavish all his light,
> And chaunted tearful strains with dulcet tone;

> Who from Pirene's spring and Helicon
> Drank copious hallowed draughts; and ransomed quite
> From earthly thrall, did change these waters bright
> Into divine, with culture all his own;
> The man, who roused Apollo's envious pique,
> Because, in union with his *Light*, his fame
> From springing till the dying day did fly;
> The well-beloved of Heaven, on earth unique,
> Turn'd into dust by his consuming flame,
> Beneath this frozen stone in peace doth lie."

The name of the lady to whom Herrera was so devoted was the Countess of Gelves. Quintana says:— " He gave to his affection the heroism of platonic love, and under the name of *Luz*, of *Sol*, of *Estrella*, and *Eliodora*, he dedicated to her a passion, fervid, tender, and constant, but accompanied with such respect and decorum, that modesty could take no alarm nor virtue offence."

His friend Pacheco gave to the world his collected writings in 1619, accompanied by a superb portrait of the "divine" poet, designed by himself.

NOTE 15. PAGE 41.

And thou as well, Don Juan de Jáuregui. This celebrated man, renowned both as a painter and a poet, was highly appreciated by Cervantes, and not the less so, perhaps, for having painted his portrait. This fact he himself communicates in the prologue to his *Novelas*. Jáuregui was born at Seville about the year 1570, and his chief title to poetic fame rests on his translation of Tasso's *Aminta*, which his countrymen are never tired of extolling, as the most perfect in all respects of any translation from the Italian, that has ever been made; as equal to the original in most passages, and superior in some. He also appeared before the public as a purist, in his celebrated attack on Gongora: "Poetic discourse against cultish and obscure speech." Even his admirers, however, confess that in his latest work, a translation of Lucan's *Pharsalia*, the old polemic succumbed to the fascinations of Gongorism, and reproduced it too in its weakest form. Cervantes here makes an allusion to this translation, although it was not published till 1684, forty-three years after the death of Jáuregui. As an evidence of the estimation in which the "Aminta" was held in its day, we give the following striking sonnet by Alonso de Acevedo; of whom Cervantes makes such curious mention at the end of his "Journey:"—

On *the Aminta of Don Juan de Jáuregui.*

Upon the famous banks of foaming Po,
   Aminta sprang to life, a noble maid,
   Whose youth in bloom to Love its homage paid,
And felt the smart of his compelling bow.
Her sombre life she passed, in friendship's glow,
   With Tirsis, famous shepherd of the glade,
   And, through her sounding Tuscan lyre conveyed,
Her fond complainings never ceased to flow;
Till from the banks of Betis forth did rove
   A gallant youth of wit and grace supreme,
   And lured by that Sevilian's potent wile,
Aminta left her country and first love;
   And now on Betis, in the Spanish style,
   She sings forgetful of her tongue and stream.

It is somewhat surprising that Cervantes, who eulogizes so many of the poets and artists of Seville, should have omitted to mention D. Francisco Pacheco, whose studio was the central point of attraction to the gifted in that modern Athens, and where Cervantes himself must often have been an honoured guest. For Pacheco was a poet as well as a painter, and in his " Art of Painting," he gives us specimens of his powers, chiefly in the form of epigrams. One of these for its neatness and point (in the original) has almost immortalized him. We give it as a curiosity.

THE PAINTER AND THE COCK.

A scurvy painter drew a cock,
When to his side a live one flew,
'Twas so unlike the cock he drew,
It gave the painter quite a shock.

The brute he slew, with little ruth,
To hide the scantness of his skill;
And so the cock, against its will,
Became a martyr to the truth.

See Stirling Maxwell's " Artists of Spain," where another version is given.

Note 16. Page 45.

Is Pedro de Morales. The man to whom Cervantes consecrates this short eulogium, one of the most delicate and touching in the poem, was a famous comedian and also a writer of comedies. He seems to have befriended Cervantes in the deepest hour of his need, and Cervantes was not the man to forget either a friend or a kindness.

He represents him further on as being one of the few who welcomed him on his return from Parnassus:—

> My heart and hand I gave and warm embrace
> To Pedro de Morales . . . .

Lope de Vega praises him in his *Peregrino en su Patria*, Sevilla, 1604, as a "ready, elegant, and sympathetic actor;" and Morales was still alive in 1636 to throw a little flower on Lope's grave, in the shape of a touching sonnet contributed to Montalvan's " Fama Posthuma de Lope de Vega."

NOTE 17. PAGE 45.

Is Espinel the grand. Espinel was the Nestor of Spanish poets in the time of Cervantes. Born at Ronda about the year 1544, he reached the age of ninety, as Lope informs us in his " Laurel de Apolo : "—

> Noventa años viviste,
> Nadie te dió favor, poco escribiste.

Cervantes and he were staunch friends in their youth, and in their old age were fellow-pensioners of the Archbishop of Toledo. Espinel did two famous things in his day. He invented, or rather perfected that form of Spanish versification usually called *Decimas*, or, after himself, *Espinelas*. He also added a *fifth* string to the guitar, by which he earned the thanks of a music-loving people. It is to this that Cervantes punningly alludes in the text when he says, "en la guitarra tiene *la prima*," the *prima* being the first or principal string. Espinel was also noted for a kind of peevish and sarcastic humour. In

Notes and Illustrative Pieces. 351

his book of chivalrous adventure, *El escudero, Marcos de Obregon*, published in 1618, he goes out of his way in his preface to exalt his own work at the expense of *Don Quixote;* thus playing "the part of Zoilus" to his old friend, when he was dead and gone.

Note 18. Page 53.

Now four appear. In the time of Cervantes poetry was quite *à la mode;* and the gravely humorous way in which he here eulogizes the courtly poets is highly entertaining. Of the Conde de Salinas or the Conde de Saldaña we know little as poets. The Marquis of Alcañices contributed a laudatory sonnet to the *Novels* of Cervantes, which contains at least one happy thought, when he praises Cervantes as one

> Whose genius sought, by means of art,
> To conjure hidden truth from fabled lie.

The Principe de Borja y Esquilache was a man of a different stamp. He was at once a great statesman and a great poet. He is called by some the "Prince of Spanish lyric poets." He even attempted the heroic style, but his epic poem, "The Recovery of Naples," brought him little renown. He is, however, unrivalled for the exquisite taste and elegance of his minor poems; and he shone especially in the *Letrilla*. We give a translation of one of these, which is both simple and beautiful:—

The Maid of Betis.

Lucinda, thy home was the mountain brown,
'Tis more than a year since thou camest to town;

With none art thou friendly, on none hast thou smiled,
If starving thou diest, how livest thou, child?

In Andalusia was never such chill,
'Tis found on the ridges of frozen Castile.

Thy cradle in Tormes, the snows on its plain,
Are one and the same with thine icy disdain.

The streams of Sevilla were ne'er drunk by thee,
Which flow by its portals, and down to the sea!

A truce to thy rigour, thy coldness, and spleen,
If thou care not to see, be glad to be seen!

To the sound of my lute-strings, at breaking of day,
I sang thee these verses, wert sleeping, I pray?

Thine eyes, Maid of Betis, O do not remove,
Let them but look loving, if thou wilt not love!

NOTE 19. PAGE 55.

Most famous Villamediana. This nobleman, of commanding presence and brilliant parts, lived the life of a gallant and spendthrift at Court, and died at last by the hands of an assassin. Those who are curious about the details may consult the "Memoirs of the Countess D'Aulnoy." As a poet he belonged to the school of Gongora, but his imitations of the affected style of that master are long ago forgotten. His epigrams, however, were very celebrated, and deserve to be remembered. We give the following one, not for its excellence, but because it refers to one of the poets mentioned in this satire :—

España swears, without a lie,
He never sups at home, for why?
His supper he must go without,
When nobody invites him out!

Notes and Illustrative Pieces. 353

This poor poet, Juan de España, is the man whose works Cervantes sarcastically eulogizes as " more worthy of divine than human praise, for in his verses he is all divine ! "

Note 20. Page 57.

Scarce can Francisco de Quevedo. The familiar, yet not unkindly way in which Cervantes here alludes to Quevedo's lameness (which amounted to positive deformity), and the warm eulogium he bestows upon him, show the existence of very friendly relations between these two great men. Quevedo himself was not oversensitive in regard to his deformity, which did not prevent him from being a very expert and deadly swordsman. In his first Satire, addressed to a lady, he alludes to his well-known defects in this curious way:—

>Como tu alma, tengo la una pierna
>Mala y dañada ; mas, Belisa ingrata,
>Tengo otra buena que mi ser gobierna.

The complete works of this wonderful, many-sided poet and politician have at length been given to the world in the *Biblioteca de los Autores Españoles*, in three portly volumes. They form a perfect mine of wealth to the Spanish student, which has still to be explored. Our space only allows us to extract one satirical piece, which, bearing the taking title of *Testamento de Don Quijote*, may find an appropriate place in this volume. There is no indication as to the circumstances under which it was composed, so we may take it, if we please, as an amusing rejoinder to the humorous personalities of

A A

Cervantes in the text. It has not hitherto been translated, and we give it in an abridged form. It runs thus:—

THE LAST WILL OF DON QUIXOTE.

All his members bruised and battered,
    Black and blue with sticks and stones,
Don Quijote de la Mancha
    Stricken lies, and feebly groans;
With his target for a cover,
    With his buckler for a bed,
Craning out, like any tortoise,
    From between the shells his head.
With a thinnish voice, and cheeping,
    As the notary to him comes,
In despite of absent grinders
    Thus he spake from out his gums:
"Jot thee down, good knight, I pray thee,
    (God thee keep in quiet still!)
This the testament I tender
    As my last and latest will.
Put not therein 'sound of judgment,'
    As thou oft hast put before;
Write it rather down 'bed-ridden,'
    For, in sooth, 'tis sound no more.
To the earth I give my body,
    Let the earth my body eat;
Scarcely will there be a mouthful,
    For its leanness is complete;
Let them bear it forth to burial
    In the scabbard of my brand,
For by reason of its thinness
    Such a coffin will be grand!
I to Sancho leave the islands
    Which I gained with toil unbated
If therewith he be not wealthy,
    He'll at least be isolated.

Notes and Illustrative Pieces. 355

Item, to good Rozinante
    I the fields leave with their fruits,
Which the Lord of Heaven created
    For the grazing of the brutes;
I bequeath him misadventure,
    And an old age full of bother,
And therewith a peck of troubles
    In the place of oats and fodder.
Of the many sticks they gave me,
    I to Dulcinea good,
For her fuel in the winter,
    Leave a hundred loads of wood.
Buckler, lance, Quixotic visor,
    And whate'er my stock in trade is,
I bequeath for pious uses
    In the ransom of high ladies.
As trustees, Don Belianis,
    And the good Knight of the Sun,
And Esplandian the doughty,
    I appoint them every one!"
Up and answered Sancho Panza,
    List to what he said or sung,
With an accent rough and ready,
    And a forty-parson tongue:
"'Tis not reason, good my master,
    When thou goest forth, I wis,
To account to thy Creator,
    Thou should'st utter stuff like this;
As trustees, name thou the Curate,
    Who confesseth thee betimes,
And Per-Anton, our good Provost,
    And the goat-herd Gaffer Grimes;
Make clean sweep of the Esplandians,
    Who have dinned us with their clatter;
Call thou in a ghostly hermit
    Who may aid thee in the matter!'
" Well thou speakest," up and answered
    Don Quijote, nowise dumb,

" Hie thee to the Rock of Dolour,
    Tell Beltenebros to come ! "
Thereupon the Extreme-unction
    At the doorway lighted down ;
As his eyes fell on the parson,
    With his candle and his gown,
He exclaimed it was the wizard
    Of Niquea at his bed ;
Whereupon the good hidalgo
    To address him raised his head.
But on seeing that his judgment,
    Tongue, and sight, and life were gone,
Scribe and Curate made their exit,
    And the Knight was left alone.
            Obras de Quevedo, iii. 196.

NOTE 21. PAGE 63.

Lope de Vega. Navarrete and other biographers quote this high eulogium, as a proof of the good understanding that subsisted between Lope and Cervantes. Benjumea, however, in his *Truth about Don Quixote*, Madrid, 1878, draws attention to the fact that Lope's position in the roll of poets is not a very dignified one, placed as he is between a mere mediocrity like Antonio de Galarza, and the needy swarm of poetasters who are the subjects of Cervantes' wrath and ridicule. Be that as it may, there can be no doubt that, during his whole literary career, Cervantes did ample justice to the claims and merit of his great rival. His praise, from first to last, was given with no grudging hand. As early as 1584, when Lope was but twenty-two years of age, Cervantes thus speaks of him in his *Canto de Caliope* :—

    Experience shows how in a true-born wit,
        In verdant youth, and at a tender age,

High knowledge finds a domicile as fit
 As in a manhood ripe, mature, and sage.
Who will not truth so manifest admit,
 With such a one will I no battle wage,
 Nor need I, when he knows that I am free,
 Lope de Vega, to say this of thee.

This rather frigid, but not unflattering encomium, addressed to a precocious youth who affirmed of himself, that "his genius taught him to write verses from his cradle," was, we are told, a matter of deep offence to Lope. The same could hardly be said of the glowing laudatory sonnet contributed by Cervantes to Lope's *Dragontea*, published in 1602, though that monstrous Anglophobic libel on Sir Francis Drake hardly deserved so much honour. It runs thus, playing on the name *Vega*, which, in Spanish, means a plain :—

Within that part of Spain, the fairest known,
 There lies a *Vega*, peaceful, ever green,
 Whereon Apollo smiles with brow serene,
And bathes it with the streams of Helicon.
Jove, grand and mighty worker, there hath shown,
 To make it bloom, his science vast and keen;
 Cyllenius there disports with merry mien,
Minerva claims it henceforth as her own;
There have the Muses their Parnassus found,
 Chaste Venus rears therein her teeming brood,
 The blessed congregation of the Loves;
And so with pleasure, and the whole year round,
 New fruits it yieldeth for the general good,
 Arms, angels, saints, and shepherds of the groves.

But while Cervantes was free at all times to recognize the astounding fecundity of Lope's genius, and the brilliancy of his achievements on the stage, it is always with a certain dignified reserve, befitting one who knew he had both the right and power to act as judge and discriminator between quantity and quality, fertility and fatal facility, brilliancy and meretriciousness. Nowhere is this more visible than in the famous speech of the Canon of Toledo, on the playwrights and comedies of the day (*Don Quixote*, i. 48), which has become classical. There the utter venality and downward tendency of the dramatic school, of which Lope was the founder and main support, are depicted with a blending of sparkling raillery and grave rebuke, such as made the wits of Madrid both merry and furious. To none was it more galling than to Lope, who in his *New Art of making Comedies in our Day*, published in Madrid, 1609, but written two or three years before, bids contemptuous defiance to all his censors, with evident allusion to Cervantes in particular; and with an amazing effrontery defends the doctrine, that Art must sink itself to the level of public taste, and that poets who please to live must live to please. This attitude of contemptuous disdain or cool indifference was Lope's prevailing mood towards Cervantes. Though, after the appearance of the first part of *Don Quixote*, he had a hundred opportunities of speaking well of his chief rival, only five or six times does he allude to him, and never once with hearty or adequate praise; for the grandiose eulogy in the *Laurel de Apolo* refers only to Cervantes' verse. When he brought out his own novels in a vain attempt to snatch the palm from Cervantes, he curtly speaks of his rival's *Novelas* as "not wanting in grace or style." When he pillaged the *Tratos de Argel* to enrich his

Notes and Illustrative Pieces. 359

own *Slaves of Algiers*, he introduces a character called Saavedra, but with no mark of respect or esteem for the captive poet, who had played such a gallant and heroic part. His private letters, which have lately come to light, tell the same tale. In one of them he compares Cervantes' verses to "fried eggs badly cooked." In another, dated 14th August, 1604, just before the appearance of the book of the epoch, he says : "Many poets are in labour for the coming year ; but none are so bad as Cervantes, or so stupid as to praise *Don Quixote!*" This curious outburst of malice, born either of envy or hatred, reads very strangely now ; for the poor despised work, borne, as its author very quaintly remarks, on the crupper of Rozinante, has carried the name of Cervantes to corners of the earth where the name of Lope de Vega has never reached, or reached only to be forgotten.

Time, that has dealt so hardly with the fame of Lope's works, has also not spared the moral reputation of the man, whom Montalvan describes in later years as exhibiting the devotion of a saint, with the austerities of a monk. For the same happy accident that brought to light the letter of Cervantes to Mateo Vazquez, which reflects additional lustre on his character as a "Chevalier sans peur et sans reproche," also revealed a mass of correspondence in the handwriting of Lope, addressed to his patron, the Duke of Sessa, to whom he seems to have acted in the joint capacity of secretary and "Sir Pandarus." The collection consists of three folio volumes, containing 225 letters, each of the volumes having this title-page : *Cartas y Villetas de Belardo á Luçilo sobre diversas materias*. These were given to Sr. La Barrera, the celebrated antiquarian, to be copied out for publication; but the contents were found to cast such a lurid light on the secret history of Lope, even after he became an ecclesiastic, that the competent authorities consigned them to safe custody in the National Library. Those who are curious, however, may find a number of the letters contained in a work by Don Ibero Ribas y Canfranc, with this strange title: *Los ultimos Amores de Lope de Vega*, Madrid, 1876.

Note 22. Page 65.

A taylor there. The name of one of these poetic taylors has been preserved in a piquant MS. satire of the period, quoted by Pellicer:

> Yo Juan Martinez, oficial de Olmedo,
> Por la gracia de Dios, poeta Sastre,
> Natural de la Sagra de Toledo.

Note 23. Page 71.

The dulcet mouth. The following sonnet by Gongora so aptly reproduces the curious sentiment of the text, that we can almost fancy Cervantes intended to allude to it. It is hardly original, being an imitation of one of Tasso's, beginning thus:—

> Quel labro, che le rose han colorite,
> Molle si sparge, e tumidetto in fuore.

SONNET.

> The dulcet mouth, that shows to eager eyes
> A moisture, 'mid the pearls distilled, that might
> Outrival that sweet liquor of delight

Which Ida's boy to Jupiter supplies,
Ye lovers, touch it not, if life ye prize;
    For, 'twixt one lip and t'other crimson bright,
    Love lurks with deadly poison out of sight,
Like curled-up snake, 'twixt flower and flower that lies.
Let not the roses tempt, though seeming gay,
    As those which drop down from Aurora's breast,
    Bedewed with pearls, and scent of sweetest kind;
Apples of Tantalus, not roses they,
    That fire the blood, and vanish with unrest,
    Leaving Love's poison and nought else behind.
          Obras de Gongora, Lisboa, 1657, vol. i. 28.

NOTE 24. PAGE 71.

Valencia's plain. " Valencia del Cid," as the Spaniards delight to call this famous town, is spoken of with rapture by Cervantes in the *Persiles and Sigismunda*. He declares it notable, "for the grandeur of its site, the distinction of its inhabitants, the amenity of its surroundings, for all that makes it the fairest and richest of all cities, not only of Spain, but of all Europe : and principally for the beauty of its women, their extreme chastity, and sprightly language, which the Portuguese tongue alone can rival in smoothness and sweetness." It was also celebrated for the number and excellence of its poets who, in October, 1591, constituted themselves into that famous academy called *Academia de los Nocturnos*. It consisted of forty-five members, who all assumed names in keeping with their character as " Nocturnals." It may be interesting to give a few of those mentioned in this satire, with their designations :—

    D. Guillen de Castro .   = *Sereno*.
    D. Lois Ferrer . . . = *Norte*.

Andres Rey de Articda = *Centinela.*
Gaspar de Aguilar . . = *Sombra.*

The name of Captain Christobal de Virues does not appear on the list; nor that of Pedro de Aguilar, who was a native of Antequera. It is generally supposed that Cervantes meant Gaspar de Aguilar, who was a very prolific Valencian poet. The Academy was dissolved in 1593; but was resuscitated in 1615, under the title of *Los Montañeses del Parnaso.* Guillen de Castro, who was an influential member of the Academy, is famous especially for his great comedy in two parts, *Las Mocedades del Cid,* from which Corneille borrowed so largely. He also dramatized portions of the *Don Quixote;* and one of his pieces bears the same title as Cervantes' novel, *El curioso impertinente.* Captain Virues, who was a comrade of Cervantes at Lepanto, also shares with him the honour (if honour it may be called) of having been among the first to reduce comedies to three acts. Ticknor, however, has shown that Francisco de Avendaño in 1553 had anticipated them both.

Note 25. Page 75.

Great Andres Rey de Articda. This was a poet after Cervantes' own heart. He was a gallant soldier all his lifetime; fought gloriously at Lepanto, where he received three wounds; but was at the same time an intense student, and devoted especially to poetry. His letters and satires are famed for the exquisite purity of their language, and for the vivid trenchant style with which they lash the vices of the age, both in morals and literature. His chief work has this title: *Discourses,*

Epistles, and Epigrams of Artemidoro, Saragossa, 1605. A passage from one of his letters to the Marquis de Cuellar will illustrate the scope and tendency of his criticism. It is aimed at Lope de Vega, and expresses in a humorous way the very opinions of Cervantes himself:—

> Beneath the Lord of Delos' burning heat
> Spring little poets from the putrid pool,
> With such agility, 'tis quite a treat;
> And marvellous it is, beyond all rule,
> To see a comedy writ by some wight,
> Whom yesterday Minerva put to school.
> Since his invention is but wind outright,
> In eight short days, or in less space of time,
> The mode and matter are in keeping quite;
> * * * * *
> I've galleys seen skim o'er the desert way,
> And half-a-dozen horsemen posting ride
> From Cyprus' channel to Palermo's bay;
> The Persian Empire placed the Alps beside,
> And Famagosta planted in Biscay,
> And Germany depicted strait and wide;
> In such-like stuff Heredia doth play,
> To suit the humour of a friend of his,
> Who writes a comedy in half a day!

NOTE 26. PAGE 79.

Of Tityrus and eke Sincerus lie. Cervantes refers here to the tombs of Virgil and Sannazaro at Naples. *Sincero* is one of the chief characters in Sannazaro's grand Pastoral, *Arcadia*.

NOTE 27. PAGE 81.

The two Lupercios greet. These two Lupercios, who might with more propriety have been styled the two

Leonardos, were the famous brothers Lupercio Leonardo de Argensola, and Bartolomé Juan Leonardo de Argensola. They were born at Barbastro, in Aragon, the one in 1564, the other in 1566. The elder, Lupercio, became a statesman and historiographer of the Crown of Aragon; the younger became a churchman, Rector of Villahermosa, and Canon of Saragossa. They both, by exalted character and high attainments, enjoyed an immense authority in the world of literature. As far back as 1584 Cervantes praised them in the *Canto de Calicpe*, as "twin luminaries, twin suns of poesy." He also passes an extravagant eulogium on the dramas of the elder brother, in the Canon of Toledo's address in the first part of *Don Quixote* (ch. 48), as models of highest excellence. On account of their classical refinement, and the exquisite character of their Satires, the brothers were styled the *Horaces* of Spain. As for the matter touched upon in the text, we know little more than what Cervantes himself tells us. The elder brother had received a commission from the Conde de Lemos, Viceroy of Naples, in 1610, to found an academy of literature there, and invite the best wits of Spain to join it. The *Academia degli Oziosi* was in due time formed, but Cervantes, who had received brilliant promises, was not thought worthy to be ranked amongst the *élite*, and was left to his solitude in Madrid. He professed to be much chagrined at this neglect; but the world at large will not share his regret. Naples was to him a paradise of delight and song. In his youth "he had trodden its streets for better than a year." As one of the "Oziosi" he might have lived a merrier and more luxurious life;

but Naples might have proved to him a Capua, and the world have been the poorer for the want of his " Novels," and his completed *Don Quixote*. We know of no talent the " Oziosi " club ever evoked ; and the Spanish academies generally were rather hotbeds of display and jealousy, than nurseries of high art.

As a specimen of the powers of Lupercio Leonardo we give one of his more humorous sonnets :—

TRUTH AND BEAUTY.

> I must confess, Don John, on due inspection,
>   That dame Elvira's charming red and white,
>   Though fair they seem, are only hers by right
> In that her money purchased their perfection ;
> But thou must grant as well, on calm reflection,
>   That her sweet lie hath such a lustre bright,
>   As fairly puts to shame the paler light,
> And honest beauty of a true complexion !
> And yet no wonder I distracted go
>   With such deceit, when 'tis within our ken
>   That Nature blinds us with the self-same spell ;
> For that blue heaven above, that charms us so,
>   Is neither heaven nor blue ! Sad pity then,
>   That so much Beauty is not Truth as well !

The Canon, Bartolomé, was famous for his epigrams. The following is celebrated, though it is but an imitation of one by Catullus :—

TO ELIA.

> If, Elia, I remember true,
>   Four teeth thou hadst without a doubt ;
>   One cough thou gav'st, and two flew out,
> Another drew the other two.

>Now may'st thou cough, upon my word,
>   And all day long, without a pause,
>   For nothing in thy vacant jaws
>Will e'er be stirred by cough the third!

One of his finest sonnets is, however, in a graver and loftier line, and is thus entitled :—

TO PROVIDENCE.

>O common Father, say, since thou art just,
>   Why doth thy watchful providence permit,
>   That Fraud upon the judgment-throne should sit,
>While Innocence, in chains, must bite the dust?
>Who gave its vigour to the arm robust
>   Which braves thy laws unchecked, nor will submit,
>   Whilst humble zeal, that gives thee honour fit,
>Is trodden down beneath victorious lust?
>See how they gleam, those quivering palms of fame,
>   In vice-stained hands, while Virtue, losing heart,
>   Groans as the lying pageant onward rolls!
>Thus spake I, when a nymph celestial came,
>   And smiling said : Blind mortal that thou art,
>   And is this earth the centre of all souls?

NOTE 28. PAGE 85.

Of furious dogs. We give the four following lines from Gonzalo Perez' translation of the Odyssey, descriptive of this scene :—

>*Alli vive la Scylla, que no cessa*
>*De aullar y ladrar continuamente*
>*Con un ladrido agudo : como suele*
>*Ladrar una perilla, que aun es nueva.*
>   *La Ulyxea,* l. 12, p. 185.

NOTE 29. PAGE 87.

They found him in that man Lofraso.—In the famous scrutiny of Don Quixote's library special mention is

Notes and Illustrative Pieces. 367

made of this luckless bard and his monstrous work. We give the passage from Shelton's version, slightly amended : " 'This booke, quoth the Barber, opening of another, is *The Ten bookes of the Fortune of love*, written by *Antonio de Lofraso*, the *Sardinian Poet*. By the holy Orders which I have received, quoth the Curate, since Apollo was Apollo, and the Muses, Muses, and Poets, Poets, was never written so delightfull and extravagant a worke as this, which, in its way & veine, is the best and rarest of all the bookes that have ever issued of that kinde to view the light of the world; and he that hath not read it may make account that he hath never read matter of delight. Give it to me, gossip, for I doe prize more the finding of it, than I would the gift of a Cassocke of the best Serge of Florence. And so with great joy he laid it aside." (*The Historie of Don-Quixote*, b. i. ch. 6.) The Spanish critics make merry over a certain Frenchman, the Marquis de Argens, who on the strength of this dubious eulogium declared the work of Lofraso to be " one of the best books of Spain." They are also most unsparing in their ridicule of Pedro Pineda, a teacher of Spanish in London, who in the year 1740 reprinted it in two handsome octavo volumes, as one of the treasures of Spanish literature. (Londres, por Henrique Chapel, Año 1740.) Pineda's praise of the work is quite unbounded, and he declares himself "under constraint to print it, knowing that the English nation loves what is good, prizes what is rare, and seeks after what is curious."

Poor Pineda, who edited an edition of the *Don Quixote* for Tonson, and an edition of the *Novelas Exemplares* for

Henry Chapelle, had evidently never read the *Viaje del Parnaso;* otherwise the subtle irony of Cervantes might have dawned upon him.

Whatever may be the merits of the book, there can be no doubt of its rarity. The British Museum possesses a very fine copy of the original edition, Barcelona, 1573 ; and Salvá declares it to be *sumamente raro.*

The author's real name was Lo Frasso, and the real title of his book, *The Ten Books of Fortuna d' Amor,* written in imitation of Montemayor's *Seven books of Diana.* The heroine's name is Fortuna, and the hero's Frexano, under which latter the author has disguised his own ; *Frasso* in the Sardinian dialect being equivalent to *Fresno* (ash-tree) in Spanish. The whole book forms a curious, unsavoury mess of maudlin verse and stilted prose, which goes jogging along, ofttimes through four pages, without a single stop. The unbounded conceit of the man (which seems specially to have roused Cervantes' wrath) is shown in a delectable poem, towards the end of the book, in the form of a huge acrostic. It consists of no less than 168 lines, the initial letters of which, when put together, were destined to immortalize the name of the author, the title and date of his book, and the name of his patron. Cervantes, however, was probably not aware, while making merry over the Sardinian bard, that Lo Frasso had almost (if not quite) anticipated himself in the invention of the immortal name of DULCINEA ! Amongst a number of disdainful damsels mentioned in the tale occurs the name of DULCINA ; and one of the rejected lovers bears the sweet appellation of DULCINEO. As a specimen of Lo Frasso's powers, we give the following octave which Deyfebo addressed to Dulcina, on returning her ring and pledge :—

> A ring, Dulcina, thou me gav'st one day
>   To mock me, and to wound my heart right sore;
> What matters it, since Love hath flown away,
>   And on thy beauty I set little store :
> If, ingrate, thou didst mean to jilt me, say,
>   Why didst thou seem to love me more and more?
> Well, since thy love was such a feigned thing,
> I rid me now of it, and of thy ring.

Nothing whatever is known of Antonio de lo Frasso save what he himself tells us; viz., that he was born at Lalguer, a seaport town of Sardinia, had served in the army, and was resident in Barcelona. Before the issue of his great work he published, in 1571, a little brochure with this title, " Here commenceth the letter which the Author sends to his sons, and a thousand two hundred discreet counsels and warnings—*Virtus post funera vivit.*" This information we owe to Salvá, who declares the copy in his possession to be unique, so far as he knows ; which gives that sapient bibliographer occasion to arraign the wisdom of Providence, in ordaining that the scarcest books shall be the stupidest.

This letter is addressed from Barcelona to " My dearest sons, Alfonso and Scipio de lo Frasso," informing them and the public that " he addresses to them these warnings and counsels because he is far from them, and cannot visit them without fear of death, owing to the intervention of the fierce Gulf of Lyons ; for that crossing the sea is a matter involving the uncertainty of snatching short life from its fury !" This is a sentiment hardly worthy of "Mercury's boatswain," as Cervantes wittily dubs him. This same volume of Salva's contains a poem in octaves on the battle of Lepanto, and a Sonnet by Lo Frasso, "al muy serenissimo S. Don Joan de Austria" with a wretched woodcut on the reverse, representing a naval combat.—Was Lo Frasso, after all, a comrade in arms of Cervantes?

NOTE 30. PAGE 89.

Th' Acroceraunian, fatal name. This is an allusion to the *infames scopulos Acroceraunia* of Horace (Carm. I. 3, 20).

NOTE 31. PAGE 88.

A cantimplora acostumbrados. The *cantimplora*, or water-cooler, plays an important part in Madrid during the summer months. Gongora introduces it in this witty stanza:—

>El medico y cirujano
>Sean para mi govierno,
>Calentador en invierno,
>Y Cantimplora en verano.

>The doctor and phlebotomist
>Be each for me in turn my ruler;
>My warming-pan in winter-time,
>In summer-time my water-cooler.

NOTE 32. PAGE 95.

Don Juan de Arguijo. This famous *veinte-cuatro*, or Alderman of Seville, though no very distinguished poet himself, was a man of such refined taste and unbounded munificence, that he was celebrated throughout the length and breadth of the land as the "Apollo of all the poets of Spain." It is to this fact that Cervantes here alludes. Arguijo's palace, and Pacheco's studio in Seville, were the common haunts of the poets, artists, and dilettanti of the town.

NOTE 33. PAGE 101.
Those of Alcinoüs. Cervantes' description of the garden of Parnassus reminds us in one or two points of the garden of Alcinoüs described in the Odyssey; especially in these lines :—

> It changeth not at all with changing-time,
> For all the year Spring offers, in her glee,
> Not hopeful blooms, but fruits in all their prime.

The corresponding phrases in the Odyssey are thus rendered by Gonzalo Perez :—

> Su fructa no se pierde, ni se daña
> Ni falta en el ynvierno, ni en verano,
> Mas dura todo el año : porque siempre
> Reyna en la huerta el Zephiro suave.
>
> *La Ulyxea,* l. 7, 105.

NOTE 34. PAGE 105.
With which fair Galatea. This was the first venture of Cervantes on the field of literature. He calls it *las primicias de mi corto ingenio.* It is generally supposed to have been published in Madrid, in September, 1584, just before his marriage, and presented to his bride, as her marriage-gift. The first extant edition, however, bears this title : " First Part of the Galatea, divided into six Books, composed by Miguel de Cervantes, &c.—printed at Alcalá, by Juan Gracian, 1585." The second part was never completed ; though till the very last year of

his life Cervantes did not despair of giving it to the public. It is a simple pastoral tale, framed after the model of Montemayor's *Diana*, and though written in pure limpid prose, interspersed with very melodious verse, it gave his countrymen no foretaste of what was afterwards in store for them. He himself had yet to learn where his true strength lay, and it was the stern pressure of the times that drove him at last from Arcadia to La Mancha. Even in these early times, however, Cervantes was well known and appreciated in literary circles. As a slight evidence thereof we give the following "laudatory Sonnet" contributed by one of his friends to the *Galatea*. It is full of the extravagance belonging to such compositions; and most likely the author of it never dreamed how much prophetic truth lay beneath his friendly flattery. It is thus entitled:—

DON LUIS DE VARGAS MANRIQUE

To the Author of "Galatea."

The sovereign gods in thee have made display,
  O grand Cervantes, of their greatness dread,
  And, nature-like, have showered upon thy head
Their gifts immortal without stint or stay.
Jove gave his bolt, that lambent vivid play
  Of words, which lend a soul to matter dead;
  Diana gave a style, light as her tread,
Chaste as herself, of more than mortal sway;
Hermes, his cunning tales and happy phrase,
  Mars, the strong vigour that inspires thine arm,
  Cupid and Venus, all their tender loves;
Apollo lent his sweet harmonious lays,
  The Sisters Nine, their science and its charm,
  And Pan, in fine, his shepherds and his groves.

NOTE 35. PAGE 107.

Don Quixote. So much has been written about the *Don Quixote* of late years that it seems unnecessary to say more now. We, therefore, merely direct attention to the peculiar estimate which Cervantes gives of the use and intent of his great work. It almost seems as if he meant to warn off the field all future hunters after hidden truths and mystic meanings. His words are few and simple, but they contain much in little compass. To purge the human breast of melancholy; to be a perennial spring of delight to the world in all seasons, through all ages; this is what *Don Quixote* was specially created for, according to the testimony of its " wise begetter." Could grandeur of idea be better embodied in plainer words? We are reminded forcibly of the self-same language used by Sir Walter Scott (the only humorist of the Cervantic type that Britain has produced) when dedicating the collected edition of his Waverley Novels to George IV.: " Sire, the Author of this collection of works of fiction would not have presumed to solicit for them your Majesty's august patronage, were it not that the perusal of them has been supposed in some instances to have succeeded in amusing hours of relaxation, or relieving those of languor, pain, or anxiety." To produce a book of universal pastime (*pasaticmpo*), to lessen, even by a few drops, the ocean of human pain and melancholy, may seem poor objects of poetic ambition; and yet two great geniuses combine in declaring these to be the sum and substance of their life-work!

We may note also, as a curious coincidence, that the

two most wonderful poetic creations of the seventeenth century saw the light of day almost at the same time. The second quarto of Shakespeare's *Hamlet* (the full-orbed conception) was published in London in 1604; the first edition of Cervantes' *Don Quixote* appeared in Madrid early in 1605. Such a planetary conjunction is very rare in the literary universe. We have deemed it worthy of commemoration in the following sonnet :—

LONDON AND MADRID,

1604-1605.

> From two great minds two madmen drew their birth,
>   Seers rather, who on this our human stage
>   Have held men's hearts enthralled, from age to age,
> Now thrilled with horror, now convulsed with mirth.
> The Danish prince, whose mind the woes of earth
>   Unhinged, and touched the brain with finest rage :
>   The Spanish Don, whose soul the knightly page
> With follies fired, to brighten many a hearth ;
> Hamlet and Quixote ! Names that will not die,
>   While those of Shakespeare and Cervantes live;
>   While Life and light with Death and darkness strive,
> And Truth in arms confronts the rampant Lie !
>   Grand teachers both ! We welcome in the twain
>   The power of England, and the wit of Spain !

NOTE 36. PAGE 107.

I penned the sonnet with this opening strain. There is a curious notice contained in a contemporary manuscript entitled *Sucesos de Sevilla*, 1592-1604, which tells us when and where this sonnet was published. It runs thus :—

Notes and Illustrative Pieces. 375

"On Tuesday 29th December of said year (1598) were celebrated the funeral rites of His Majesty, and it appears that the Inquisition was condemned to pay for the wax consumed during the first day, and the town for the masses. And on that day, while I stood in the holy church, there entered a roguish poet who recited an *octave* on the grandeur of the funeral pile:—

> I vow to God such grandeur stuns my brain!
> I'd give a crown its wonders to detail;
> For such a grand machine on such a scale
> Beggars description, makes invention vain.
> Now, by the living Christ, each piece, 'tis plain,
> Is worth a million! Pity it should fail
> To last an age! Hail, grand Sevilla, hail,
> In wit and wealth a second Rome again!
> I'd wager that the soul of the deceased,
> On such a sight as this to gloat and gaze,
> Hath left its joys eternal in the skies.
> A listening puppy answered: "I at least,
> Sir soldier, doubt not what your honour says,
> Who dares to think the opposite—he lies!"
> On this, to my surprise,
> The stripling stinted, fumbled with his blade,
> Looked sideways, vanished, and no more was said.

For full particulars regarding this astounding catafalque of Philip II., see Espinosa de los Monteros, *Historia de Sevilla*, foll. 1111-1118; Stirling Maxwell, *Annals of the Artists in Spain*, i. 403.

As a pendant to this famous sonnet we may as well give the other, equally famous, which Cervantes made two years before. It commemorates the relief of Cadiz, July 1596; and the exploits of the awkward squad of Sevilian volunteers who, under the command of the

Duke of Medina-Celi, entered Cadiz—after the Earl of Essex had sacked it, and evacuated it. The Bull-calf (*Becerro*) represents Captain Becerra, who drilled the doughty band :—

SONNET.

This July saw another Holy week,
  When certain brotherhoods made quite a blaze,
  Well-known as squads—in military phrase—
Which made the mob and not the English shriek!
So many feathers waved from peak to peak,
  That in some fourteen, or some fifteen days,
  Their Pigmies and Goliaths winged their ways,
And all their pageant vanished like a freak.
The Bull-calf bellowed; placed his squad in line;
  The sky grew dark; a rumbling seized the ground,
  Which threatened total ruin as it shook;
And into Cadiz, with a prudence fine,
  Soon as the Earl had left it safe and sound,
  In triumph marched Medina's mighty Duke!

NOTE 37. PAGE 107.

P've of Romances. Of the infinite number of romances which Cervantes penned, very few are now extant. These few, though some are very doubtful, may be found in the *poesias sueltas*, appended to the volume of Cervantes' works in the *Biblioteca de los Autores Españoles*. Among the rest is one entitled, *Los Celos* (Jealousy), which is supposed to be the very one alluded to by Cervantes, as his masterpiece in this department of song. If authentic, it is certainly curious, though not very striking. The most charming of all his romances is that given in his novel, *La Gitanilla*, as sung by the gipsy maiden on the streets of Madrid. It is too long to quote here; but it is worthy of a better translation than any that has yet been published.

NOTE 38. PAGE 109.
To rival Phyllis my Phylena. The *Phylena* is supposed by most Spanish critics to have been a youthful performance of Cervantes, written probably before he went to Italy as *camarero* to Cardinal Áquaviva, and never published. Mr. Duffield, following in the wake of Sr. Asensio, informs us that *Filena* is a misprint for *Silena*, one of the shepherdesses introduced into the *Galatea*. This notion seems very far-fetched. The *Galatea* has already been mentioned in this oration; and, moreover, it requires but a single glance at Cervantes' own words, *Al par de Filis mi Filena*, to see that the one name is suggestive of the other.

NOTE 39. PAGE 113.
A wondrous being. Readers of *Don Quixote* will remember the delectable address which the immortal Hidalgo gives in the house of Don Diego de Miranda, on the nature and uses of poetry and poets, for the benefit of his hopeful son, a student of Salamanca (Part ii. ch. 26). There they will find, in a more practical shape, the essence of this wonderful description of True Poesy. Whatever may be thought of Cervantes' claim to be a great poet, no one will question the grandeur of his conceptions, regarding the worth and power of True Poesy in the economy of the universe.

NOTE 40. PAGE 116.
Campo y vereda. The reading, in the first and subse-

quent editions of the *Viaje*, is *compa y vereda*. This is a manifest blunder, which makes the whole passage unintelligible. *Compa* and *vereda* are thus reckoned amongst the other odorous herbs sacred to Bacchus, which False Poesy scatters. But *compa* is not found in Spanish Lexicons, and *vereda* is a bridle-path. The slight alteration of *compa* into *campo*, as suggested by Sr. Gayangos, gives at least a glimmering of sense.

NOTE 41. PAGE 121.

I spied six persons of a clerkly kind. This amusing description of the ecclesiastics, and their flirtation with the Muses, is quite Cervantic. We can well fancy what a fluttering there would be among the black cloaks of Toledo, when it was first published. Of five out of the six shame-faced but ambitious aspirants to the honours of Parnassus, whose names are given, but little is known, and that little is hardly worth relating. More interest attaches to the sixth, whose name is not given. It is supposed that Cervantes here satirizes that famous writer of comedies, Fray Gabriel Tellez, who, under the pseudonym of Tirso de Molina, enjoyed a popularity on the stage second only to that of Lope de Vega. He was born in Madrid, studied at Alcalá, and became a priest in 1613. He composed no less than 300 comedies, the most famous of which are the *Burlador de Sevilla*, the prototype of all succeeding Don Juans, and *Don Gil de las calzas verdes*, whose sappy humour was the delight of the common people. (See Ticknor, vol. ii., ch. 21.) Cervantes very aptly characterizes Molina's not over-chaste delineations of the manners of his time; for which he had to suffer at sundry times the lash of the Inquisition.

NOTE 42. PAGE 205.

Is Arbolanches. This redoubtable commander-in-chief of the heterodox army, Hieronymo Arbolanche, as he styles himself, was a native of Tudela, in the province of Navarre; and with this single fact (vouched for by himself) begins and ends his recorded history. Such immortality as he enjoys is, therefore, due to Cervantes, and in some measure also to the fact that his work (*The Nine Books of the Havidas*, Saragossa, 1566) is one of the rarest in Spanish literature. Salvá, who thought himself the happy possessor of the sole copy in existence, was surprised to find that Don Pascual de Gayangos (whose library is noted for its rarities) describes it in the notes appended to his translation of Ticknor's *History of Spanish Literature* (Madrid, 1851-56, vol. iii., p. 537), and also extracts from it five little gems as proofs of its high quality. Fortified by the opinion of this distinguished authority, Salvá is not disposed to submit to the indignity of having one of his pet rare volumes consigned (like that of Lo FRASSO) to the limbo of the stupid. He therefore roundly charges Cervantes with having depreciated a book he had never seen. Cervantes, it seems, calls it "a very breviary in bulk," whereas it is the smallest of small octavos; he also calls it a *melange* of prose and verse, whereas it is written throughout in blank verse, interspersed with little poems of different kinds and measures. These be blunders unpardonable in the eyes of matter-of-fact bibliomaniacs, who know nothing of poetic licence or sly sarcasm. Cervantes no doubt looked upon blank verse as but disguised prose. But it seems to us that the title-page alone was quite sufficient to call forth the peculiar humour of Cervantes. Arbolanche has planted a woodcut representation of himself right in the centre of it, and, not content with this, has reproduced it on the reverse side, with this absurd inscription :—

Ebro me produzió, y en flor me tiene,
Mas my rayz de rio Calibe viene.

which we can only render thus :—

Ebro produced me and keeps me fresh ever,
But my stock hath its root on the Calibe river.

Arbolanche's portrait represents a man with a massive head, set on a thick short neck ; a rather sensual mouth with protruding lips (*muso por la vida*) ; a slightly aquiline nose ; a crop of matted hair curiously foliated (if we may use the expression) so as to take the form of laurel leaves ! The whole expression of the face is smug and self-satisfied, and we do not wonder that it called forth a little of the sarcastic raillery of Cervantes. As to the merits of his book, since no one seems to have read it through, it would be unseemly to judge. From an abstract of it given by the author himself, we infer that its subject-matter is totally out of the range of human interest. But the most entertaining and characteristic part of the whole book is the introductory letter, addressed by Arbolanche to his pedagogue. The singular mock-modesty with which he repudiates all pretensions to poetic skill, and anticipates all adverse criticism, is very

Notes and Illustrative Pieces.

amusing. Singularly enough both Gayangos and Guardia represent this letter as addressed by the master to the pupil. The title, however, runs thus :—

EPISTLE OF HIERONYMO ARBOLANCHE TO DON MELCHOR ENRICO, HIS MASTER IN ARTS.

O master mine, my will was never free
    To find in printing books a great delight,
But she who has the power hath ordered me
    To bring this ill-sung Book of mine to light;
I grant I am not versed in poesy,
    And only know that I know nothing right;
And know as well that many know as little,
So care not, if they praise me not, one tittle.

I never chaunted on Parnassus' height,
    Nor ever drank the waters Cabaline :
What Octave is or Sextain beats me quite,
    Nor have I dealings with the Muses nine ;
Not mine the gift, like improvising wight,
    At every step to vomit forth a line ;
I cannot verses on my fingers measure,
Nor mouth two thousand fooleries at pleasure.

I do not hire me Sonnets to indite
    For books that go to press in this our time :
I do not ballads spin, or tercets write,
    Nor have one notion of impromptu rhyme :
With echo-songs, in sooth, I'm puzzled quite,
    To make them to the full note curtly chime :
I do not medleys make, nor things at all
That may be dubbed with name of Madrigal.

I cannot use strange words or obsolete,
    Nor am I read in books of chivalry :

> Nor can the names of blustering knights repeat,
>   Nor tell the tale of each stale victory;
> I know not what is meant by " broken feet,"
>   For mine own limbs are sound as sound can be;
> I cannot make some short, and others long,
> Some very sweet, and others very strong.

In the succeeding twelve octaves Arbolanche reveals an unexpected vein of coarse sarcasm, not wanting in point or vigour. All the most famous Spanish authors and books of his time, and before it, come in for their share. He is not ashamed to quiz such venerable men as Juan de Mena and Juan del Encina, and is even impudent enough to let fly a shaft at Garcilaso and Boscan. But we must allow him to speak for himself :—

> Tampoco sé yo hacer que cosicosa,
>   Como el de las *Preguntas* y *Respuestas*,
> Ni como Garcilaso de la prosa
>   Del Sanazaro coplas hago prestas;
> Ni sé yo hacer mi pluma muy famosa
>   Llevando el hurto italiano á cuestas,
> Como el Boscan, que tanto se me entona,
> Porque llevó el Amor en Barcelona.

The whole Epistle winds up in this wonderful way :—

> Ne'er wished I, 'mong the Wits, to find my name
>   Within the *Cancionero General;*
> Nor ever strove the foremost place to claim,
>   As many do whose names are there withal;
> I never sought to rank with men of fame,
>   Nor even thought of such a thing at all:
> But, lest I may, O lend me wit of thine,
> Señor Melchor Enrico, master mine!
>
> I do not evil speak of men so high,
>   As if I thought I had sufficient grace

Notes and Illustrative Pieces. 383

> To reach unto their lofty blasonry,
>   Still less to give myself a higher place;
> But since without much bitter raillery
>   None ever came off victors in the race;
> And since such famous men their weird must dree,
>   What will the dolts and envious make of me?

It is quite evident that such a man was fair game for the shafts of Cervantes, and quite as evident that his rhinoceros hide was quite impervious to any amount of contempt. But the whole matter is of little interest to the present generation: and such is the irony of Fate, that the priceless First Edition of the *Don Quixote*, and the tiny tome of Arbolanche, have equally achieved the honours of the "glass case" in the British Museum. *Requiescant in pace.*

Note 43. Page 215.

La Picara Justina. This, the most scandalous novel of its time, was written by the Dominican, Fray Andres Perez, under the *nom de plume* of Francisco Lopez de Ubeda. Its title is: "Book of Entertainment of the Rogue Justina, in which under merry conversations are concealed useful counsels, &c. Medina del Campo, 1605." It receives here the most stinging reprobation from Cervantes: though its contents were the delight of a not over-squeamish age, which demanded edition after edition. It appeared in the same year as the *Don Quixote*, most likely a little before it: and, what seems wonderful, it not only mentions that as yet unpublished work in the body of the text, but does so in a stanza of the curious kind of verse (*versos cortados* = docked lines) which Cervantes first made popular in the *Don Quixote*, and of which he esteemed himself the inventor. The stanza is this :—

> I'm the Quee— of Picardi—
> Famous mo— than Dame Oli—
> Than Don Quixo— and Lazari—
> Than Alfarach— and Celesti—

The wonder ceases, however, when we consider that the *Don Quixote* was well-known in the literary circles of Madrid long before it was printed. Lope speaks of it contemptuously in a letter already quoted, dated Toledo, August 14, 1604. The wily Dominican had, therefore, ample opportunity of knowing its contents. It is thought that Cervantes, in the eighth chapter of the *Viaje*, roundly accuses him of plagiarism, when he introduces the Muses as dancing to the "sweet sound of instrument of mine" :—

> Mine, did I say, I do but lie perchance,
> Like him who calls another's verse his own,
> If it be fit his honour to advance.

To Spanish students of the *Don Quixote* the mysterious poem of *Urganda la desconicida*, which introduces the work, and whose metre Perez imitated, is well known. It has hitherto been regarded by English translators as a farrago of nonsense verses, unfit for serious rendering. In Duffield's new translation of *Don Quixote*, we attempted for the first time a translation of it in plain metre. As a curiosity we give it here again ; but with its full complement of "broken feet." It is written in a style of versification hitherto uncultivated by English rhymesters; perhaps it may become popular. Benjumea, in his "Truth about Don Quixote," declares it to be the key which unlocks most of the mysteries that follow.

We commend it, therefore, to all ingenious searchers after the occult sense of the plainest book in Creation. Perhaps the Oracle will give forth a more certain sound, when uttered in something like the original "docked lines:"—

URGANDA THE UNKNOWN

TO THE BOOK OF DON QUIXOTE DE LA MANCHA.

I.

O Book, if it be thy inten—
   To rise and rank amongst the goo—
   'Twill not be said by any foo—
Thy fingers are not tipped with sen—
But if thou cook what is not mean—
   To please the taste of every boo—
   Thoul't find it handled by a broo—
Of silly folk, of high preten—
   Who bite their nails, and look askan—
   To shew that they are dilettan—

II.

If it be true, as saith the stan—
   "Who to a goodly tree repai—
   Will surely find a goodly sha—"
Here in Bejar thy lucky plan—
Presents a royal tree and gran—
   Whose fruit are princes of the Sta—
   Their chief, a Duke of noble na—
A second, mighty Alexan—
   Come to its shade without a ca—
   For Fortune favoureth the bra—

III.

Thou hast to tell the adventurous fea—
   Of that Manchegan knight and no—
   Whose wits were turnèd out of doo—

By dint of much and idle rea—
Arms, ladies fair, and cavalie—
   Inflamed his brain in such a mo—
   That like Orlando furio—
Transformed into a lover swee—
   By strength of arm he reached the goa—
   Fair Dulcinea del Tobo—

IV.

Engrave not thou upon thy shie—
   Devices strange and hiero—
   When picture-cards are all we ho—
We brag with points that court defea—
If in the preface thou be mee—
   Thou'lt hear exclaim no blatant foo—
   "Behold! Don Alvaro de Lu—
Or Hannibal the Carthagi—
   Or else King Francis, he in Spai—
   Is railing at his doleful fa—"

V.

Since Heaven's wisdom hath refu—
   To turn thee out a Classici—
   Like that black linguist, Juan Lati—
Be chary of the Latin mu—
Launch not us thy biting hu—
   Nor din us with philosophi—
   Lest one, who careth not a whi—
For learnèd ways or literatu—
   Should twist his mouth, and give a shrie—
   "What mean to me your flowers of spee—"

VI.

Of others' lives make no pala—
   Nor peer into thy neighbour's hou—
   What comes not straight into accou—
Pass by; it is the wiser pla—
For foolish words at random ca—

Fall often on the jester's crow—
So burn the lamp, and strain thy pow—
To gain good fame throughout the la—
For he who prints a stupid boo—
Consigns it to eternal doo—

VII.

Take warning from the ancient pro—
That if thy house be made of gla—
It is a most imprudent pla—
To pelt the passers-by with sto—
Compose such works as men of no—
May pleasure find in every pa—
For he who takes his pen in ha—
And brings to light a portly vo—
Mere idle damsels to amu—
Writes for the silly and the stu—

END OF NOTES AND ILLUSTRATIVE PIECES.

CHISWICK PRESS:—C. WHITTINGHAM AND CO., TOOKS COURT
CHANCERY LANE.

www.ingramcontent.com/pod-product-compliance
Lightning Source LLC
Chambersburg PA
CBHW031954300426
44117CB00008B/750